Dumbth

Books by Steve Allen

Bop Fables

Fourteen for Tonight

The Funny Men

Wry on the Rocks

The Girls on the Tenth Floor

The Question Man

Mark It and Strike It

Not All of Your Laughter, Not All of Your Tears

Letter to a Conservative

The Ground Is Our Table

Bigger Than a Breadbox

A Flash of Swallows

The Wake

Princess Snip-Snip and the Puppykittens

Curses!

What to Say When It Rains

Schmock!–Schmock!

Meeting of Minds (First, Second, Third, and Fourth Series)

Chopped-Up Chinese

Ripoff: The Corruption That Plagues America

Explaining China

Funny People

The Talk Show Murders

Beloved Son: A Story of the Jesus Cults

More Funny People

How to Make a Speech

How to Be Funny

Murder on the Glitter Box

The Passionate Nonsmoker's Bill of Rights (with Bill Adler, Jr.)

Dumbth

And 81 Ways to Make Americans Smarter

by Steve Allen

PROMETHEUS BOOKS
Buffalo, New York

Library of Congress Cataloging-inPublication Data

Allen, Steve, 1921–
    Dumbth and 81 ways to make Americans smarter / by Steve Allen.
        p.   cm.
    ISBN 0-87975-539-3 : $21.95
    1. United States—Intellectual life—20th century.
2. Inefficiency, Intellectual. 3. Thought and Thinking. I.   Title.
E169.12.A3755   1989   89-10647
973.92—dc20   CIP

Table of Contents

Should the human race not be extinguished by a nuclear war it will degenerate into a flock of stupid, dumb creatures under the tyranny of dictators who rule them with the help of machines and electronic computers.

This is no prophecy, just a nightmare.

—Max Born,
Bulletin of the Atomic Scientists,
November 1965

There is no expedient to which a man will not resort to avoid the real labor of thinking.
—Sir Joshua Reynolds (1723-1792)

I think the world is run by C-students.

—Al Maguire

I know from my own experience that in the last twenty years the world has moved a very long way towards conformism and passivity. So long a way that the distance is, to me, both frightening and disconcerting. I have been all the more sensitive to it because I have spent this time in the isolation of a contemplative monastery, and have only recently come back into contact (through certain discrete readings and conversations) with the America which I used to know as a rather articulate, critical and vociferously independent place. It is certainly not so any more. Not that the people do not complain and criticize, but their complaints and criticisms, indeed their most serious concerns, seem to be involved in trivialities and illusions—against a horrifying background of impending cosmic disaster. It seems to me that for all our pride in our freedom and individuality we have completely renounced thinking for ourselves. What passes for "thinking" is mass-produced, passively accepted, or not even accepted. We simply submit to the process of being informed, without anything actually registering on our mind at all. We are content to turn on a switch and be comforted by the vapid, but self-assured slogans of the speaker who, we fondly hope, is thinking for the whole nation.

—Thomas Merton
Preface, *Disputed Questions*

Foreword

by Norman Cousins

The world knows Steve Allen as a musician and as an entertainer. In addition, his friends know Steve Allen as someone whose thought processes are always working as a student of history and world affairs, as a philosopher, and, finally, as someone who takes pains to get the most out of his own capabilities. Certainly no one I know has thought more carefully about the use of his time and skills—or his relationships to other people. I first became aware of these special propensities when, in the middle of conversation, he whipped out a mini tape-recorder and dictated notes to his secretary by way of following up on a point that emerged from our discussion. When I visited his office for the first time, I was enormously impressed with the organization of his files, which I learned he designed himself. I was consumed with envy at his ability to maintain access to, and stay in possession of, his past. I was to discover that he organizes his memories no less systematically than he does his papers.

Everything in this book is Steve Allen-tested. That is, he doesn't theorize about the way an individual perceives the world; what he says flows out of actual personal experience. His is the inner view, conveyed with uncommon wisdom and felicity of expression. No man who knows as much about comedy as he does can fail to know a great deal about life. What we have, then, is a book that only a lifetime lived by Steve Allen can produce.

John Dewey once said that the test of an educated person is the ability to come into possession of all his/her powers. This book is dedicated to that proposition.

Acknowledgments

I must, first of all, express profound gratitude to the hundreds of my fellow Americans who, by their striking ineptitude in performing certain services for me over the last few decades gave me the idea for this book in the first place and kept my enthusiasm for the project constantly vigorous by almost daily replenishing the store of incidents that illustrate my thesis. The examples of what I call dumbth have not, of course, been drawn only from personal experience. The journalistic record has provided a good many, all of considerably more importance than the daily they've-lost-my-luggage-again sort of frustration now so common.

I must also thank Cristina Gutierrez of my office staff for listening to endless hours of dictated cassette tapes (I do not use a typewriter) and doing a very good job of transcribing my remarks, often to the distraction of such background noises as airplane engines, New York street traffic, the chattering of grandchildren, and other sounds natural to the scores of places through which I happened to be moving when many of the observations that follow occurred to me.

Special thanks go to Karen Hicks, whose magical touch at typewriters and word-processors and whose natural gifts for organization have greatly facilitated the task of bringing the present work to the point of completion. I'm extremely grateful, too, to Doris Doyle for her invaluable editorial recommendations. Although I have written thirty-one books, I have never, perhaps unwisely, worked with an outline or any sort of pre-planned structure. I simply dictate random parts of a manuscript, in no particular order, and although such an approach has the virtue of producing a large volume of material in a relatively short time, it does lead to reliance on an astute editor experienced at making orderly something that had at least certain elements of chaos about it.

I am indebted, too, to Paul Kurtz, editor-in-chief of Prometheus Books, for encouraging and agreeing to publish yet one more plea for reason of the sort that his company has so repeatedly distinguished itself by bringing out.

Lastly I must thank my personal secretary, Pat Quinn, and my wife, Jayne Meadows, for maintaining order in the office and in the home, and thus creating a climate in which it is possible for me to concentrate on matters creative.

The Problem

Introduction

On February 15, 1983, the NBC television evening news carried a feature about the incredible ignorance of students at the University of Miami concerning matters of simple geography.

A survey of more than one hundred *geography students* showed that 42 percent didn't know where London was! Several thought Quebec was in Alaska. One student believed the Falkland Islands were off the coast of England. More than half couldn't find Chicago! Many weren't too sure what part of Europe France was in. Greenland was mistaken for Iceland. And half of those polled didn't know where Baja California was. But the final insult was that 8 percent of these students in Miami couldn't place Miami on the map!

My wife and I were watching the dinner-hour newscast on which these distressing revelations were made. "Perhaps," she said, "since that school is in Florida, a lot of the students may be immigrants, who wouldn't know much about American geography and might have difficulty speaking English."

A moment later, as the camera showed some of the students in class, and others being interviewed, we realized that Jayne's charitable thought had no relevance to the situation: The faces shown were almost entirely Anglo; there were no Hispanic students.

An isolated exception?

On the contrary, it is all too typical.

A 1984 survey showed that 75 percent of the *high school* students questioned could not even locate Vietnam on a map, and approximately a third of them literally did not know that the United States had been involved in a war in that country!

In 1982, a poll of opinion on public issues among high school students revealed that more than 25 percent actually believed that the American landing on the moon had never occurred and was a matter of propaganda, fake photography, or CIA machinations.

An American teacher recently used the term "forbidden fruit," and all of her third-year high school students drew a blank.

In another instance, a teacher of juniors and seniors in a high school raised the question of what tribes had invaded England. Among the guesses were the Aztecs and the Jews.

The Progressive magazine, in their September 1984 issue, printed a letter from a David Carleton of West Lafayette, Indiana. The information he supplied was so shocking, I quote it here.

> I am a doctoral student in international relations at Purdue University, and during the past spring semester I taught an introductory course in international relations. As part of that course, I decided to require the students to take a simple geography test. Each student was given a list of U.N. member nations and a map of the world that was divided into ten regions—North America, Central America, South America, Western Europe, Eastern Europe, North Africa, Sub-Saharan Africa, the Middle East, Asia, and Oceania.
>
> The students were asked to specify the region in which each nation was located; in other words, they simply had to place each nation *within several thousand miles* of its actual location. Each student, moreover, was given a copy of both the list and the map *two weeks before the test.*
>
> The following nations were identified as being in Central America: Liberia, Burma, Malawi, Bahrain, the Seychelles, Niger, Gabon, Nepal, Cape Verde, Comoros, Nigeria, the Philippines, Iceland, and, in an act of poetic justice, Vietnam.
>
> Costa Rica was placed in Sub-Saharan Africa, Haiti in Western Europe, and Grenada—this was five months after the U.S. invasion—in Asia. (Italics supplied.)

More recently, in a survey of a cross-section of high school *graduates,* 26 percent of those responding could not identify Mexico as the large country on the southern border of the United States.

And as of the beginning of 1989, approximately one-third of America's high school students could not locate the United States on a map of the world.

According to the December 1988 issue of the *Washington Monthly,* a recent survey of American eight- to twelve-year-olds found that they could name 5.2 alcoholic beverages but only 4.8 presidents.

The bare fact is shocking enough, but when we stop to consider that the great majority of American children are at least familiar with the names of George Washington and Abraham Lincoln, and presumably at least know the name of the president of the moment, the conclusion is that our nation's eight- to twelve-year-olds know the name of only one or two additional presidents.

And it doesn't stop at the schools. Martin Mand, vice-president of the DuPont Company, recently told me that when he tells people he's from Delaware sometimes he is asked, "Delaware? Which state is that in?"

Another Wilmington resident told me the following day that a national study revealed that 24 percent of Americans believe that Delaware is a city.

Mountains of evidence—both in the form of statistical studies and personal testimonies—establish that the American people are suffering from a new and perhaps unprecedented form of mental incapacitation for which I have coined the word *dumbth.*

I do not mean to suggest, by concentrating on the increasingly common ignorance about the kind of basic elements of national and world geography that not too many years ago were well within the grasp of the average American twelve-year-old, to suggest that knowledge about towns, states, nations, continents, and oceans is either the only or at least the chief area in which we are now lamentably uninformed. Would that it were so. But we are becoming equally dumb about history, politics, the rudiments of the marketplace, religion, the sciences, and, in fact, every significant category of human knowledge. There are obviously scholars and experts who are minding the store in these separate areas, but the gap between their knowledge and that of the average citizen is so hopelessly wide that there is at present almost no communication between the two camps. An early-1989 study, "A World of Difference," conducted by the Educational Testing Service, compared the science and mathematics performance of thirteen-year-old students from the United States and twelve other countries. Korea's students ranked number one. To the surprise of few informed people, United States students came in dead last.

So far we are talking, of course, about ignorance, and it is at least theoretically possible to be strikingly poorly informed and yet to reason fairly well. But I argue that there is a great deal more than ignorance troubling us at present. Side-by-side with this historically unfortunate factor, we are now, in a broad statistical sense, also guilty of a form of stupidity that, although also an ancient human problem, now threatens to swamp our efforts to conduct the affairs of an at least generally rational society and one also capable of dealing with dramatic new opportunities made possible by modern technology.

Ignorance about events in space and time is bad enough. But increasing numbers of today's young people are ludicrously uninformed about the long-standing American rules of social and political conduct. Most frightening is the way many young people have embraced intolerance. There is a rise in racially based violence on college campuses, a proliferation of the "skinhead" groups, and the alienation that brought less than 17 percent of America's eighteen- to twenty-four-year olds to the polls in the last election. Hate-related violence—harassment, vandalism, arson—has been documented on campuses from Columbia to the Citadel, from the University of Vermont to the University of Michigan. Reports Arthur Kropp of People for the American Way:

- A rabbinical student was fatally shot in Pittsburgh.
- A cross was burned on a University of Alabama campus.
- At the University of Vermont, fraternities were disciplined for spray-painting derogatory slogans that threatened homosexuals.
- At a community college in California, where Hispanics won seats in the student government for the first time, Anglos harassed their Mexican-American classmates, and two masked white men assaulted a young Mexican-American woman in a campus rest room.
- Outside San Francisco, young "skinheads" threw a teenage boy through a plate glass window when he tried to stop them from displaying anti-Semitic posters.

Concerning the narrow problem of ignorance, I leave its solution to others. But this particular report will concentrate on the general sort of poor thinking and inefficiency that is now endemic.

The fact that you have already picked up this book suggests that you are prepared to at least entertain the possibility that, at present, Americans do not think as well as they should.

Indeed, they do not.

After absorbing the eighty-one suggestions on the following pages, however, we may be able to do something about it.

To forestall one possible objection, I want to make it clear that this book is not intended to help people become rational about what might be called the dramatic aspects of their lives. While such a result would obviously be highly desirable, there is simply no manual, no combination of suggestions and aphorisms, however wise, that could produce such an effect.

Consider, for example, the case of a married man with an attractive, intelligent wife and three children. He becomes romantically involved with another woman, someone who, let us assume, would be judged by any disinterested party as considerably less appealing than his wife. We would all agree that the man in question is behaving both dangerously and foolishly. He is risking not only his own happiness, but that of his wife and children—not to mention that of the other woman. He is, in a word, behaving irrationally. But the compressed, condensed wisdom of all the wisest philosophers and theologians would be unequal to the task of advising our unfortunate subject how to promptly put the other woman out of his mind and resume a more sensible mode of behavior.

Just so, there is nothing whatever that sound advice alone can do to change the mind-set of the millions of unfortunate individuals suffering from phobias, neuroses, psychoses, and addictions.

It is perfectly reasonable to include the component of rationality as part of an assortment of arguments designed to change the behavior of the confused individual. My point is that we ought not to be deluded that a course in rationality is, in itself, sufficient.

Now, back to dumbth.

Beginnings have always fascinated me, whether related to trivial or important subject-matter. But often, even in our personal lives, we literally do not recall the precise moment at which something eventually important to us first became part of our experience. As regards my interest in dumbth, oddly enough I do recall the instance in which the enormity of the problem became crashingly clear.

It was back in 1948 that I came across a series of articles in the *New Yorker* written by humorist James Thurber, in which he reported what an extended study of radio soap-operas had revealed to him. After so many years, Thurber's series has gone out of focus for me, except for one particular. He reported that whenever a character on a popular soap-opera died, had a baby, became engaged, or was married, thousands of listeners across the country would send the sort of letters and gifts it would be reasonable to send to real-life rather than make-believe characters.

If a soap-opera character had a baby, she would receive enormous quantities of booties, little caps or jackets, supplies of diapers, cards of congratulations, and so on. I was very young when I learned this, but I have never forgotten how the news depressed me. It still does. This particular aspect of the larger problem, in fact, is now worse than ever. And it was bad enough in the 1950s, when actor Robert Young, who played the title role in the popular television series "Marcus Welby, M.D.," received an average of five thousand letters every week seeking *medical* advice!

In 1968, when actor Leslie Nielsen played a brutal sheriff in the television film *Shadow Over Elviron,* he received more than two hundred poison-pen letters. In addition to the naked hatred and anger the letters expressed, Nielsen noted, the language was shockingly vulgar. Perhaps the most surprising factor is that the majority of letters were written by women.

A classic instance of dumbth on a nationwide scale occurred in July 1982, when the ABC television network carried a program titled "Pray TV," on which actor John Ritter played the role of an evangelist. Incredibly, the stations affiliated with the network received some 22,000 calls, many from people who wanted to pledge financial contributions. When I read about this in a column by Marvin Kitman in the New York newspaper *Newsday,* I found it difficult to believe. But a check with Peter Durlin of ABC's publicity department established that Kitman's information was reliable. Durlin reported that the various telephone companies involved had monitored and logged the incoming calls. Just after a scene in which the evangelist said, "We need your prayers," a fictitious toll-free number was flashed on the screen. Many viewers around the country tried to phone the number to offer prayers and money.

More recently, Spuds MacKenzie, the dog introduced in television commercials in mid-1988, was receiving an average of five thousand letters a month. Not the trainer, not the sponsor, not the agent, not the handlers. The dog herself was getting the letters.

It is odd, of course, that in the latter half of the twentieth century so much is being written about intelligence when, at the same time, there is no clear consensus as to what it is. One reason for this, I suppose, is that intelligence is not just one thing. But the absence of a clear-cut definition acceptable to the intellectual jury clearly does not mean that there is no such thing as intelligence, nor does it mean that we may not, to our benefit, continue to speculate about it. We have never been able to get the physical phenomenon of electricity into clear focus either, but no one doubts its existence. In any event, I argue that it is helpful to consider intelligence in its various aspects. We know from all too much daily experience that there are people who, according to certain criteria, are fairly well educated (at least they formally graduated from high schools and colleges) but, to use another metaphor, do not know enough to come in out of the rain. Then there are those who are in a certain observable sense reasonably bright—alert, quick-thinking, quick-speaking—and yet are staggeringly ignorant about significant people, places, events, and ideas that distinguish their individual cultures and societies and hence are lacking many tools—words and ideas—with which to reason.

Again, ignorance and stupidity are two of the chief factors comprising dumbth. But there are other elements, such as incompetence. In early 1983 the Ford Foundation, the Gannett Company, and other groups solicited responses from approximately 200 corporations and labor unions and 125 school administrators concerning the basic skills of American workers. Three-quarters of the corporations responding said they had had to institute programs of remedial training for their employees. The

Center for Public Resources, the nonprofit organization that conducted the survey, reported that "businesses may lose millions of dollars annually because their employees cannot read, write, or add well enough to handle basic tasks."

Nor should it be assumed that only lower-level workers are so poorly equipped. Half the corporations surveyed reported that their *managers* and *supervisors* could not write paragraphs free of grammatical and spelling errors.

In 1986 an enterprising publisher brought out a book, aimed chiefly at business executives, instructing them how to write simple business letters. According to the latest reports it was selling well.

The primary difficulty facing the writer of this sort of analysis is that almost as soon as research is initiated, one is swamped—I must repeat it—by a flood of corroborative evidence. I stress this because I would not want the reader to think that I have buttressed my case with a few laboriously sought-out bits of data. On the contrary, there is so much evidence that there is room here to refer to only a tiny fraction of one percent of it.

Many people, of course, report the vague sense that some of those with whom they now come into contact are not as intelligent or well informed as they might have been twenty years earlier. Such a widespread feeling must have some evidential basis. And, indeed, as soon as we look into the situation in our schools, where careful measurements can be taken, we find the painful thesis confirmed resoundingly.

In the mid-1960s the International Project for the Evaluation of Educational Achievement, with the help of UNESCO, made a comparative study of schools to determine how well, or poorly, mathematics was being taught. One of the major discoveries was that the United States was doing a poor job of teaching children how to add, subtract, and deal with problems in calculus. A deep and disturbing gap between Japan and the United States was one of the findings. Japan placed 76 percent of its thirteen-year-olds in the upper half of the international test group, the United States only 43 percent. Thirty-one percent of the Japanese children ranked in the upper tenth percentile. The American figure was 4 percent. As the study stated, the top tenth "is a very critical index, since it is likely to be the source of national mathematics and science talent."

Could such information relate to the increasing dominance of Japan in the electronic and automobile fields some twenty-five years after the study?

There is no necessity—since this is not a scholarly report—to specify the date at which a decline in reading, writing, thinking, and computing skills became precipitous. I arbitrarily use the year 1960 as a starting point. It was then that the relative inability of American children and young adults to write coherent English in any form—letters, essays, newspaper articles, poems, short stories, song lyrics—first became apparent on a broad scale.

In an article published in late 1979 in the Phi Delta *Kappan,* W. Timothy Weaver, associate professor at Boston University School of Education, reported that the Scholastic Aptitude Test scores of the nation's high school seniors were continuing a decline that had begun years earlier. Since 1963, both mathematics and verbal scores had dropped a total of 42 and 51 points, respectively. Weaver wrote:

> High school seniors planning on *teaching careers* were scoring lower than such students formerly did on the Scholastic Aptitude Test. In 1979 future teachers averaged only 420—on a 200-800 scale— in mathematical skills. Students taken altogether scored 467! All students averaged 427 in verbal skills; the future teachers and school administrators averaged only 392.

In July 1976 school officials in Pinellas County, Florida, gave examinations to applicants for teaching posts. If the results surprised them, they do not surprise me. *Some of the teachers scored lower in math and reading than the school system's eighth graders.*

A 1974 survey asked graduating high school seniors which of four countries—India, Israel, Egypt, or Mexico—was Arabic. Half the high school graduates taking the test could not answer the question!

In 1976 teacher Don Dunlap of San Jose, California, stated in a letter published in the November 13 *Saturday Review,* "Most of my students come to college unable to distinguish an adverb from a noun. They simply lack the vocabulary, the elemental points of reference needed to talk intelligently about writing and to respond with understanding to specific indications of common weaknesses in writing."

According to Mary M. Stover Thomas of South Harpswell, Maine, only two students—in a classroom of some thirty juniors at a well-known university—could remember ever having *heard* of then-Secretary of State Henry Kissinger.

David Anson, reviewing the film *The Twilight Zone* for *Newsweek's* June 27, 1983, issue, reported that for him the most frightening moment in the film's first section came not from anything on the screen but from something that took place in the audience.

When actor Vic Morrow first entered his "Twilight Zone," Anson reported, "he finds himself in Nazi-occupied Paris, surrounded by Swastikas and German soldiers. 'Wow!' exclaimed the awed teenager behind me. 'It's Vietnam.' "

As of 1977, 13 percent of all seventeen-year-olds in the United States were functionally illiterate.

There would appear to have been no significant improvement since that time. Lawrence Uzzell, writing in the *Wall Street Journal* of May 10, 1989, referred to the following extemely simple test question, given to seventeen-year-old high school students:

Which of the following is true about 87 percent of 10?
(A) It is greater than 10.
(B) It is less than 10.
(C) It is equal to 10.
(D) Can't tell.

Half of the students tested answered the question wrong, obviously having failed to grasp the point that 87 percent—of anything at all—cannot possibly be equal to all, or 100 percent, of it. The horror stories and statistics are endless. Uzzell mentions that in 1988, in the entire continental United States, only 986 high school seniors scored above 750 on the SAT's verbal section—fewer than half as many as in 1981, and probably the lowest number ever.

His purpose was not simply to add more bad news to the veritable Mt. Everest of it already available. He was making, in a sense, the more gloomy point that such miserable results have followed after a great deal of rhetoric and even significant attempts at "educational reform."

During the last several years of research for this book, much of it quite casual, I have heard from and spoken to dozens of teachers, all of whom report that while there was once a time when a good many American high school and college students enjoyed reading, or at least were willing to do it even if they were not particularly thrilled by the exercise, we have at present a generation whose majority has little or no interest in reading. This one factor alone would absolutely assure us a nation of dummies, even if everything else was working quite well, and we know that practically nothing is.

In an effort to examine the scope of their political knowledge, 145,000 American teenagers were surveyed in 1970, 1972, and 1976. The findings showed that during the first half of the 1970s understanding of the democratic process itself declined among America's thirteen- to seventeen-year-olds. The simple ability to explain the basic concept of democracy—that the people elect their leaders—had fallen among seventeen-year-olds, from 87 to 74 percent. Among thirteen-year-olds it declined from 53 to 42 percent. More than 96 percent of both age groups knew that the president of the United States (in 1976) was Gerald R. Ford, but only 32 percent of the thirteen-year-olds and 71 percent of the seventeen-year-olds were aware that he was a Republican! Only 20 percent of the thirteen-year-olds and 48 percent of the seventeen-year-olds could name *any* of their representatives in Congress.

In April 1978, the *New York Times* arrived at the sobering estimate that "as many as one out of every five *adults* do not possess the minimal reading, writing, and calculating skills necessary to function in modern society" (italics supplied).

The decline in mathematical ability, though exceedingly unfortunate and certainly dangerous for a modern society, nevertheless is perhaps understandable. But the decline in the simple ability to speak coherently, to read, to write, to spell, to communicate, is even more depressing, and surprising, since modern Americans live in the most talkative, talked-to, and talked-about culture in history.

Churches, too, are becoming concerned about the problem and its effects on their members.

According to a 1980 Gallup Poll, 57 percent of Americans believe in unidentified flying objects, 19 percent believe in witches, 28 percent in astrology, 39 percent in devils, and 54 percent in angels.

By 1988, 74 percent of American teenagers polled by the Gallup organization said they believed in angels, and 29 percent believed in witchcraft, up 25 percent since 1978. Fifty-eight percent of those teens polled accepted the legitimacy of astrology even though scientists have repeatedly described it as worthless. Twenty-two percent of the youth in the 1988 study believed in ghosts.

Those who believe in witches, angels, and devils are, of course, chiefly Christians, since belief in the literal reality of such creatures is part of Christian orthodoxy. But assuming the statistics are reliable, there is obviously a serious problem for the churches revealed by the percentages believing in such beings. The figures for church members—according to Christian doctrine—are supposed to be 100 percent in all categories.

The Christian churches have now had a relatively unimpeded opportunity to preach the Gospel for some two thousand years. For the past five centuries the availability of printing presses and the greatly increased literacy that resulted have considerably facilitated their task. New editions of Bibles leap immediately to bestseller lists, the number purchased usually running to the millions. There are religious television and radio programs, Sunday-school classes, university courses, adult-study courses, books, pamphlets, tapes, lectures, and sermons, ad infinitum. Incredibly enough, despite this vast effort, engaged in not only by thousands of individual clergymen but by members of hundreds of separate Christian congregations, a general state of biblical illiteracy exists. As long ago as 1959, the Reverend Thomas Roy Pendell, a Protestant pastor of what he described as "quite a proper congregation in a boulevard church located in the college section of a rather large city," prepared a simple test about Jesus' life for the members of his flock. Reports Dr. Pendell,

> The results were staggering. Nearly one-fourth of the adult members of that Sunday's congregation could not identify Calvary as the place of Jesus' death. Over one-third did not know that Nazareth was the town where Jesus was brought up. Gethsemane rang no bell for 43 percent, and Pentecost had no significance for 75 percent. Only 58 percent could identify the Gospels.

There was complete confusion as to the number of converts baptized by Jesus, ranging from none (correct) to 300,000. Jesus was variously listed as living under Julius Caesar, King Saul, and King Solomon.

Concludes Pendell, "It seems plain that Biblical ignorance is the rule among members of one particular congregation. If other Protestant congregations are like ours, Christian education still has a long way to go."

It does indeed. And Catholic church leaders have long conceded—and lamented—that Catholics know even less about the Bible than do Protestants.

In this connection, I recommend "American Catholic Intellectual Life" by Father George Hunt, editor-in-chief of *America* magazine, in that periodical's May 6, 1989 issue. In referring to works distributed for a sixty-year period by the Catholic book club, Father Hunt says:

> Up to 1970 or so, the most popular offerings were Catholic biographies (saints or other heroes, or converts for the most part) and Catholic fiction. . . . Only a handful of books on theology were offered and *none on biblical scholarship*. (Italics supplied.)

This was, of course, in keeping with the longstanding general lack of interest, among the Catholic laity, in the Bible. It is encouraging to note that during the 1980s quite a different picture emerged. It remains to be seen whether the upsurge of Catholic Bible scholarship and lay interest will lead more to religious doubts or renewed faith; but whatever the outcome, it is good that more and more Catholics are taking a serious interest in Scripture.

As a Christian I am grieved to report that some of my fellow Christians, though chiefly of the fundamentalist persuasion, have been responsible for more than their share of publicly exhibited stupidity in recent years. Members of the white supremacist group, The Arizona Patriots, some of whose members consider themselves Christians, were arrested for conspiring to bomb an IRS complex and rob a bank to fund a paramilitary encampment. In Shelby, North Carolina, several men affiliated with the White Patriot Party entered a gay-oriented bookstore where they shot five men, killing three, in order to, according to an informant, "avenge Yahweh on homosexuals."

Another notable example of this was the rumor that the famous household products company, Procter & Gamble, is connected with devil worship. Because I perform comedy for a living, the reader might take the preceding sentence as a joke. It is not.

During the 1981-1982 period, Procter & Gamble was obliged to go to great and expensive lengths to stamp out the rumor, which had taken a variety of forms. The most common alleges that an executive of P&G appeared on either the Phil Donahue or the Merv Griffin show and admitted that the company logo—a crescent moon with the outline of a man's face looking at a group of thirteen stars—represented the company's formal connection with Satan worship.

To the extent that the realities may be of interest, no executive of the company had ever appeared on either television talk-show and the trademark itself is merely a picture of the traditional childhood symbol, the man in the moon, facing toward thirteen stars that represent the thirteen original American colonies. The logo has been used on P&G products for more than a hundred years.

I stress that I do not refer here to a casual comment from an at-liberty mental case or two. In fact, the company began receiving an average of *twelve thousand telephone calls a month* concerning the rumor. In the early stages of this nonsensical drama, P&G responded by issuing press releases and answering phone calls and letters with factual information.

A new phase was reached in mid-1982, however, when P&G employees and their families in the Cincinnati area were threatened and harassed by fanatical Christian fundamentalists. According to the *Los Angeles Times* of June 25, 1982, "Employees reported that paint had been thrown on their cars, tires slashed, and workers challenged to fist fights. Children of P&G employees have also been harassed at school."

Once the company learned that certain fundamentalist ministers had actually been spreading the rumor from their pulpits, P&G enlisted the aid of two fundamentalist leaders—the Reverend Jerry Falwell, of the now-defunct Moral Majority, and the Reverend Don Wildmon, executive director of the National Federation for Decency—in an attempt to put an end to this bizarre campaign. Said Falwell, "It is unfortunate that such false accusations are made in the first place, but even more disconcerting that they can be spread as rumor by people who call themselves Christians."

Added Wildmon, "The facts are that this is a vicious, unfounded rumor, and I hope we can help stop it."

One way that the Reverends Falwell and Wildmon can make such displays of irrationality less likely is by encouraging a respect for reason and evidence across the board.

Since the United States, in the ninth decade of the twentieth century, is facing a longer list of social problems than ever before in its history, do we really need to direct our attention to yet one more?

You had better believe it. And, given that the issue at hand is that of a serious erosion in simple intelligence, we have no choice. The problem exists. Because it is real, it must be faced. To say that Americans in recent years have become less intelligent obviously is not intended to suggest that we have become a nation of mental incompetents or that all Americans are less intelligent than they once were. There is no need to exaggerate the dimensions of the problem; the actuality of it is serious enough.

Again, part of the problem is that we *think* very poorly. But how could it be otherwise when few of us have been given any instruction in that difficult task?

Do schools teach us how to think? They do not. They teach us *what* to think.

But it's odd that at a time when "consciousness raising" is at least relatively popular, thinking itself has nevertheless enlisted the support of relatively few defenders, even though it is one of the chief means of raising one's consciousness.

When people use that now-common phrase, they usually refer to consciousness about specific issues—abortion, civil rights, women's rights, environmental pollution, and so on. But simply to learn seventeen new facts about these important social questions is hardly an adequate method of achieving the desired end. What one wants is the addition of a philosophical component. It is necessary to *think* about such issues, intelligently speculate about them, reason about them, communicate articulately about them.

This by no means excludes increased awareness of emotional factors.

It is good, for example, to be aware of the sufferings of those who fall on the uncomfortable sides of such social dramas. Our hearts should bleed for them, and the injustices they suffer should serve to fuel our energy in the cause of social justice. It would be foolish to choose between (a) being angry or moved to tears about such issues, and (b) thinking intelligently about them. Both avenues should be busily traveled. What we often see at present, by way of contrast, is a combination of apathy and ignorance at one extreme and belligerent fanaticism at the other.

Specific Problems We Reason About Poorly

Even many who perceive the problem do not, it seems to me, often proceed to relate the relative collapse of our literary and reasoning powers to the depressingly long list of troubles our society faces.

We don't have time to consider here all the dilemmas that make this moment in history the most dangerous we have ever known. There are just too many. But some tentative conclusions might suggest themselves on the basis of a random sampling of serious difficulties. (I do not list these problems, by the way, in order of importance.)

1. The international Marxist challenge is an issue that must be considered not as an isolated phenomenon but in relation to worldwide poverty, disease, overpopulation, and hunger.

I sometimes get the impression that a number of Americans imagine that our planet was some sort of economic paradise in which social justice, happiness, and prosperity were common, until some strange creatures from outer-space called Communists landed in our midst and, out of sheer perversity, began to stir up trouble. This view is, of course, absurd. Communism came into existence in Europe because of the relative failures of Christianity and capitalism. In my personal capacity as both a Christian and a capitalist it causes me discomfort to face such a reality. But I must, because it is a reality. If we can't understand that much then we're going to be at a considerable disadvantage in the competition with the Marxist powers for the minds of people all over the world. What we have to show now is that our prescriptions for the world's ills are better than those the Marxists propose.

A brief word about anti-Communism: Some misguided people act as if they believed that Communism is the only real problem we have. Or, if they do not go quite that far, they imply that we are entitled to give other difficulties short shrift until we find the solution to the dilemma that Communism poses. But if that were true, then our only real political virtue would be anti-Communism. Responsible anti-Communism is—in my prejudiced view, at least—a necessity. But it is certainly not enough to establish political virtue or wisdom. Adolf Hitler was perhaps the most energetic anti-Communist the world has known, but he succeeded in plunging our planet into a war in which some forty million people were killed and which, in the end (by greatly increasing the power of the Soviet Union), placed additional millions into the Communist camp. Anti-Communism alone, therefore, is not enough. One wants to know not only what a man is against but also what he is for. Misguided, irrational anti-Communism is actually harmful to our national and international interests.

2. The nuclear weapons dilemma remains unresolved. Few Americans seem really aware that a true scientific revolution has occurred in our lifetime. The bomb that burned some hundred thousand mostly civilian men, women, and children at Hiroshima—like the one at Nagasaki that left 75,000 casualties—was not just a somewhat larger weapon than the World War II blockbuster. It had the explosive power not of a pound of TNT—enormous in itself—not of a hundred pounds of TNT, a thousand pounds of TNT, but of twenty thousand *tons* of TNT. And that amount of power, compared with today's hydrogen bombs, is now considered in the small or tactical class.

If we develop a scale according to which the blockbuster is represented by a one-foot ruler, then the Hiroshima and Nagasaki bombs would be represented by a line as high as the Empire State Building, and a full-power H-bomb by a line running as high as the orbit of Sputnik I.

3. The black American's struggle for civil rights and social justice continues.

4. Problems of education are worsening. You know what they are: underfunding, not enough good schools, low salaries for teachers, a rising number of underqualified teachers, and so on. In this connection I draw your attention to a tragic paradox. The Communists are—in my opinion—mistaken in their premises and frequently brutal in their

methods. But they are not ignorant. If we are, relatively speaking, on the side of virtue, but ignorant, isn't there some terrible irony in that?

5. Economic injustice, the poverty problem, continues. Ours is the richest nation in history, but about thirty million of us live a life characterized by squalor, crime, danger, poor housing, inadequate medical care, bad education, and a general collapse of family life. Hundreds of thousands are now living on the street, as if we were a poverty-stricken Third-World country.

6. Our migratory farm workers, in particular, live lives of deprivation, and their poverty, ignorance, disease, and discouragement are being handed down to their children.

7. Most of our big cities are being strangled by slums and ghettos, becoming more dangerous, and suffering a general deterioration of services.

8. Our prison problem is a national disgrace.

9. The ever-growing narcotics traffic is another.

10. The condition of Native Americans should be a source of deep shame.

11. Problems of our elderly citizens are growing more severe. Because of dramatic medical advances, many more people are living to what was once called a ripe old age. But in their very advanced years, they can no longer work. The majority, therefore, cannot afford the heavy medical and drug expenses that are inevitable (except in cases of sudden death). For a very long time our conservative friends, and the American Medical Association, told us that, while it was no doubt very sad to be old and poor, there was nevertheless nothing whatever that the federal government need do about it. History eventually marched past such bastions of selfish resistance, but sniping from the rear continues. Mr. Reagan and his associates told us that nothing they were doing would hurt the "truly needy." That's nice to know. But conservatives, for the past hundred years, have obstructed every single federal effort to help the truly needy. All the humane social legislation of which our nation may now rightfully boast was accomplished "over the dead bodies" of earlier generations of such obstructionists. So while we welcome our conservative friends to the cause of the truly needy, we lament that they are arriving about a century late.

12. The problem of mental illness remains. You're probably familiar

with the statistics: 10 percent of Americans will have some form of mental or emotional illness in their lifetimes. That's more than twenty-three million people. But even the least knowledgeable person can see that the problem of mental illness is directly related to such other social dilemmas as crime, narcotics addiction, alcoholism, juvenile delinquency, the divorce explosion, compulsive gambling, sexual anarchy, child-abuse, child-pornography, bigotry, political irrationality, and religious fanaticism.

Christian Scientists don't believe in illness or formal medicine, but at least they tolerate them. They do not picket doctors and hospitals. Some American rightists in recent decades have actually attacked the mental-health movement itself.

13. The problem of world hunger is potentially explosive. Most of the world is hungry. That's threatening for us as well as tragic for those who suffer.

14. The population explosion continues. There are now four billion of us on this planet. In thirty years there may be six billion. We can't feed everybody now. Thousands die of malnutriton every day.

15. We claim to be concerned with law and order, but are unconcerned about the open anarchy that prevails among nations in the absence of a World Law that all nations are prepared to respect.

16. The daily pollution of our air, water, and soil continues. The Reagan administration formally decided to weaken some of the pitiably few protections the public had achieved. We now have acid rain, depletion of the planet's ozone layer, and the greenhouse effect, all seriously dangerous.

17. The power of organized crime is undiminished. Many published studies document that such crime is our nation's largest industry.

18. Our Spanish-speaking population continues in a difficult predicament. In some respects they lag behind black Americans.

19. The old-fashioned problem of alcoholism demands a high price. Many of the 25,000 traffic deaths a year are related to drinking.

20. There is now an incredible degree of corruption of the so-called law-abiding or majority segment of American society, a society increasingly on the take and on the make. (See my book *Ripoff*, Lyle Stuart, 1979)

21. Almost twenty-thousand Americans are killed each year by guns,

but we can get only weak gun-control legislation, despite the fact that the American majority wants it.

22. The struggle of women for social justice and equality continues.

23. Crimes of a revoltingly sadistic nature are on the increase.

The list could be continued, but let us arbitrarily stop at this point. These are just some of our problems. What are our chances of solving them?

The answer naturally will vary, depending on the particular issues involved, but the overall case for optimism is not at the moment very strong. Again, one reason is that we don't like to think. We mentally respond on the basis of our conditioning but don't feel comfortable thinking. We distrust science, prefer illusion to reality, and prefer the dangerous status quo—and twenty-three reasons why it is dangerous have just been cited—to the changes necessary for our salvation. Catholic author and social critic G. K. Chesterton once said that Christianity has not been tried and seen to fail, but that it has been found exceedingly difficult and consequently rarely tried. The same thing is true of the scientific, rational, humanist approach to life. We delude ourselves that we are a scientifically advanced people. The astounding technical achievements of our age were made not by the mass of us but by a tiny fraction of one percent of the population, frequently against the apathy, inertia, or bitter opposition of the other 99 percent.

True, we boast of skyscrapers, space shuttles, and dramatic cures for diseases. But this proves only that a few of us live intellectually in the twentieth century. Most of us live in earlier times. We may have skyscrapers, but we are still so ignorant and superstitious that we will not permit their thirteenth floors to be labeled as such. They're there, of course—like all our problems—but we deny their existence and call them the fourteenth floors. Most of us, instead of approaching a new problem rationally, will fall back on our cluttered file of superstition, nonsense, prejudice, and misinformation. Is it any wonder we so often fail?

The brain is a computer. Those who have even slight experience with computers are aware of the saying "garbage in, garbage out." This means that although a computer will perform its function with near perfection, it nevertheless cannot be responsible for erroneous answers if confused data are fed into it.

Now again—perceiving the human brain as a computer—consider just a few common beliefs:

Opposites attract.

As Maine goes, so goes the nation.

It always rains on Good Friday.

Fish is brain food.

Raw oysters have aphrodisiac value.

There's nothing new under the sun.

The murderer always returns to the scene of the crime.

If an expectant mother suffers a fright, her baby may be marked as a result.

The mental-health movement is a Communist plot.

The movement to flouridate public water supplies is either a Communist or a Jewish plot, and probably both.

It's unlucky to walk under a ladder.

A horseshoe or a rabbit's foot brings luck.

Eating pickles and milk in combination will make you sick.

The New England colonies offered freedom from religious persecution.

The earth is flat.

The physical universe is approximately five to ten thousand years old.

"President Eisenhower was a dedicated, conscious agent of the Communist Conspiracy" (Robert Welch of the John Birch Society).

But this list, too, must be cut off. We don't have the space to enumerate all the nonsensical ideas that are fervently believed by millions in our time. But if so much foolishness abounds, one might think, would not the world warmly welcome the occasional individual who brought some nugget of new truth? Those who specialize in history know that the answer to that question is in the negative.

Bertrand Russell has reminded us that when anesthetics were discovered more than a century ago, the Scottish physician Sir James Simpson recommended their use in childbirth. He was quickly rebuked by many clergymen who reminded him that God had said to Eve, "In sorrow thou shalt bring forth children" (Genesis 3:16). If a woman was under the influence of chloroform, the clergy inquired, how could she properly sorrow?

Dr. Simpson was clever enough to argue that since God had reportedly put Adam to sleep (when he extracted the rib from which woman was made) there would seem to be nothing wrong in principle in administering anesthetics to men, at least. Believe it or not, it took some time before its benefits could be extended to women.

Inventor Charles Kettering has recalled that when he was a twenty-year-old teacher he took some of his students to a railroad-car traveling exhibit that included a then-new X-ray machine, a device that provoked protests from fundamentalist clergymen shocked at the thought of "stripping the decency of clothing" by peering beneath it. Presumably, the gentlemen had not seen the object they were criticizing, since, if they had, we would have to assume that they considered the sight of skeletal bones erotically stimulating.

But the plot-line is an old one. We know what happened to Christ, Socrates, Copernicus, Galileo, Darwin, Freud, Pasteur, Frank Lloyd Wright, Susan B. Anthony, Florence Nightingale, Margaret Sanger—to the countless artists, scientists, composers, prophets, saints, and seers who broke through the traditional, who expanded the horizons of their art or science or philosophy. Were they applauded by their associates? No, they were usually condemned—sometimes literally to death.

But now let us approach our own time. Today no good conservative, or even reactionary, would dream of urging a return to the seventy-two-hour or sixty-hour work week. The forty-hour week is part of the economic status quo. It's the American way, one of the glories of our free-enterprise system. But the older reader can remember that those who first recommended the forty-hour week were called Communists, socialists, radicals, and agents of the devil.

Another example: Today it does not seem very radical or even progressive to suggest that young children of eight or ten ought not to work in dirty, dark, dangerous factories for twelve or fourteen hours a day to earn just a few pennies. And yet there was a time in this nation when exactly that occurred! The reformers who first were so bold as to suggest that this was an immoral and inhuman practice were called radicals, subversives, revolutionaries.

You miss my point altogether if you suppose that what I am trying to demonstrate is that our ancestors were sometimes stupid. They were indeed, but that is not what I'm getting at. My point is that you and I are just as stupid, and we will make precious little social progress until we admit as much.

A leading Los Angeles heart specialist has reported to me a conversation he had with one of his patients not long after one of the disastrous hillside fires that destroy homes in that city every few years. The woman, who was wealthy and reasonably well educated, said, "Tell me, doctor, do you have any doubt that the Communists did it?"

What is wrong here is not the alleged fact. We have no way of knowing what caused the fire. What is wrong with the woman's non-sensical question is the inadequate method of problem-solving. She was apparently unable to distinguish a remote possibility from either a probability or a fact. But let the person who has never committed that sin cast the first stone. We are all guilty of this offense at certain times.

Usually what makes us function so stupidly is a prejudgment, a prejudice, an ego-commitment. Sometimes the issue itself, as in the instance of the Los Angeles fires, is a relatively simple one to deal with.

What is fascinating is that so much of this haphazard substitute-for-thinking comes from people who have had a high school or college education. Again, this suggests that there may be something radically wrong at the very heart of our educational process in that it concentrates on teaching us what to think but rarely gives us the slightest instruction in how to think.

This is not a matter of making an either/or choice. We do indeed have to be taught what to think about, taught facts. But the "whatness" is beginning to drown us. Those who specialize in a scientific or technical field have observed that so much is being learned today that one doesn't have time to keep up with all the informative literature pertaining to one narrow field of specialization.

Fortunately, even though we consciously forget most of the facts we are taught, we are at least instructed in how to look up information in libraries and reference works and by means of computerized data-storage banks.

What we desperately need now—as individuals and as a society—is instruction in how to think, in logical reasoning.

It's no panacea. It won't introduce us at once into paradise. But we'll be better off than we are now, so often ruled by ignorance, prejudice, superstition, anger, and fear.

We must also learn our limitations. I sometimes suspect that nobody can correctly report anything. Therefore we must be skeptical and as scientific and objective as possible about what we read and hear. No two people agree completely on anything.

Do not be deluded, incidentally, that all that is needed is a return to good old-fashioned common sense. That there is a shortage of common sense no one would deny. But we need much more. Common sense might be compared to playing a musical instrument by ear. It's nice if you can do it, but it's better if you can also read music and know something about the theory behind it. Common sense, after all, for long centuries made human beings very comfortable in their certainty that the earth was flat, that the sun goes around the earth, that the sun and the moon are the same size, that the sky is blue.

We start—if we are fortunate—with some degree of common sense, but to it we must add the applied power of reasoning, aided by the observations and methods of science.

How Did We Get So Dumb?

The present phenomenon is considered by many educators, social scientists, parents, and journalists as something of a national disaster. The crisis in education has at last come into focus for the nation. In 1983 even Ronald Reagan finally mentioned it. Most—perhaps all—of the reasons for it are evident enough.

Concerning ignorance, the simple lack of knowledge, it is the most characteristic feature of our initial state, rather than something essentially foreign or unusual to us—in the sense that having a certain rare disease may be said to be uncharacteristic of humans even though a few do suffer from it. On the contrary, ignorance and poor judgment are typical of the state into which we are born. Whatever small amount of innate instinct we may have, it is clear that during our first two years we know very close to nothing and therefore have to be taught almost everything. Considering the blankness of our original slate, it is quite remarkable that we have such a striking ability to learn, particularly during our first five years.

We can see the naturalness of our originally pitiable condition dramatized in the tragic cases of those individuals who are mentally retarded. Indeed, we measure the degree of retardation by reference to specific chronological periods. If we say, for example, that someone has the mental development of a normal two-year-old, this is very pleasant news indeed to the parents if the offspring is in fact two years of age, but crushingly tragic if he or she is twenty-two.

We are dumb today partly because we have always been dumb. Supportive evidence may be found on every page of history.

In China, for centuries women's feet were tightly bound in infancy (for vaguely sexual reasons) so that by the time they were adults they were effectively crippled and could only hobble about—a remarkably stupid practice, as all now agree, including the Chinese themselves. But, for all its inherent absurdity, the custom flourished for a remarkably long time.

Lest Americans or others in the West feel superior in this regard, the women of my mother's generation deliberately injured themselves by wearing shoes much too small for them, thus suffering hideous deformations, painful bunions, and corns, all because of vanity. Many of us today have not bound feet but bound brains. Some things are actually done to our minds—early in our lives, though not only then— that stunt our mental growth and inhibit our potential.

We must now examine such factors. Only by doing so can we diminish their ugly power. The problem of ignorance and stupidity— the point must be often repeated—is especially serious at present.

Among the causes of the diminution of our intelligence is some forty years of television watching. I have elsewhere described most commercial television as junk-food for the mind. The point is not that watching just thirty minutes of "Charlie's Angels" reruns will make a little piece of your brain fall out of your left ear. This will not happen, any more than eating one piece of white bread will make a tooth fall out. But, by God, forty years of eating mostly white bread, white sugar, or the equivalent, will cause you physical harm. And forty years of watching television of the most mindless sort must have a destructive effect on the intelligence.

But can it not at least be said that by watching television people know about more things today than they did fifty years ago? Indeed it can, simply because more things are brought to their attention. An unfortunate result of this process seems to be that, as time passes, they know less and less about more and more until, at last, they will know almost nothing about almost everything.

This relates directly to the ever-shortening attention-span problem, for which television bears the primary—but by no means sole—responsibility. Even television itself suffers from this process, in that programs of a charming but leisurely pace are all but ruled out of the ratings race. Today, if there is not some outrageous reference, socko joke, or dramatic plot twist every few minutes, situation-comedy storylines are considered boring and are consequently discouraged.

One practical, unfortunate result of the attention-span problem in recent television history was the early demise of nothing less than the best variety program in the history of the medium, NBC's 1980 "The Big Show." No earlier television series of its kind approached its all-around excellence. But even before the program went on the air, a network programming executive had called me in for consultation on the prospect of another experiment with the variety formula.

"What you should be putting on the air," I said, "is a sketch-comedy program, of the sort that was so popular in the 1950s. I don't think the variety show, as such, is likely to work now."

"Why not?"

"Such shows could succeed in the 1950s because, even though an individual viewer might not care for what he was watching at a given moment—an opera singer, an ice skater, a marching band, or whatever—he knew that in two or three minutes something else would be on the screen and there was a chance that he would like that. Today the ability of most television viewers to concentrate their attention is so weak that they seem unwilling to put up with more than thirty seconds of something that does not amuse or fascinate them. Also, you now have the technology of those channel-switching devices people can manipulate from their chairs or beds."

"So you don't think variety will work at all?"

"I didn't say that. Variety of the traditional sort won't work. But if you do a program with some variety elements, but where the chief emphasis is on comedy—that could work."

I was eventually given the job of cohost and head writer of the first of "The Big Show" series, and in that instance the emphasis was definitely on comedy. Critical response was enthusiastic. The program was of excellent quality, but the attention-span factor did lead to ratings problems. In television, if you have a serious ratings problem, you go off. Quality is irrelevant. A short attention-span is one indicator of low intelligence. By itself it proves nothing, but in America today it is not encountered by itself.

Radio and the music market are also at fault. As a people, we devote far too much time to listening to popular music. I have nothing against the art; I contribute to it, even writing a certain amount of rock music. Some modern songs—whoever writes them—are of a high order. But there is no serious questioning of the fact that, compared to the Golden Age of popular American songs, the music of the early 1980s reached a revolting culmination in the form of what is called "punk rock," although the style called "heavy metal" had earlier almost obliterated the song-form itself.

At every moment of your life you are, in a literal sense, both living and dying. Old cells of your body reach the end of their time and are replaced by new ones. The same thing, in a sense, is true of societies. Not only do some individuals die while others are being born, but institutions, customs, and practices, too, come into being, evolve, grow, and die. The changes are more dramatic at certain times.

As regards American popular music, its greatest period, approximately thirty years in length, stretched from 1920 to 1950. This obviously is not to say that there was little or no worthwhile music written before or after that time. But it is clear that America's most gifted popular composers and lyricists—Jerome Kern, Victor Herbert, Sigmund Romberg, Rudolph Friml, George Gershwin, Richard Rodgers, Cole Porter, Harry Warren, Irving Berlin, Harold Arlen, Vincent Youmans, Oscar Hammerstein, Hoagy Carmichael, Johnny Mercer, Ira Gershwin, Jimmy McHugh, James van Heusen, and others—did their greatest work during the twenties, thirties, and forties. An incredibly rich profusion of beautiful melodies, inventive and fresh harmonies, and intriguing new rhythms characterized the music of the period. Suddenly, at mid-century, perhaps because of the strains on society caused by two international wars and a long, crushing financial depression, there was a general collapse of cultural standards in American music.

The reasons were also partly economic. As it became evident that teenagers comprised an ever larger part of the audience for music, and as recordings became more popular in the marketplace than sheet music, which implied the ability to read notation and play the piano, more and more music began to be created for the relatively uninformed and illiterate new audience. Bobby-sox and bubble-gum songs, sung by new young performers, became popular. White singers and musicians appropriated an initially vigorous and creative art form—rhythm-and-blues or rock—and began to weaken its currency. The young were no longer interested in the rich harmonics of a Jerome Kern, the sophisticated or witty lyrics of a Gershwin, Porter, Hart, or Hammerstein. A decidedly inferior brand of merchandise became increasingly available in the musical marketplace.

Children are adorable, and I am prejudiced in their favor. But because their conscious experience on Planet Earth has been brief, even the brightest of them know very little. It is an enormous compliment to say of an eight-year-old that he has the intelligence of a twelve-year-old. But who in his right mind would place a society in the hands of its twelve-year-olds? Such inexperienced humans are not only comparatively ignorant but they exercise notoriously poor judgment, which is precisely why they are not permitted to marry, vote, drink intoxicating beverages, drive a vehicle, or do any number of things that require a certain minimum sense of responsibility.

Even in the best of societies, children are poorly qualified to speak with an authoritative voice, but in our increasingly dangerous and irresponsible culture children are now being corrupted, stunted, and psychologically and educationally ruined at a far earlier age than in previous periods of our history. Yet, as they become, statistically speaking, dumber, more delinquent, even more criminal, they continue to have a strong vote in the cultural marketplace.

It would be irrelevant here to expound further on the collapse in musical quality. Its relevance to the case I present is that some forty years of exposure to the newer, more mindless, repetitive, ungrammatical, poorly constructed songs has inevitably had an effect on the public consciousness itself. The words—of many songs, at least—became so cheapened that in time they came to have relatively little importance. It was no longer a lyric of near-poetic quality that the new audience demanded. What it wanted was "a sound." Whatever became hot in the marketplace was immediately copied. Since this was often inferior material, market factors quickly extrapolated it, thus debasing the cultural currency even more dramatically.

A French thinker once said he would not care who wrote the laws of a country if he were permitted to write its songs. He was aware that a great deal can be learned about a people by simply observing the material they sing or listen to.

What little quality there has been in American music during recent decades is attributable to the personal gifts of a few talented artists. The South American composers who wrote in the bossa nova or samba style deserve great credit since most of their songs are highly melodic, original, and totally nonrock. Much of Marvin Hamlisch's work, too, is of such high quality that it sounds as if it had been written in the 1940s. Burt Bacharach and Henry Mancini also made important contributions, chiefly in the 1960s, as did Jim Webb with songs like, "MacArthur Park," "By The Time I Get to Phoenix," "Didn't We?" and "Wichita Lineman." Stevie Wonder, too, has written some interesting material, although it is hardly to be compared to the songs of Duke Ellington or Eubie Blake. Carole King, Joni Mitchell, the Beatles, Rupert Holmes, and Billy Joel deserve praise for helping keep quality alive. But it is significant that their output is modest indeed compared to that of the dominant composers of the twenties, thirties, and forties. And it must be acknowledged that for every good song the Beatles created, they wrote several that were innocuous.

We are not simply referring to a generation gap here; some of the most brilliant jazz instrumentalists of all time are young men and women now in their twenties and thirties. But it is significant that they are playing jazz, not black-leather-jacket, punk-rock, heavy-metal, acid-rock garbage, which is distinguished more often by electronic amplification, recording tricks, and deafening volume than by musical beauty of the sort that has sustained the human heart and spirit for centuries. Taken all together, some four decades of brainwashing with such music is one more reason for the deterioration of intelligence in the United States.

But the erosion of standards and of simple quality is by no means restricted to radio, television, or recordings. The situation of the Broadway theater is summed up in the following lines of a *Life* magazine article by Jennifer Allen about playwright Lanford Wilson:

> But only after a six-year stint in Chicago as a commercial artist did he write a play and move to New York. He arrived in 1962, *unaware that Broadway had closed its doors to serious drama.* "I expected to see *Long Day's Journey* playing next to *Death of a Salesman* playing next to *Hamlet.* I saw everything—*Bye, Bye, Birdie* and *Do Re Mi*—such a lot of crap." (Italics supplied.)

Among the numerous causes of inefficiency at present—oddly enough— the factor of sexuality must be listed.

Since many people have special difficulties in thinking about the problem, this paragraph may require a rereading. I do *not* suggest that either homosexuals or heterosexuals are more or less efficient. I know of no correlation whatever between sexual preference and efficiency. The inefficiency to which I refer results from both gay and straight employers hiring on the basis of sexuality rather than competence. So far as the factor of inefficiency is concerned, this is no worse than nepotism, which leads to jobs being given to people simply because they are relatives of the employer. But I know of several businesses and institutions in which serious inefficiency has become the norm largely because of the hiring of increasing numbers of professionally inefficient homosexuals and heterosexuals simply because of their sexual preference. Lastly—and again, so as not to be misunderstood—I personally don't care if those who attend to my professional needs are heterosexuals, homosexuals, or, for that matter, kangaroos. I am concerned only that they perform their professional services competently.

While it is well known that patterns of immigration both from for- eign countries and from less educated portions of our own country—

chiefly southern rural areas—were among the factors responsible for the deterioration of academic achievement in the past thirty years, I was unaware until I read Frances FitzGerald's *America Revised* (Vintage, 1980) that a similar process had occurred earlier in our history. Fitz-Gerald—who in turn refers to Richard Hofstadter's *Anti-Intellectualism in American Life*—relates that the abandonment of rigorous standards of academic achievement was caused by patterns of social migration during the latter part of the nineteenth century. Originally the most influential leaders in American education had been affiliated with elite private academies and universities. By the end of the 1890s, however, the rapidly expanding high-school population had greatly enlarged the numbers of less educated teachers and administrators. Perhaps perceiving that their personal and professional interests were not identical with those of university professors, the teachers formed their own organizations, founded special colleges to train new crops of teachers, and in time, largely by the power of sheer numbers, took control of the secondary-school establishment.

Their educational theories, formally stated in a series of official pronouncements by the National Education Association, were what might have been expected, given "the background of the people who wrote them," as FitzGerald puts it.

> The teachers in the common (or elementary) schools of the nineteenth century had always been poorly paid and minimally educated. And when the system of public secondary schools expanded, so, too, were the mass of new teachers. Toward the end of the century, those concerned with the curricula of the high schools began to adopt a utilitarian philosophy. Administrators and teachers put increasing faith in the notion that vocational training was the democratic alternative to the academic elitism of the European secondary schools. The idea that academic education might be made universal and therefore democratic had very little appeal—and not unnaturally since the high-school teachers would have been incapable of putting it into practice. The ideology of the teachers, however, merely reflected the fact that *the community at large had no interest in providing intellectual training for the mass of high-school students; its concern was to train skilled workers for industry.* (Italics supplied.)

At this stage of the development of her argument, FitzGerald provides especially important information. The defenders of the old order, which emphasized a more classical training, had, by chance, picked a particularly inappropriate moment to advance their cause. The 1890s were the years of a new flood of European immigration.

Although FitzGerald does not mention it, I believe it was not simply a matter of the arrival of millions of new Europeans *per se* that caused problems in the public schools. More important was the fact that the majority of the newcomers were peasants or people of poverty-stricken urban backgrounds. Not only did many of them and their children not know how to speak English—which would have been the case even if most of them had been well-to-do in their homelands—but their very poverty, ignorance, and illiteracy, even in their native languages, understandably led to a degree of chaos in the American schools to which they flocked. "Of necessity," FitzGerald observes, "the city schools became generalized social-welfare agencies, offering courses in English, home economics, and health care to adults as well as children. The educationalists thus had some reason to assume that the goal of education was health, vocational training, and citizenship training rather than academic studies."

It is easy to see how similar the schools' predicament in the 1890s was to the present situation in which large numbers of Mexicans, Puerto Ricans, Cubans, Africans, Asians, and others have taxed the resources of our northern school systems.

In the 1950s and 1960s there was a great migration of poorly educated blacks from mostly rural sections of the southern states, a movement that in its time put strains on northern schools in mostly urban areas. That particular migratory pattern, however, has been reversed during the 1980s, as almost 100,000 more blacks have traveled south than moved north, according to the census bureau. The reasons for this otherwise surprising reversal are not difficult to fathom. One is that living conditions in America's large northern cities have become much more difficult and unpleasant than they were. Another is that the racial tensions and animosities that made southern life miserable for so many black Americans in earlier days have now improved considerably. The Ku Klux Klan mentality, though it still exists, no longer has nearly the social dominance in the South that it had fifty years ago. Consequently, many blacks, having been disillusioned by the realities of life on the mean streets of New York, Philadelphia, Chicago, or Detroit, are heading back to the part of the country they still regard as a cultural home.

All social problems, of course, have roots in history. The idea of universal education is quite modern.

I want to make it particularly clear, however—to the point of risking repetition—that it would be a serious error to ascribe all of our present troubles to such factors as immigration and poverty. We would be relatively fortunate indeed if the situation were so simple, since, in that event, we would at least be able to narrow our target areas and concentrate our resources in particular ghettos and barrios. But the fact is that the middle-class—a good many of whom have had the benefit of elementary, high school, and college education—is also getting dumber.

In August 1976, the *Los Angeles Times,* in a four-month investigation into what it termed "the widespread erosion of academic standards within the American education system"—which had produced "declining achievement and rampant grade inflation among students"—traced the roots of the decline to a shift in social and educational values during the 1960s that led to a massive cut in the number of basic academic classes, less strenuous graduation requirements, and an overall emphasis on less demanding elective courses.

Other factors were:
- a rising emphasis on vocational education
- serious student absenteeism
- disagreement among educators as to the mission of education itself
- addiction to television, which undermines the desire to read
- changes in the structure of the American family, including a sharp rise in the number of working mothers.

Concluded the *Times:*

Collectively these trends served to undermine the rational and intellectual foundations of education, leading some to question the importance of formalized learning in institutions which themselves were confused about it.

The anguish of teachers themselves had become increasingly heard. Novelist-critic Francine Du Plessix Gray, who teaches at the City College of New York, wrote:

> There's so little continuity in our lives. We don't want to change the world anymore. We just want to teach one child to read properly, so that he can have something to hang onto, so that his center will hold.

And on March 19, 1978, the *Los Angeles Times* quoted Associate Commissioner of Education John H. Rodriguez:

> Teachers make a difference but we don't know what the difference is. We need to know that. We just can't go out and give advice when we don't know what it is that makes for success or failure.

Something was "destroying the atmosphere required to learn."

The rise in the number of single-parent households and the increase in violence, drug use, and alcoholism among the young were also among the causative factors.

Busing was not seen by the *Los Angeles Times* as a factor contributing to the decline in educational standards. According to the paper's study, the changes in school curricula were primarily responsible for the crumbling standards, falling test scores, and growing illiteracy. "It is the fundamental and massive shift from basic academic requirements to a vast array of electives which seems to be the most direct contributor to the achievement decline in both schools and colleges." According to the *Times,* in areas where curricula have changed the least—in science classes and in primary schools—performance has risen.

The major indicator of the massive decline in achievement is, of course, standardized achievement test scores. In 1964-65 and 1974-75, as math and English requirements were dropped or substantially weakened within higher education, student scores on the Graduate Record Examination (GRE)—aimed at assessing achievement levels of students prior to entrance into graduate schools—fell in those areas: Math scores dropped 25 points, English 18 points, during that ten-year period.

By contrast, in the natural sciences, where the least change in school curricula took place and where course requirements were most stringent, the *Los Angeles Times* study showed that scores on the GREs had risen. In biology, between 1965-66 and 1975-76 scores on the GREs increased by 14 points, while scores on the history subtest dropped nationally by 41 points.

There are, of course, some who would take issue with the *Times* study, finding questionable the use of achievement test scores as a measure of learning. There are also questions about the ability of the public schools, as now set up, to deal effectively with what is seen by many as primarily a problem of motivation. Perhaps the public school is neither capable of being, nor intended to be, parent, psychiatrist, sociologist, and medical doctor to the youth of America.

Observes Ashley Montagu:

> The United States has more educational institutions, more colleges and universities than the rest of the world put together, and practically no education whatsoever. What passes for education . . . is not education at all, but instruction—instruction in the 3 R's. You go to school, where you are instructed in the higher 3 R's—remedial arithmetic. You end up with those invidious distinctions, the degrees, which enable you to go out then and perform similar operations upon the delicate minds of other creatures.

Montagu reminds us that the root origin of the word *education* is *educere,* which means to care for, nourish, cause to grow. To educate, then, does not mean merely to inject with knowledge but to help to master the process of investigating what knowledge is for.

The architecture of the school day places stress on students. Classroom size—too small for lecture but too large for discussion—a class day consisting of constant interruptions, where a teacher rarely gives a child more than a couple of minutes of consistent time and discipline takes precedence over instruction, contributes to the pressures that impede real learning.

One writer speculates that individual attention to a particular student may average a mere six hours a year. Notice is usually given to the more vocal members of a class, so that perhaps two-thirds of the students, those who may need the most instruction, are largely ignored.

In such a situation, some failures are not surprising.

If, as Montagu suggests, the only true knowledge, the only true science, is "love, is goodness, is the ability to confer survival benefits in a creatively enlarging manner upon others," then reading, writing, and arithmetic are important, not as ends in themselves but as means. The failure in our schools, then, comes not only from an inability to read or do long division, but from the loss of awareness of the reasons these tools were once thought important. Back-to-basics must mean more than a return to academic structure; it needs to mean a reinvestment in nourishing those qualities in human nature that allow human beings an understanding of what it is to be human.

Similar trends can be found within secondary education; a decline in enrollment in strict academic courses has been most strongly felt in the basics—U.S. history and English fundamentals. Concludes the *Los Angeles Times:*

> Electives in and of themselves are not bad, of course. When used to supplement or enhance knowledge gained in a basic history or English course they provide for both a more sound and complete education than could otherwise be obtained.
>
> . . . But when they are used in a wholesale manner to replace basic courses, as they increasingly are . . . and are innovative in name but marginal in content, as many are in high school, then their worth at the very least is questionable. And it is this latter type of elective which has gained an unprecedented foothold in American education.

The elective came about, of course, not randomly as an out-of-the-blue experiment, but as a response to student unrest and boredom with the traditional curriculum; it provided a convenient way to lure disinterested young people back into the classroom. The social turmoil of the 1960s led the faculties of many schools to remove themselves from positions of authority because of the then-prevalent if absurd assumption that authority itself was questionable.

In today's classroom, according to the *Los Angeles Times,* there is a hesitancy on the part of the teacher to demand excellence, there is scarcely half the assigned homework of former times, and high grades are often bestowed upon students as rewards for whatever level of performance they achieve. Such factors further erode academic standards. Many students graduate from high school with a high grade-point average and proceed to college, where they promptly experience the shock of being placed in remedial instruction because they cannot read or write adequately.

Ronald Reagan's cuts in public monies for education—as governor and as president—came at the end of the general collapse and therefore did not cause it, though they led to further damage.

As I stated earlier, a depressing aspect of our list of society's serious problems is that so many of them, and perhaps all, have some sort of effect on the other listed items. It is obvious enough that for those living below the poverty level the possibilities of getting even a fair education, much less an adequate one, are minimal. We can see this, for example, in the recent recommendations for welfare reform, which are usually expressed in terms of "getting people off the welfare rolls and on to the payrolls."

Part of such programs is referred to as job-training. But, points out Andrew Hacker in his informative article "Getting Rough on the Poor" from the *New York Review of Books* of October 13, 1988, "as it turns out, much of the training has less to do with specific jobs than with basic literacy, and with such matters as dress and deportment, with knowing how to fill out forms or use an alarm clock."

To recapitulate, the recent weakening of American education and intelligence is part of a larger, depressing social picture, the general outlines of which are now all too familiar: the nihilism of such popular musical forms as punk or heavy-metal rock, the popularity of the most vapid television programs, the increasing number of failures of magazines and newspapers, rising rates of violent crimes of a particularly mindless or cruel sort, the irresponsibility of those who sell guns, drug dependence and the gang wars it causes, the rising indulgence in superstition and fanaticism, the staggering increases in white-collar crime and corruption, the rise of racism among the young, of which the "skinheads" are only one example, and so on. A case can be developed for the argument that, on some level below the conscious, we are, as a people, *choosing* to become dumber, and more insensitive because the world has come to seem too dangerous and complex. There is a growing sullen contempt for traditional values, rules of the game, and social standards, even among the wealthy and successful. There are hints of this, I think, in the ugly adolescent sneers seen in the photographs of punk rockers, the grating, pounding menace of the music, the pouting, almost sadistic stares of some high-fashion models, the menacing macho tones used in certain radio and television commercials.

As I observed in *Ripoff,* a study of white-collar crime in America, distorted values that have traditionally been associated with individual criminals and criminal subcultures are now characteristic of the American social ethic itself. Success, however achieved, is given enormous respect, talent and virtue very little. A lack of compassion for minorities, immigrants, the old, the poor, the destitute, the psychologically troubled, becomes ever more evident as those most guilty of it smilingly deny their insensitivity.

It is fascinating that, although our fundamentalist clergy of the Far Right campaigned passionately for conservative Ronald Reagan on the grounds that he would bring a higher moral tone to the White House, more than one hundred highly placed members of the Reagan administration resigned from office in one form of ethical disgrace or another, and there was a greatly increased emphasis on the get-rich-quick-by-whatever-means philosophy.

Dishonesty and corruption are now the norm; the worst crime is getting caught. Adam Smith, the founding father of capitalist philosophy, quite properly identified greed as the energy-source of the free enterprise economy, but Smith was wise and compassionate enough to recognize this as the heart of a moral dilemma for capitalist cultures. Would that his followers were equally wise and moral.

It's interesting that George Bush, when he came into office, said that he would like to become known as the "education president." Certainly Reagan, who was one of the least well informed presidents in our nation's history, could not have done this. American conservative intellectuals were well aware of Reagan's unbrightness, but for understandable reasons did not refer to it publicly since Reagan, in his capacity as an experienced radio announcer and film actor, was an extremely effective salesman for conservative programs.

But if Ronald Reagan and the general mind-set that he encouraged are to be added to the long list of causative factors of our present predicament, we nevertheless ought not to think that the problem is uniquely modern.

Although the present degree of popular American ignorance may be unprecedented, the underlying problem dates from the age of Plato, and may well go back to an even earlier time. The Greeks, in any event, understood that since citizenship was a high honor and a responsibility, it went without saying that one had to be prepared—which is to say *educated*—for it. Not every citizen has to be a philosopher, and obviously not every citizen is qualified to hold political office. But, by God, every citizen ought to know enough to vote intelligently.

As for reason, until recently we have not bothered to defend it because we assumed it had come to be more or less the norm, just as we have often failed to realize the precariousness of our freedom because we assumed it represented the natural state of affairs historically.

There is no ground for the latter assumption. Taking the long view of history, it is tyranny that has been the norm, and freedom the rare exception. Of the some 160 nations on Planet Earth at present, only a handful are real democracies. Civilization is a quite modern, and fragile, invention. Reason is central to it.

No one, of course, has ever recommended complete democracy as a means of conducting the affairs of a modern nation. Even in theory total democracy can function only in a small community, and in practice seems at best to be a qualified success even there. But the sensible alternative is certainly not a steady, even precipitous, erosion of popular competence to take part in democratic procedures. The American people are now running just such a risk, as ignorance about political philosophy and practice increases.

Conservatives, among others, speak repeatedly, and correctly, about the necessity to uphold intellectual standards. Yet in their two relatively recent opportunities to select presidential candidates, they have offered us men of modest intelligence, such as Barry Goldwater and Ronald Reagan. Let the conservative reader waste no time on the assumption that to so characterize these genial gentlemen is merely to express liberal bias. I repeat that almost every conservative intellectual in the country will concede the point, if not for personal attribution. Indeed, in 1982, one of the nation's best-known right-wing polemicists said derisively, at a small dinner party, "Do you know what our esteemed president has on his mind these days?"

"No," said a table companion, playing the conversational game, "what does he have on his mind?"

"Absolutely nothing," said the conservative leader, to the amusement of all present.

It would be fortunate for the country if all recent Democratic contenders for the presidency were noted for their intellect. Alas, they are not.

Incidentally, readers should by no means infer that, in writing such a book, I am presenting myself as a supremely reasonable authority, any more than they should assume that a clergyman who delivers a moral sermon is necessarily himself saintly. But I am, at least, sensitive to the irrational in my own thought and behavior, and feel uncomfortable about its all too frequent outbreak.

Most of us wince when we hear a musical tone that is too high or too low. Just so, such modest rational powers as we possess should make us wince when we hear blatant examples of unreason.

Inefficiency

The Collapse of American Efficiency

One of the first indicators of weakening intelligence in a people—as in an individual—is a marked decrease in efficiency. When the abilities to reason, to concentrate, to remember, to care, and to perform begin to deteriorate—for whatever reasons—it is obvious that one will less ably attend to personal or professional tasks. Accordingly, one of the first clues I had to the growing seriousness of the problem of dumbth was a sudden sharp erosion of efficiency in the world in which I move. Because of the circumstances of my life—activity in several professions, much travel, meeting large numbers of people—I am in a better position to note instances of this sort than the average individual might be. Early in the 1960s I began to notice that certain things were beginning to crumble a bit around the edges. It obviously didn't happen overnight, and no doubt it had been going on for some time before an accumulation of evidence brought the hypothesis to my conscious attention.

It can have escaped the attention of no observant person that, since at least as far back as the early 1960s, this gradual erosion has been taking place in every part of our nation. Services, attitudes, and degrees of competence once the norm, and hence taken for granted, have become increasingly rare. Indeed, it is now noteworthy when almost any complex social function is properly conducted.

Airlines

Any busy traveler could write a book of his own about examples of goofing by airlines. There have been problems of airplane dumbth going back perhaps as far as the Wright Brothers.

A few illustrative instances:

On Monday, October 15, 1973, I was scheduled to fly from New York to Cincinatti, on TWA flight 225, at 12:00 noon. Much to the discomfiture of the passengers, the flight was canceled because the airline had decided that inasmuch as there was a fuel shortage, that particular plane should not take off with a relatively small number of passengers.

TWA then scheduled us on an American Airlines flight later that day. After waiting around for several hours, passengers were advised that that flight, too, would not be taking off after all. The reason: "We cannot seem to locate the pilot and copilot."

On a TWA flight to Dayton, Ohio, on October 28, 1974, when dessert was being served, the stewardess said, "Would you like chocolate sauce or pineapple sauce on your ice cream?"

Since I have a slight allergy to chocolate, I requested the pineapple. Naturally the stewardess gave me chocolate.

I was lucky to be on the flight at all, however, because the young woman in charge of TWA's VIP waiting room, though she said she would advise us, had neglected to tell passengers that the 4:00 P.M. plane was boarding and leaving. I was sitting in the lounge at 4:05 P.M.—assuming departure time had been delayed—when a harried airline official came racing in to tell me and another passenger that the plane was about to pull away. He had to ask the loading-ramp attendant to unlock his door so we could get on the craft.

On a recent luxury-class airline flight, a young woman serving dinner wanted to know if, regarding a dinner-roll, I would prefer "plain or kirdwent." Unable to make any sense out of the second word I said, "I'm sorry; what was that second category again?"

"Kirdwent," she said.

"What does that mean?" I said.

"I don't know," she said, turning to another attendant for help.

It turned out that the roll in question had *currants* in it. The woman simply had not the slightest idea what the word meant.

Another instance:

November
Twenty-Fifth
1974

Miss Rosemary Aurichio
Customer Relations Manager
TWA
605 Third Avenue
New York, New York 10021

Dear Miss Aurichio:

I wrote to you a few months ago to point out that a door through which foot-traffic passes from your New York baggage pickup area directly to the sidewalk and street outside was out of order.

Not only did the "automatic" door not function properly but I observed that it swung back in toward the person using it so that he was given a sharp blow on the side of the right shoulder as he exited through the door.

When I arrived in New York this past Tuesday, November 19th, traveling on your flight that arrives at Kennedy Airport at 4:39 P.M., I observed that the door was either still or once again out-of-order. It is now, however, in considerably worse condition.

This is probably not TWA's direct responsibility. But since I do not know to what office of airport authority to communicate this information, and inasmuch, secondly, as it is only TWA passengers who are either inconvenienced, startled or injured by the out-of-order door, I am sure you will agree that it is to the best interest of TWA to do what it can to see that the necessary repairs are made.

Cordially,
Steve Allen

Although the subject is fraught with controversial overtones, the reality must nevertheless be faced that all over the planet the general intellectual level falls off as one moves from urban to rural areas. The slower pace of rural and village life, a requirement in such environments to concentrate on the simpler elements of life, a relative lack of educational opportunities, the tendency of the brighter rural individuals to move to larger communities—these and other factors account for the phenomenon. It is obvious enough that there are individuals who are exceptions to the rule, but the generality itself is commonly acknowledged.

There is also a general drop-off of efficiency and quick intelligence from big cities to smaller towns. In one western city of about 250,000, I arrived at the airport not long ago after a pleasant three-day working visit, turned two bags over to a porter, told him I was leaving on a United Airlines flight, showed him my United ticket, and followed him as he promptly took my bags to the *Republic* Airlines counter. He did not take them to the weigh-in scale, as is usually done, but simply stood with me at the end of a line of eight or nine people.

Acting on what proved to be the groundless assumption that he knew more about the matter at hand than I did, and knowing that there are instances in which one airline counter will service customers of another company, I asked, "Is this also a United counter?"

"Oh," he said, staring—apparently for the first time—at the enormous printing of the word "Republic" on the wall directly in front of him. He then pushed his luggage cart about twenty-five feet to the right, directly toward an equally large printed sign that read *Frontier* airlines.

I naturally did not follow him but stared in fascination, waiting to see how long it would take to have the word "Frontier" register on his internal computer. To his great credit, it took only about a minute and a half. By now, evidently feeling some slight embarrassment, he said, as he passed me, going to the left and—finally—in the direction of the clearly identified United counter: "They've been changing these counters around recently. We've got some—uh—construction or something going on."

This I took to be a simple lie, advanced in an attempt to avoid being perceived as guilty of a serious instance of dumbth.

The clerk behind the United counter, a pleasant, middle-aged man, quickly extracted my ticket from its paper folder and then said, "Smoking or nonsmoking?"

"Definitely *non*smoking," I said. "In fact, I have been told that aisle seat 1-C had been reserved, as of several weeks ago."

"Very good," he said, as he started to check my information by punching keys on the computer before him.

"Actually," I said, "it doesn't have to be seat C, specifically, as long as it's a *first row* seat on the aisle."

"All right, sir," he said, looking up pleasantly. "We have you in seat 8-A. Will that be acceptable?"

"I cannot answer that question," I said, "until you tell me at which row your smoking section starts, since my entire purpose in having reserved a seat in the *first* row was to get as far from cigarette smoke as possible."

"Smoking starts in Row 14," he said.

"Well," I said, "since you are suggesting that I sit in the eighth row, I assume that somehow there has been a mix-up as a result of which all the aisle seats in rows 1 through 7 have already been taken. Is that indeed the case?"

"No," he said. "There are plenty of seats available in the first seven rows."

"Then it is not clear to me," I said, "why you are attempting to put me in the *eighth* row when I have twice told you that not only (*a*) do I want to sit in the *first* row, but (*b*) I believe I have a *reservation* for the first row and (*c*) the reason for the specification of that factor is that I want to be far indeed from cigarette smoke."

"I'm sorry, sir," he said, still pleasant. "I'll be very glad to put you into the first row. Seat 1-A it is. All right?"

"No," I said. "It is certainly a good deal better than row 8, but it is not 'all right' because—if you'll forgive me for pointing this out— I have now three times attempted to make it clear that I prefer to sit on an aisle. The reason I prefer that is it relieves me of the inconvenience of having to climb over the feet and legs of others if I wish to stand up and move about."

"No problem at all, sir," he said. "I'll just put you down for row 1, seat C."

As I strolled toward the plane gate, I dictated this account of the two conversations.

The plane itself was—not at all to my surprise—about forty-five minutes late. This happened during early December 1981. All through that period—so far as I have been able to conclude from personal experience—almost every plane in the country was late because Ronald Reagan had dismissed almost all of the experienced, professional air-traffic controllers. Reaganites, perhaps, were generally pleased by this since it was an instance of a leader doing what is called "being firm." It harmonized well with the grim, tight-lipped set of Reagan's jaw characteristic of his expression immediately following his occasional angry, make-my-day pronouncements. So on the one hand we had an instance of some emotional satisfaction and a slight racing of the blood, and on the other hand the reality of the airplane fleets of the world's mightiest nation no longer being able to adhere to flight schedules, not to mention the greatly increased danger to millions of travelers.

On this subject, Harry Bolikoff, in a letter to the *New York Times* (May 1, 1982) said: "Last January, my grandson at Ithaca College called Empire Airlines, during a snowstorm, to find out whether his flight from Syracuse to New York City had been canceled. He was told that there was only a one-hour delay and therefore fought the storm to get to Syracuse for the flight—only to learn that *Syracuse and LaGuardia airports had been closed all day.*"

Adding dumbth to dumbth, Bolikoff reported, "When I complained of this misinformation to the [Civil Aeronautics Board], it replied: 'The Board is no longer involved in detailed regulation of airline services' and—instead of making 'sure' that [my letter] reached someone in the airlines . . . the CAB [would you believe it?] sent me a copy of an outdated *Guide to Air Travel* published in June, 1980." (Italics supplied.)

In early November 1977, at Washington, D.C.'s Dulles Airport, it took me twenty minutes to get through the security clearance gate. Once inside the passenger waiting area those who entered at that time discovered that their number greatly exceeded the number of seats. I cannot even imagine the justification for a then new, modern airport facility, in the most important capital in the world, keeping a large number of its passengers standing about, as if they were in some rural airport, before they could get on a plane. Indeed, come to think of it, I've never had to stand in rural airports. In those remote outposts there have always been sufficient chairs available.

When, a few minutes later, I decided to make a phone call, I had to try phones in four booths before I found one in working order.

In September 1983, six years later, I noted that the phones at Dulles were in an even worse state of disrepair.

Hotels

It would be fortunate if weary travelers, exhausted by airline inefficiency, could at least count on reliable service at hotels. American hotels were, in fact, once world-famous for their general level of efficiency. Sometime in the 1960s, it seems to me, things began to fall apart. A few examples from personal experience:

On one trip, Jayne and I stopped at the Mall Motor Hotel in Dayton, Ohio. Since both of us were exhausted, before retiring we left the customary "Do not disturb" instruction on our telephone line, "until further notice." Jayne had come in on an earlier plane and retired early. I got to the hotel close to 1:00 A.M. and fell asleep about 2:30. At 7:00 A.M. the phone rang, insistently. Thinking that there must be some sort of emergency I got out of bed and answered it.

"Good morning, sir," the cheerful operator said. "It's 7:00 A.M."

"Why are you telling me that?" I asked, half-asleep and honestly puzzled.

"Because you left a wake-up call, sir."

"I left no such call," I said. "Hang on a minute." Turning to Jayne, also awakened by the phone, I said, "Did you by any chance leave a wake-up call?"

"God no!" she said, justifiably disturbed. "I left a *do-not-disturb!*"

"Are you sure you have the right room?" I asked the operator.

"Yes," she said. "This is 1007, isn't it?"

"Yes," I said, "but neither my wife nor I left a wake-up call. Both of us, however, left damned important *do-not-disturb* instructions. I suggest you take up the matter with your manager before we do."

Later that morning the room-service breakfast order—again, not at all to our surprise—was not correctly delivered. I had asked for a *large* amount of jams, jellies, and marmalades, but got the usual two tiny plastic containers. Asked for half a grapefruit, but got grapefruit *juice*. Asked for extra hot water with the coffee, but got none.

When we sent the waiter back for the missing items we also told him to bring whole wheat toast. A moment later, when the telephone operator at the coffee shop called to reconfirm the order, we discussed the toast at some length. To be helpful, the woman brought the rest of the order up herself. She brought *no* toast.

At the Desert Inn Hotel in Las Vegas at six o'clock one evening, as I was having a snack in the coffee shop, I heard a page. "Telephone call for Mr. Steve Allen. Mr. Steve Allen, telephone, please."

I picked up a nearby phone. The conversation went as follows:

OPERATOR: Yes?

S.A.: This is Mr. Allen.

OPERATOR: Yes?

S.A.: I say, this is Mr. Allen. I was just paged.

OPERATOR: Yes, sir. What is your *name?*

S.A.: The very same name I've given you twice within the last ten seconds—Allen.

OPERATOR: *Steve* Allen?

S.A.: Yes.

OPERATOR: All right, Mr. Allen. Just a moment.

SECOND OPERATOR: It's six o'clock, Mr. Allen.

S.A.: I don't doubt that for a moment, since it confirms the information available from my own wristwatch, but why are you telling me this?

SECOND OPERATOR: Well, you left a wake-up call for 6:00 P.M., sir.

S.A.: I don't too often sleep in the coffee shop, and in any event, I did not leave a wake-up call.

SECOND OPERATOR: I have a message that you *did*, sir.

S.A.: Despite the reality of that message, the call was almost certainly from *Mrs.* Allen, who at this moment is upstairs in our room, asleep, and would probably appreciate being awakened.

SECOND OPERATOR: Well, we rang the room and nobody answered.

S.A.: I suggest you ring again.

In 1975, at the swank Arizona resort Mountain Shadows, Jayne and I, having arrived exhausted, retired about one o'clock in the morning, and—again—left a *do-not-disturb* call on the phone line, giving the clearest possible instructions that we wanted to receive *no* calls except long-distance emergencies until 11:30 in the morning. At 10:00 A.M. the phone rang. It was the manager himself, cheerfully "welcoming" us to his establishment.

At a comfortable hotel-motel lodge in the civilized city of St. Louis not long ago, I was surprised to be asked, "What *is* marmalade?" after requesting that the confection be served with my breakfast toast. The person who posed the question was a pleasant young man who did not appear to be retarded.

Not long ago, at a hotel in Orlando, Florida, I encountered another individual who had never heard of marmalade. The relevant part of our conversation went as follows:

S.A.: . . . And to go with the toast I'll have a large supply of marmalade.

ROOM SERVICE: Of what?

S.A.: Marmalade.

ROOM SERVICE: Omelade?

Since the young woman had evidently never before heard the word, she was apparently attempting to relate it to the word *omelette,* with which she would naturally be familiar.

S.A.: No. The word is spelled m-a-r-m-a-l-a-d-e. It's made of ground-up oranges and sugar. Now that we've established that, do you have any?

ROOM SERVICE: I don't know. (*Calling to someone else*) We got any omelade?

VOICE: Any what?

ROOM SERVICE: Man wants omelade for his toast.

VOICE: Oh, marmalade? No.

I ran into yet another instance of this specific sort not long ago at an attractive and well-run hotel in Nashville, Tennessee. A request that marmalade, rather than the conventional jellies and jams, be served with the breakfast toast seemed to produce instant consternation.
"You said what?"
"I said I'd like marmalade and not the other jams and jellies."

"Wait just a minute, sir."

At that point I could hear the young man checking with another source. A moment later he said, "Okay, we do have the marmanade."

"Fine," I said, figuring that unless there turned out to be some obscure substance called *marmanade,* of which I personally had never heard, I was likely to get what I wanted. "And I'd like skim milk, not regular milk, served with the meal."

"Okay," he said cheerfully, "that's *skin* milk. And do you also want skin milk with the second oatmeal?"

Again, rather than correct him, I told him that yes, I did.

On the evening of November 18, 1978, I checked into the Capital Hilton Hotel in Washington, D.C. A representative of the organization on whose behalf I was visiting the city had assured me that a message would be left at the hotel explaining certain details of my local schedule. After the necessary preliminaries had been attended to at the reception counter, I said, "I believe there's a message here for me."

"I'll check, sir," a young man behind the desk said. A moment later he reported that there was no message.

Since I was aware that the efficiency-level in American hotels had fallen sharply, the thought of making an experiment occurred to me. After having been shown to my room, I used an outside line to call the hotel itself. When an operator answered, I said, "I'm calling a Mr. Steve Allen, who is a guest at your hotel."

The operator absented herself briefly, after which she said, "I'm sorry, sir. We have no Steve Allen registered."

"May I speak to your supervisor?" I asked. In a moment another woman said, "May I help you, sir?"

"Yes," I said, "I would like to speak to a Mr. Steve Allen—the television entertainer—who is registered in your hotel."

"Just a moment, sir. I'll check."

In less than thirty seconds she was back on the line. "I'm sorry, sir. There is no Mr. Steve Allen registered here."

"I see," I said. "May I then speak to the manager of your hotel?"

The next voice I heard was that of the manager. "Yes, sir, can I help you?"

"I'm sure you can," I said. "I have just placed a call here to the Capital Hilton to speak to a Steve Allen, and both your operator and your telephone supervisor, after presumably checking through normal channels, have absolutely assured me that no one named Steve Allen is registered at your hotel."

"Yes, sir, and what is the problem?"

"The problem," I said, "is that there *is* a Steve Allen who is not only registered in your hotel but whose reservations were confirmed some *ten days ago*. I, in fact, am Steve Allen and am calling you from my room. We need waste no more time, therefore, on the question of whether there is a Steve Allen registered here. What we should discuss now is how we can stop your operators from telling people who call for me that I am not here when, in fact, I am here."

"I see, sir. You're absolutely right. I'll check into the situation immediately."

"Thank you," I said.

"And I apologize for the inconvenience, sir."

"That's all right. It's not your fault personally. But I thought there might be a problem when I was told, at your reception desk, that there were no messages for me."

"Oh? And what is the problem there?"

"I have reason to believe that extremely important messages *have* been left for me. Or at least that people have called here attempting to leave them. Of course the reason there may be no messages is that those who called and tried to leave them were probably told that no one named Steve Allen was registered. They may well have been told that I was not even expected."

The punchline of the story is that when, three days later, I checked *out* of the hotel I was handed the message that I had assumed was waiting on my arrival. The date and time marked on the piece of paper showed clearly that the message had come in before my arrival.

A friend, author Cleveland Amory, recently told me the story of an acquaintance of his who stayed at what is actually one of the country's better establishments, the Beverly Hills Hotel, and one afternoon looked through the room service menu to see what he might order. The Russian sandwich struck his fancy. As the reader may know, this is a sandwich that usually includes turkey, cheese, and sliced ham. The gentleman asked to have the Russian sandwich "without cheese." It was delivered as requested, but the bill for it read as follows: "Russian sandwich, $9.95. No cheese, $3.00."

Hollywood Reporter columnist George Christy has told the story of a film writer and his female companion who were pistol-whipped and bloodied in a famous luxury hotel—"the bed and the carpet were pools of blood"—when criminals broke in by posing as room-service waiters. Because the attack happened on a weekend night, neither manager of the hotel was available. According to the staff, they could not be disturbed! "When the screenwriter asked to be driven to a hospital, the hotel staff suggested calling a cab, rather than drive him and his friend to an emergency room. And when the managers finally did hear about it, they offered to deduct a night's lodging from the tab. The screenwriter is filing suit for 2 million."

The application of even a modest amount of reason could have made such a lawsuit highly unlikely.

The collapse of efficiency in the city of New York—once vaunted for its know-how and expertise—has become notorious. As a Manhattan socialite recently put it: "In hotels that used to be world-famous for their efficiency—the Plaza, the St. Regis, and a few others—the service now ranges from fair to deplorable. You're constantly being plagued by mistakes. You make a reservation for a dining room and when you show up, they have no record of your name. The main reason for this terrible state of affairs, I think, is that many of the good old hotels have been bought by hotel chains. That means that top management is no longer on the premises to insist on efficiency, to fire those who are inefficient, and to maintain staff discipline."

While in New York not long ago, my wife stopped into the swank Ritz Tower apartment building where, she had been told, an interior decorator named Levee was occupying the apartment of Mr. and Mrs. Norman Lear. A concierge explained that unfortunately Mrs. Levee was not in residence. When Jayne asked if she could be put on a telephone line to the apartment, the woman said that the Lears' daughter was using the phone at the moment. Jayne later found that Mrs. Levee and *her* daughter—*not* the Lears—were not only using the apartment but had been present for several days.

Then there was the adventure of the French toast in one of Tennessee's more interesting hotels, at the Chattanooga Choo-Choo Station. Reporting to the dining room one morning, I decided to order the French toast referred to in the menu.

Since I do not eat white bread, I said, "Oh, one small detail. Would you please tell the chef to make the French toast with *whole wheat* bread?"

"Certainly, sir." A few minutes later I was served three pieces of fried white bread with—so far as close inspection could attest—not the slightest trace of egg.

Since French toast is made by simply dipping bread into an egg-and-milk batter before frying it, I assumed that only some momentary carelessness had delivered the tasteless pieces of eggless starch to my table.

Having, with some difficulty, attracted the attention of a waitress, I said, "I'm sorry to trouble you, but something seems to have gone wrong with the French toast. Could you just ask the chef to give me *regular* French toast, of the sort that has been popular in this country now for over half a century?"

"Very well, sir," said the cheerful young woman.

A few minutes later I was served three warm pieces of fried white bread—not whole wheat—somewhat darker brown in color, but again, with not a speck of egg. I checked this very carefully by eating a piece. The inside was standard rather dry junk-food bread.

At that point I decided that the explanation of the difficulty might be that the young man with the tall white hat visible in the cooking area was new on the job and had never actually made French toast before. Acting on this hypothesis I strolled over to him and in a pleasant voice said, "Say, I hope you won't mind, but it's occurred to me that you might not have had much experience in preparing French toast. Might I therefore suggest that all you have to do is crack an egg, whip it just for a moment with a fork, add a little milk, and then soak three pieces of whole wheat bread in the mix?"

The young fellow took this advice with more than a touch of surliness, but at least had the good grace to follow my instructions. French toast of the proper sort was finally served, although I was now half an hour behind a busy morning schedule.

Perhaps I should not have been surprised, because the day before, when I had checked into this establishment, I had taken three shirts to the front desk myself to make absolutely sure that all hands clearly understood I was entering the shirts into the hotel's laundry-handling process on the "one-day service" arrangement. To a pleasant young man at the counter I said: "I must stress—so that there will be no possible misunderstanding on the point—that the shirts absolutely must be delivered back to me tomorrow *morning*. There are two reasons for this. First of all, I have to wear one of the shirts tomorrow and, secondly, I am leaving town tomorrow afternoon."

"Very good, sir," the young man said. "I'll take care of that myself."

The shirts did not reach me until three weeks later, by long distance mail.

The late comedian-parodist Allan Sherman once checked into the Sheraton-Rochester Hotel and a short while later was being interviewed by two journalists and a television cameraman when a bellhop came to pick up his laundry.

Sherman interrupted the interview and said to the bellman, "I must have this back tomorrow because I'm leaving town."

"Yes, sir!" the bellman answered. "No problem."

The next day Sherman sent an aide to get the laundry. The man returned shortly with the original bag of dirty laundry. "When I had said, 'I must have this back by tomorrow,' " Sherman later recounted, "the bellhop had taken it literally. The hotel figured I gave it to them for safe-keeping, so they kept my dirty laundry and returned it safely."

Next, a word-for-word transcript of a conversation that took place recently when I spent a night at a good hotel in a Pennsylvania city. Having arrived very late, dog-tired from work and travel, I left a no-calls order, "till 12:00 noon." At 10:00 A.M. the next morning, I was awakened by a call, which I refused. An hour later, this exchange took place:

OPERATOR: Mr. Meadows?

S.A.: What?

OPERATOR: Er—Mr. Allen?

S.A.: Yes.

OPERATOR: We have a message for you, sir, from a gentleman at Station WOMT in Wheeling, West Virginia.

S.A.: Before you give me that message, may I ask why I am getting any message at all since I left a do-not-disturb on this line last night?

OPERATOR: Oh, I'm sorry, sir. I just came on duty and we didn't have any word to that effect down here.

S.A.: Would you take the matter up with whoever it was that forgot to leave that important message, since this is the second call I've received this morning?

OPERATOR: Yes, I will, sir.

S.A.: Very well. Since I'm already awake, I'll accept your message now.

OPERATOR: All right. (*She hangs up.*)

S.A.: (*Calling back*) Is this the young lady I spoke to a moment ago?

OPERATOR: Yes, it is.

S.A.: You may recall my saying, I will *accept* your message now.

OPERATOR: Yes. (*Very long pause.*)

S.A.: Very well, what *is* the message?

OPERATOR: Oh. It's just that somebody called you from a Wheeling, West Virginia, radio station.

One part of the explanation of such incidents is that many of today's hotel employees appear to be able to absorb information only in the sequence in which they are trained to receive it.

For the past forty years or so, when giving information to room service, housekeeping, a front desk, or a bellman's station, I have *first* given the number of my room. For over three decades this presented no problem whatever, but in recent years an increasing number of such conversations conclude with the employee saying something like, "Very well, sir, and now—what is the number of your room?"

Performing at a hotel in a California city on December 31, 1981, I had made arrangements to have dinner served in my suite at 6:30 so that I could take a nap when the meal was concluded and be in good shape for the New Year's Eve performance, which was scheduled to start at 10:00 P.M.

As it happened, however, the afternoon's music rehearsal ran much later than I had expected. At 4:30 I decided to change the time of my dinner—which had been set several days earlier—to 7:00 P.M., thus allowing thirty minutes more for relaxing before dinner.

The following conversation took place when I attempted to make this simple change in the evening's plans.

OPERATOR: Room service.

S.A.: Hello, this is Steve Allen in room 326. I'd like to leave a message with someone there about the time my dinner is to be served this evening.

OPERATOR: I'm sorry, sir. Room service is closed right now.

S.A.: That's quite all right, since I don't want to have anything served at the moment. I simply want to leave a message *for* the folks in room service.

OPERATOR: Could you hold on a minute? (*Long pause*) Now, you wanted to place a breakfast order?

S.A.: No. I have said nothing about breakfast. I'm trying to change the time at which my *dinner* will be served—by Room Service—*this evening.*

OPERATOR: I see. And what is the message you want to leave?

S.A.: Simply that the time should be changed from 6:30 to 7:00.

OPERATOR: Just a moment, sir. (*Incredibly long pause*) Now, then— you're leaving a breakfast order for 7:00 in the morning?

S.A.: No. I think perhaps we should not use the word *breakfast* any more. May I explain? About a week ago it was arranged—with the management of this hotel—that I would have *dinner* served in my room, *this evening,* at 6:30. I am simply trying to change that plan by thirty minutes. I wish to have dinner served at 7:00 P.M.—half an hour *later.*

OPERATOR: Just a moment, sir. (*Sound of discussion with others in the operator's area, during which the word "breakfast" could occasionally be clearly distinguished.*) All right, sir. No breakfast. You just want to have your dinner served at 7:00 tonight?

S.A.: That is correct.

The dinner arrived at 6:45, on the dot.

Perhaps the most unusual instance of hotel-operator dumbth was this brief exchange, which occurred in September 1981.

OPERATOR: We have a message for you to call Celia Black at (number).

JAYNE: I'm sorry; what was that name again?

OPERATOR: They didn't leave a name.

All busy travelers have such stories to tell. One of the officials at a recent American Hardware Dealers' convention told me that, after having left do-not-disturb-under-any-circumstances instructions, he had been awakened at the ungodly hour of 5:45 A.M. that morning by a hotel employee who said that a member of the convention group had just charged a continental breakfast—totaling $3.95—to the executive's account. The employee wanted to know if the transaction was authorized.

Other Services

The collapse of efficiency is not, of course, limited to the nation's airlines and hotels.

One of the first areas in which the deterioration impressed itself upon me was that of limousine service. I never hire limousines myself but am frequently provided with them by employers. If a prominent entertainer—Bob Hope, let's say—goes to Cleveland to do a concert performance, he does not get off the airplane, go out to the sidewalk, and try his luck at the taxi-stand. A limousine is reserved for his use, presumably a week or so before he arrives. And so it is with most people of prominence. But early in the 1960s I began to notice that goof-ups on the part of limousine companies were becoming more common. In many cases the limousine simply wouldn't show up. There was always an excuse, of course. The man had a flat. There was an error in scheduling. "The car we expected to use didn't come back from the garage when promised," and so on. But before this stage the limousines had always shown up, and on time.

The situation finally became so unmistakably clear that my secretaries began to incorporate reference to it in letters and memos going to various employers, simply by way of alerting them to the possibility that their local limousine contact might not be as dependable as it had been some years earlier. This led, on one visit to Chicago, to a tragic–comic incident. As I walked through the airport, after getting off the plane, I suddenly saw running toward me a distracted young woman, breathless and almost in tears.

"Mr. Allen," she said, "I'll be waiting for you out front because I parked out there in a no-parking area. You were absolutely right about the limousines."

"I'm sorry," I said. "I don't quite follow you."

"Well, your secretary wrote last week telling us that we ought to double-check on limousine service for you. And, sure enough, when I called this morning to make certain the limousine would arrive on time, they told me they didn't have any record of my placing the order and that all their cars were already out. So, rather than calling another limousine service, and maybe running into the same sort of problem, I decided to pick you up myself, so that there wouldn't be any slip-up."

"That's very nice of you," I said.

"But," she cut in, "I couldn't get my own car started this morning. The battery was dead and by the time the Auto Club came and charged it up I was forty-five minutes late in getting here. Thank God I got here in time to see you, but I didn't have time to put my car in the parking lot so I'm illegally parked out there. The policeman told me not to park but I told him I was picking you up and he said he didn't care and—"

"Well," I said, "don't worry. Why don't you just go back out to your car and wait there? I'll get someone to bring my baggage out as soon as it's available."

When, about twenty minutes later, I met the woman on the sidewalk she was in an even more agitated state.

"My God," she wailed. "They hauled my car away and I have to go to some other part of town to get it back."

"That's terrible," I said. "Well, listen, don't worry about us. We can take a cab."

When—about thirty-five minutes later—I finally had collected all of my luggage and arranged to have it deposited on the sidewalk, along with my wife's luggage (Jayne had arrived at about the same time, on another plane), a taxi dispatcher flagged a cab for us. The driver jumped out and began putting our bags into both the front and back seat compartments rather than in the trunk.

Since not only Jayne and I, but also the young woman who had met us, were to be seated in the back, I said to the driver, "Chief, I think we have some kind of a problem here. As you see, we have a lot of luggage and it seems to me that you're not going to be able to fit all the bags in the interior of your cab, at least if we three human beings try to get in at the same time."

"Yeah," he said, "I guess you're right."

"May I ask then why you don't do what cab drivers have been doing for the last forty years or so?"

"What's that?" he asked.

"Put the luggage in the compartment that the manufacturer has provided specifically for that purpose."

"I'm sorry," he said, "I don't put no luggage in the back."

"You don't?" I said.

"No," he said.

Since I saw no way that I could force the man to do something that was perhaps against his religious principles, or explained by the presence of a Mafia rub-out victim in the trunk, Jayne, our welcomer, and I simply climbed into the back seat and let the fellow wrestle with the problem, which took him quite a few more minutes. We made the trip to downtown Chicago in very cramped space, since two large bags had been placed in front of us on the floor. One smaller one was on my lap.

Sometimes institutions pay an immediate price for inefficiency. In May 1983, the debut of the *Star Wars* sequel, *Return of the Jedi,* nearly became a sequel to *The Wild Bunch* when moviegoers threatened to riot in a packed National City, California, theater because a film reel was omitted, interrupting a chase scene. Two No. 2 reels and no No. 4 reel had been delivered. Each of the 70-millimeter reels provides about twenty minutes of screen time.

"I've been with this company thirty-five years," the manager said, "and never have I seen anything like this, and I hope I never will again."

If I'm any judge, he will.

And with increasing frequency.

A few more random beauts:

The November 1979 edition of *Learning* magazine revealed that the words *minimum, remediation,* and *explicit* were misspelled in the printed text of a bill approved by the New Jersey Senate. The purpose of the bill: *to deny high school diplomas to those who cannot pass writing-proficiency tests.*

In October of 1979 the Federal Reserve acknowledged a $3.7 billion error in estimating the nation's basic money supply. Before a week had passed, the Fed discovered another error, of $800 million. The mistakes were blamed on faulty reporting by Manufacturers Hanover Trust of New York.

In 1979 I wrote a book on the subject of China. The publisher, a prominent old-line house, simply *lost* a box of color slides—the best I had taken in China—intended for inclusion in the book. Later they lost my only copy of a colored poster brought back from the mainland, also meant to be included. We had to settle for the use of more than one-hundred pictures in the "second-best" category.

Speaking of the Orient—in Los Angeles not long ago, I agreed to narrate a film about China for a local museum. When I reported for duty, I learned that the cue-cards commonly available for such narrations had not even been thought of. Over an hour of everyone's time was lost on this detail.

When I got to the section of the museum set aside for the video-taping, I immediately perceived that, because the area was relatively dark, the bright flood-lights necessary to enable the camera to take any sort of picture would close down the iris of the human eye to an extent that would make it impossible to read the cue-cards unless they were independently lighted.

The same production unit that had neglected these, among other standard details, had also made arrangements to tape the audio portions of my narration at another location in the building but had not thought to have anyone on hand to run the audio-taping equipment.

Lastly, I noticed that the signs installed to describe the most important displays of priceless Chinese antique objects were situated exactly nine inches off the ground. Since the print was extremely small, it was impossible to read these descriptions without either kneeling, squatting, or bending very low.

(This last factor, by the way—small print and odd placement—is now common. I have written to the presiding officer of two of the nation's leading museums to point out the problem.)

In exploring the question further, I discovered another reason it was extremely difficult to read explanatory captions in the Los Angeles museum. Some of the cards were printed with white print on a very pale background.

In the great world capital of New York City, one hears more and more complaints from people who cannot get a simple phone number from the telephone company's information department, when some of the numbers sought have been listed for years.

During the summer of 1981, I had the pleasure of meeting an unusually bright young man in his early twenties. He was educated and trained in what I will describe only as a somewhat unusual scientific discipline. The subject of my PBS network television series "Meeting of Minds" came up. This is a program on which all of the guests are actors and actresses portraying important personages from history. While making a number of complimentary remarks the young fellow said that he had particularly enjoyed the program with "Madame Chiang Kai-Shek." The woman who had, in fact, been represented as a guest on the program in question was not the wife of the Nationalist leader of China in the 1940s, but Tz'u-hsi, that nation's long-dead Manchu dowager empress. To state a rough equivalent in the American context, it would be as if someone had watched a program in which Dolly Madison was interviewed and later told me that he had enjoyed the program with Eleanor Roosevelt. And I am saddened when I think of the dozens who had seen either one or both of the "Meeting of Minds" programs on which Attila the Hun was interviewed and later complimented me on my exciting discussion with Genghis Khan.

Then there was a letter I received from a man in Memphis, Texas. He had a suggestion as to a suitable guest for "Meeting of Minds." (Again, all the program's guests are important personages from history being played by professional actors and actresses. Among those who have been interviewed are Aristotle, Plato, Socrates, Darwin, Martin Luther, St. Thomas Aquinas, Sir Thomas More, Karl Marx, Galileo, Cleopatra, Marie Antoinette, Susan B. Anthony, Leonardo Da Vinci, and Francis Bacon.)

My Texas correspondent wrote a three-page neatly-typed message arguing that Mary Tyler Moore would make a fine guest. He did not mean as an actress to play the role of some illustrious personage. He meant that she should appear as herself.

It is not, alas, only viewers of television who think rather flakily. Every production office, too, has internal horror stories to tell.

Several years ago I did a series of national radio programs for the B. Dalton bookstore chain. The programs, titled "Hooked on Books," consisted of two ingredients: (*a*) reviews and comments about books, and (*b*) interviews with authors. About a year after the show went off the air, it occurred to me that so large a body of recorded material could be reconstituted and remarketed. When I instructed members of my staff to count the number of tapes, I was shortly informed that they could not be counted because they could not be located. Nor did anyone connected with the B. Dalton company or the original recording studio have any idea what had happened to the tapes. The entire series had been lost.

A friend with whom I not long ago discussed the growing incidence of dumbth told me a story about the secretary of an advertising woman. The executive's father phoned her office one day. "She is not here right now," the secretary said, "but I'll tell her you called. What is your name, sir?"

"I'm her *father*," the man explained again.

"Yes, sir, but I would like to have your name."

The man gave the woman his name.

"How do you spell that?" the secretary asked.

"The spelling doesn't matter," the man said. "I'm her father. She *knows* how to spell my name."

The absurd conversation actually continued at some length.

A proprietor of a live-poultry shop in Washington, D.C., recently told a National Public Radio interviewer that one of his customers, who had purchased three chickens, called him back to complain that there were only six legs in the package. The woman honestly believed that chickens had four legs.

In early February of 1989, I entertained an audience of more than one hundred of America's leading corporate executives and university presidents. The purpose of this convention was to explore ways to improve education, to increase efficiency, and to encourage critical thinking.

The first bit of information the group's associate director gave me was that, in addition to my formal performance, I was invited to attend a black-tie dinner the evening before. When I presented myself at the dinner, the first thing I noticed was that I was the only man present wearing formal attire.

The second nugget of information concerned the starting time of the dinner. I was told that a cocktail reception would begin at 6:30 (I have no idea whether it did since I do not enjoy cocktail parties) and that the dinner service was scheduled to commence at 7:30.

Accordingly, a few minutes after 7:30 I walked into the dining room to find it absolutely deserted except for a sizable symphony orchestra already in position and waiting for its audience. When I raised the question of the starting time with the dining room's maitre d', he told me that the event was scheduled for 8:00. All-in-all, it was not a very auspicious start for a convention at which efficiency was to be stressed.

For the past thirty years or so, in my various comedy-and-music performances, there is a simple comedy prop I've used, always to good effect. The relevant instructions, which are sent to my employers, read as follows. "There should be, on a small table downstage of Mr. Allen's piano, a transparent glass or plastic pitcher full of orange juice and, next to the pitcher, two drinking glasses, each covered by *paper envelopes* of the sort commonly used in hotels in recent decades." Twenty or more years ago I literally never encountered any problem about this, no doubt because of the very fact of its simplicity. How, the reader might wonder, can anybody past the age of seven possibly fail to understand such an instruction? Well, as of five or six years ago, stage managers and production assistants in some of the nation's leading concert halls and hotel ballrooms began to misunderstand them.

The situation has continued to worsen so that at present the task is almost never done right, without a good deal of discussion and clarification during the rehearsal period. Even then, after personal meetings and shared rereadings of the memos, I often still walk on stage to find that the detail has been improperly attended to. If the reader still is in doubt as to how anything so simple can get so loused up, I will here specify some ways in which errors have been made:

1. The pitcher is sometimes metal and therefore not transparent, which naturally prevents the audience from seeing that it contains orange juice.

2. Sometimes there are no glasses, sometimes one, sometimes five or six.

3. Frequently the glasses are not covered by anything whatever.

4. They are sometimes covered with transparent plastic.

5. They are sometimes covered with those little circular cardboard covers that simply touch the top of the glass and do not cover the rest of it at all.

There are, alas, other instructions connected with my concert performances that aren't followed either, but I select this one as an example because of its utter simplicity.

I am not, needless to say, alone in my perception that people in general are not as bright as they used to be. Chuck Ross, a Los Angeles writer, in 1979 sent a manuscript of Jerzy Kosinski's novel *Steps,* with the author's name changed, to fourteen publishers, all of whom turned it down, including Random House, which had published the book several years earlier. Emboldened by this triumph, Ross in 1982 made 217 copies of the original screenplay of the classic film *Casablanca,* starring Humphrey Bogart and Ingrid Bergman. Ross made only two minor changes in the script. The title he changed to "Everybody Comes to Rick's," and the name of the piano playing character called Sam ("Play it again, Sam") was changed. Of 217 agents to whom the script was submitted, 184 rejected it, giving no indication that they had recognized it. Some sent it back with such comments as "The subject matter, World War II and all that—you're talking big budget." An agent named Allan Nicolette commented, "Too wordy." Another alleged expert, Ross reports, wrote: "Not very interesting. Make something happen." So far as Ross could tell, only 33 out of the 217 agents recognized the script, though eight others thought it seemed somehow familiar.

In mid-August 1983, Army Chief of Staff General John Wickham, Jr., publicly blamed private industry for producing weapons and other military equipment constructed partly of faulty materials and with careless workmanship. "There are some things I can get emotional about," Wickham said, "and quality control is one of them. The Department of Defense could save billions if we could have better quality assurance."

Among the problems Wickham drew public attention to was that the electronic weaponry of the Patriot ground-to-air missile had failed so often that the Army had temporarily decided to stop testing it. The Copperhead guided artillery projectile, too, did not live up to expectations. The Pershing II missile had failed in five of its sixteen practice firings. Wickham said that every one of the misfires resulted from quality-control problems.

The foregoing should not be viewed as merely a collection of accounts of isolated incidents mostly peculiar to my experience. No, I have discovered that whenever the subject comes up in conversation, others are prepared to deluge me with similar stories. Again, inefficiency—once rare—has become the norm. What is startling now is when things go as planned.

In addition to individual instances of inefficiency and dumbth there are examples of mass-dumbth. Consider:

Let's say that tomorrow night Dan Rather, Tom Brokaw, and Peter Jennings announce on their separate newscasts that the Surgeon General's office has just released the shocking information that bananas have been identified, beyond any doubt, as among the leading causes of cancer. Included in the announcement is the statistic that eating bananas is already responsible for approximately 340,000 deaths in the United States annually.

What do you suppose would be the effect of such news on the banana market? Obviously prices would tumble and the millions of bananas now in grocery markets and warehouses would turn black and rot since almost no one would be willing to eat them.

The entire process, mind you, would result from simple common sense on the part of those who had heard the news. Even though such an announcement would include the point that it was quite possible to eat bananas without getting cancer, nevertheless few would knowingly run such a risk.

But now turn from fantasy to reality. Substitute cigarettes for bananas. What do we see? That millions of intelligent Americans have indeed given up smoking and millions more are making the attempt, most of them repeatedly. But what can one say about the additional category of millions who are perfectly aware of the dangers to health, are not yet addicted to cigarette smoking, and yet—in the face of mountains of documented evidence about the harmfulness of cigarettes— simply decide to smoke anyway?

A number of people with whom I have discussed the general message of this book have suggested that cigarette smoking is not only properly included in a list of instances of dumbth, but should be considered a classic case of it. The attribution of dumbth is fair in some cases and unfair in others.

A British study discovered that children born to women who smoked ten or more cigarettes a day were later three to five months behind their peers in reading and math.

While it is obviously unfortunate that anyone on earth smokes tobacco, it is nevertheless the case that those who began smoking years ago or those who have somehow, in the modern day, contrived not to acquire relevant information about the physical dangers of smoking are guilty only of ignorance in this connection. But any person even fairly well informed about the medical realities at present who nevertheless proceeds to develop a habit of smoking may indeed properly be charged with dumbth in the extreme.

Another relevant factor establishing dumbth is that so much is risked for so little gained. If it were to be discovered, let's say, that sexual intercourse itself causes some severe disease, there is little doubt that the majority of the human race would still run the risk for the quite simple reason that the degree of pleasure afforded by the act is quite pronounced. The same, unfortunately, is true of such narcotics as heroin and cocaine, which have their strongest effects on the brain's pleasure-centers. People recognize that the pleasures are powerful and immediately available and therefore simply close their minds to the ultimate risks. In the case of cigarette smoking, however, the pleasure is available only at an extremely low level, a fact that nonsmokers may easily grasp by comparing it to the physical and psychological reactions induced by drinking a cup of coffee. It is the relation, then, between (1) the serious risk of hideously painful and deadly diseases on the one hand and (2) an extremely modest degree of pleasure on the other that justifies the accusation of stupidity on the part of those who are perfectly aware of the physical risks, but still decide to start smoking.

It is not possible to draw sharp lines of demarcation between dumbth and stupidity. A large component of ignorance, simply inadequate factual knowledge, will always be a part of dumbth. In the case of stupidity—of which we are all, of course, occasionally guilty—ignorance is often irrelevant. Consider, for example, the Great American Seat Belt Problem. Most motorists are well aware—even if they have the precise figures only hazily in mind—that the annual toll of serious injury and death from highway and street accidents—something over 56,000—could easily be cut in half if drivers and passengers would take just a few seconds to fasten seat belts. Despite the constant repetition of this information in countless radio and television announcements, newspaper and magazine editorials, speeches and pamphlets, and, even though there has been legislation on the matter, still only one in three adults uses a seatbelt most of the time.

Dumbth

If dumbth were merely annoying, it would still be a serious enough national problem. But it is much more than annoying. The essential dumbness of racial prejudice and hatred, for example, is also socially destructive and dangerous. It may be perfectly reasonable to despise an individual black, Jew, Catholic, conservative, Rotarian, brain surgeon, or circus clown. The individual may have committed a crime of which you are the victim. If a Lithuanian raped my wife, I would certainly feel strong animosity against that particular Lithuanian. But to use that incident as rationalization for hating Lithuanians as a class is the height of stupidity. Precisely such stupidity, nevertheless, is common.

Recently a middle-aged New York couple—WASPs, wealthy, and eminently civilized—made inquiries about the possibility of joining an exclusive Connecticut country club. They were invited for cocktails to the home of one of the local social powers. While making small-talk about events in the news, the New Yorkers were surprised to hear their hostess suddenly say, "Well, look what the Jews did in Beirut, killing all those Palestinians."

"The killing was done by Christian Falangist soldiers," the man from New York said.

"Well," the Connecticut woman said, "you can't trust the Jews anyway. They just always get in on what other people do and they have no real talent themselves."

This struck the man from New York as an assertion of such stupefying idiocy that for a moment he was speechless. "What about Albert Einstein?" he finally said.

"Oh, he was left-handed," the Connecticut woman answered, in all seriousness.

"What?"

"Left-handed Jews don't count. They're okay."

One of the tragic aspects of this problem is that it is partly caused by survival defense mechanisms built into us by millions of years of evolutionary experience. Man obviously must eat to survive. Over the course of eons, he has eaten a great many things, some of which were poisonous or distasteful. Since experience is an effective teacher, man learned to be wary of foods that caused him harm. Even today, if an individual is made sick by contaminated shellfish, a spoonful of mayonnaise, a pork sausage, or whatever, he may become so negatively conditioned to the offending food that he will never be willing to eat it again, even in the repeated presence of clear evidence that those about him are eating the same food with no harm and even with great relish. Mark Twain once observed that a cat that had accidentally sat down on a hot stove-lid would not only never again sit on a hot stove-lid, but would be unlikely ever to sit on a cold stove-lid either.

Such a protective response may be involved with the formation of the mindless hatreds that to the present moment in history have led to much social injustice and bloodshed. But I believe that if in childhood we were *taught to demand evidence for our beliefs before accepting them,* we would be protected, at least to a great degree, from such stupid and harmful behavior patterns.

There is a very real sense in which the history of mankind is the history of human stupidity. As Paul Tabori states in *The Natural Science of Stupidity:*

> Stupidity is man's deadliest weapon, his most devastating epidemic, his costliest luxury. . . . It is not just a sweeping simplification to say that the various forms of stupidity have cost mankind more than any war, plague or revolution.

Tabori documents with wit and detail some highlights in the history of dumbth. It was common practice for more than four centuries, for example, to put animals on trial as though they were human and, if they were found guilty after due process of law, to torture, hang, burn, or pillory them. Sometimes the offending beast might be let off with a stern warning. On other occasions, animals were actually tortured until they confessed—and confess they did, by shrieking in pain. To ensure legality a clerk appointed by the court was on hand to record the assorted squeals and brays as confessions. The entire legal proceedings were conducted exactly as though the beast were human, at exactly the same cost as well. There is a record of an executioner who came all the way from Paris to carry out the court-ordered execution of a pig—and was reimbursed at the same rate as for the killing of a human criminal.

In another case, after a trial lasting more than a year, the field mice in a small German town were legally evicted from the fields around the town for damaging the crops. If the sentence sounds unfair, bear in mind that the rights of the accused had been fully protected. An attorney was appointed by the court to represent the defendants throughout the trial.

Less amusing were the medical practices of the day. God help the injured or ill in a relatively enlightened age like the seventeenth century. Almost any ailment might be treated by bleeding—opening up the veins of the sick person and draining out the "bad blood" thought to cause the sickness. If bleeding failed one might be treated to some of the scientific medicines of the period. I emphasize that these treatments were not folk cures or old-wives'-tale remedies, but represented the wisdom of the accepted medical practice of the day. The physician spared no effort to get rare and often costly ingredients for his potions and poultices. Some of the more common included moss scraped from a human skull— but it had to be the skull of a man killed by hanging or in battle— gold or rare gems, dragon's blood, the ashes of burnt earthworms, grease from assorted (but always specific) animals, and the dung of dogs, mice, pigeons, elks, bulls, griffins, ants, and so forth.

One might have been fortunate enough to have a physician who followed the "sympathetic theory" and treated the object causing the injury rather than the suffering patient. Not surprisingly, more patients recovered after this "sympathetic therapy" than did those receiving the benefit of medicine.

One might think that as science progressed, wisdom necessarily accumulated. Wrong! Though better informed, we face the same basic problems today as did our seventeenth-century ancestors. The major change is that the stakes are dramatically higher; gross ignorance and incompetence today can cause millions of deaths rather than merely hundreds.

Dumbth is not a side-issue in today's problem-bedeviled world. Lamenting the extent of it is not an elitist preoccupation. Dumbth may be the single greatest problem facing our society today. Certainly it is close to the root of every other social dilemma: racial tensions, nuclear proliferation, environmental pollution, corruption and stupidity in high office, poverty and hunger—each is complicated by the simple inability to see and understand clearly what is at issue and to act accordingly, with basic rationality.

Dumbth is responsible for uncountable deaths, every day, all over the planet. Airline mechanics use the wrong kind of de-icing fluid and a plane crashes—or perhaps the pilot reads his instruments incorrectly. These and other cases are not simply misjudgment, nor are they mistakes resulting from ignorance. Most are instances of aggressive ignorance combined with the at least temporary inability to think properly.

As in the case of the seventeenth-century physicians, dumbth is far from being the exclusive property of the unwashed masses. It's a problem we all share: doctors, lawyers, political leaders, scientists, educators, and nuclear engineers alike.

Consider, for a moment, nuclear engineers.

Regardless of your feelings on the issue, you will agree that a nuclear power plant must first be safe, on some very basic level, before it is put into operation. Unless we can be reasonably certain that it will not blow up, fall apart in an earthquake, or leak radioactivity into the surrounding area, we should not allow it to begin operating. Otherwise we are risking millions of lives. But as the history of such plants suggests, sometimes we cannot be sure of these things.

According to the *Los Angeles Times* of June 2, 1979, "*A wrong assumption* about the water level at Three Mile Island was a major factor in the March 28 accident . . ." (Italics supplied.)

How much worse might have been the accident at California's San Onofre nuclear facility, where in November 1977 it was discovered that a 420-ton reactor vessel *had been installed backwards?* After several such incidents, the plant was closed down.

Then, of course, there was the mid-October 1983 discovery by the *Los Angeles Times* that the use of illegal drugs—including marijuana and cocaine—was widespread among craftsmen who built, maintained, and helped repair the three reactors at the San Onofre plant. Information provided by seventeen current and former plant employees, reported Daniel Weintraub and Robert Montmayor of the *Times,* "describe a working atmosphere at the nuclear plant that sharply contradicted the image of efficiency and security normally projected by the plant's operator, Southern California Edison Company."

In late June 1989, after owners of the Seabrook, New Hampshire, nuclear plant had ignored the advice of the Nuclear Regulatory Commission and the New Hampshire attorney general to close the facility, the owners of the installation fired the vice-president in charge of plant operations because of "inappropriate management actions" connected with the way in which the shutdown was conducted.

As regards complications caused by earthquakes: Although the engineers assure us that the plants are safe up to such-and-such a point on the Richter scale, can we trust their figures? Consider a few other examples of modern American engineering:

1. The town of Niobrara, Nebraska, has been plagued by flooding for most of its recorded history. In 1957 the Army Corps of Engineers built a dam to relieve the problem. Unfortunately they built it in the wrong place, and the flooding got worse. The entire town had to be moved, at a cost to the government of some $15 million.

2. A forty-year-old dam in Toccoa, Georgia, burst in 1977, killing at least thirty-eight people and injuring forty-five others. Although there had been reports of leaks for some time, the dam had never been inspected.

3. In Hartford, Connecticut, in 1978, the roof of the Civic Center

collapsed when nine inches of snow—not an uncommon amount in that part of the country—piled up. A "design error" had resulted in inadequate bracing.

4. In Scranton, Pennsylvania, a bridge collapsed, injuring several motorists. One week earlier the bridge had been inspected and pronounced safe.

5. In Norristown, Pennsylvania, a few years ago, it was discovered that someone had mislabeled two pipes in a hospital's operating room, one of which read "oxygen," the other "nitrous oxide." At least five people died as a result of the error. Four years earlier a similar mistake in a hospital in a city in Ontario, Canada, cost fourteen lives.

A special prize for engineering inefficiency goes to the U.S. Army's M-1 tank, an enormously expensive weapon. Then-senator Gary Hart reported in the *New York Times Magazine* of February 14, 1982, that the tank "has to stop for repairs every forty-three miles; the engine eats up so much fuel that it gets only one mile for every 3.86 gallons; the troops often cannot even operate, much less maintain, the computer; and the armor is ineffective against shells fired by enemy tanks."

Then there is the Viper, a light-weight rocket designed as an anti-tank weapon for American infantrymen. When the weapon was proposed in 1976, the cost was estimated to be $78 per unit. By 1982 the price had risen to $787. Moreover, the weapon turned out to be ineffective against Soviet tanks. The Army nevertheless committed itself to purchase 649,100 Vipers! According to an Office of Management and Budget official, quoted by the *Knight-Ridder* newspapers, the Viper "is peanuts in terms of the whole 90 billion dollar procurement budget. . . . The system itself is no more of a turkey than about fifteen others I could mention."

Another splendid example of military dumbth was offered by Russell Warren Howe, in the April 29, 1978, issue of *Saturday Review*. The fact that weapons and equipment of contributing nations are not standardized is costing NATO about $15 billion every year, besides doubling the time it would take to mobilize and deploy. Said Howe, "The research and development subcommittee of the Senate Armed Services Committee estimates that 'NATO loses 30 to 40 percent of its effectiveness because of inadequate standardization.' "

Consider the problem in the context of an attack by Soviet troops—all with standardized and therefore interchangeable weapons and munitions—and you begin to get an idea of the seriousness of the problem.

There are approximately two thousand full-fledged, card-carrying members of the Flat Earth Society who, in the face of overwhelming evidence to the contrary, devoutly maintain that our planet is not a globe but a disc.

A classic instance of dumbth compounding dumbth occurred in Michigan in 1973, when several thousand pounds of the powerful chemical PBB were accidentally mixed into dairy-cattle feed. Not long after, farm animals across the state of Michigan developed strangely shaped hooves, thick, ugly skin, sores that would not heal, and breeding difficulties. Michigan farm people who ate their own produce complained of pain, diminished sex drive, memory lapses, and severe fatigue. The State Health Department ascribed the symptoms to "situational stress."

It took almost a year for officials to recognize what had happened, by which time PBB had permeated Michigan's food chain. In time millions of cows, hogs, sheep, chickens, and other animals had to be killed. Hundreds of farms were placed under quarantine. Despite the fact that this was the worst man-made agricultural disaster in United States history, state officials repeatedly issued optimistic comments about the situation.

In April 1982 the *Journal of the American Medical Association* published a report revealing that approximately 97 percent of Michigan's 9.2 million residents were contaminated by the cancer-causing chemical.

According to the January 1982 issue of *Esquire*, five senior citizens in Spokane, Washington, had their teeth removed in order to get dentures under a state-funded program. After the teeth were pulled, they were told that there had been a budget cut and that no more money was available for dentures.

The General Services Administration a few years ago bought 115 electronic flagpoles. The poles, at $10,000 each, were intended to relieve government employees of the time-consuming tedium of raising and lowering the flag by hand. The problem? The poles worked too well; the photo-electric cell that raised the flag at dawn and lowered it at dusk also lowered it every time a cloud obscured the sun.

Several years ago, the Department of Health, Education, and Welfare hired a private consultant, Rockwell International, to find out how many private consultants HEW had in its employ. From an original price tag of $378,147 Rockwell's contract had reached a cost of $2,200,000.

A few years ago, Marin County, California, was suffering a terrible drought. Water had been rationed for months, citizens restricted their showers, used paper plates, etc. Further, climatologists were predicting yet more drought.

In the middle of the water shortage, the Marin County Supervisors voted to build a 600,000-gallon Olympic-sized swimming pool. They did not announce where they planned to get the water or, conversely, what good an empty pool would be.

In Bluebell, Pennsylvania, Montgomery County Community College, citing a "lack of demonstrated interest," decided early in 1982 to shut down its Library Science program and replace it with a training course in the use of lethal weapons.

While filming a television show at a New York hospital recently, I happened to hear the common word *stethoscope*. I wondered about the Greek origin of the word, so I asked a medical attendant what the word *stetho* meant. She promised to have the information shortly. Thirty minutes later she returned and said, "It means *chest*."

"Of course," I said. "I should have known."

"But," she said, "I had to call three nurses and three doctors before I could find anybody who knew what the word meant."

By mid-1985, millions of young people had literally given up on education, though naturally for a wide variety of reasons. In California, on any given day, approximately one-third of those who should have been in school were on the streets, some temporarily, others permanently.

In July of 1984, a woman with an important position in television said, during a conversation with my wife, who had just made a critical reference to communism, "I've often wondered just what communism is. What do people mean when they talk about communism?" The question was not rhetorical; the woman actually did not know, and this in the latter part of a century in which the challenge of Marxism is one of the most serious questions ever to confront humankind.

A few days later Jayne was explaining, to another group of television employees, that she had recently worked in a motion picture directed and produced by filmmakers from Finland.

"What does Finland mean, actually?" a woman said.

"Do you mean where is it?" Jayne said, puzzled by the question.

"No," the woman said, "*what* is it?"

As everyone who sends or receives mail will attest, an entirely separate study could be done on the deterioration of postal services in the United States. A young vocalist named Meredith d'Ambrosio said in a July 17, 1984, letter that she had not received a package of albums and tapes I had sent her. "It is typical of the mail service to lose things," she said. "So far, in the past four years, twenty-five albums I sent out to people were never delivered. I wonder where they do go, because not one was ever returned to me."

Bill Herz, the magician, overheard two young teenagers talking on the street in New York City. One said to the other, "Did you know that Paul McCartney was in a band before *Wings?*"

Jayne and I recently sent a congratulatory mailgram to Tova (Mrs. Ernest) Borgnine. Although the message was checked and rechecked for accuracy, since it was telephoned, it arrived as follows:

Dear Tova,

No one is more deserving of the Grace Award from the Los Angeles Girl *Scott* Council. You are certainly the most graceful Girl *Scott* we know. (Italics supplied.)

Evidently the simple word *scout* was not in the typist's vocabulary.

A twenty-seven-year-old Los Angeles disc jockey once visited the home of a proprietor of a lighting-fixture shop in the same city. The electrician, an aficionado of big band and jazz music generally, proudly showed the radio man a wall of his den devoted to a display of album covers personally autographed by music-world luminaries.

"And this one, of course," he said, "is from Benny."

"Benny who?" the disc jockey said.

I will spare the reader the rest of the conversation.

The disc jockey had literally never heard of Benny Goodman, one of the major popular-music figures of this century.

"I was appalled," the shop owner told me. "The young fellow talks about today's music but has no idea of its roots."

On New York's Second Avenue there is a stationery store in which the word "stationery" is spelled "stationary" on the front of the store in permanent lettering.

Even individuals who are ordinarily of superior intelligence are sometimes guilty of dumbth. Conservative polemicist George Will, for example, in attacking the generally conservative Supreme Court for some of its 1985 rulings concerning the American principle of separation of church and state, correctly specified that the phrase "wall of separation" comes not from the Constitution but from one of Thomas Jefferson's letters. So far, Mr. Will had not been guilty of an affront to sound thinking. In his next sentence, alas, he was. "The justices would rather construe Jefferson's correspondence than the Constitution." The statement is first of all factually incorrect. Secondly, it is an instance of the mind-reading fallacy. The simple inclusion of the word *perhaps* would have avoided the error.

Steve Harvey, staff-writer for the *Los Angeles Times,* reported in mid-February 1983 that another *Times* reporter had made a $12 cash purchase in a Radio Shack store.

"Can I see your driver's license?" asked the young clerk.

"But I paid you in cash."

"I know, but I have to see your driver's license," the clerk said.

The reporter pointed to Alexander Hamilton's face on the $10 bill and explained that there is a difference between cash and checks.

"I know, but it's the boss's orders," the clerk replied.

The reporter proceeded to ask for an audience with the boss.

It turned out that the young clerk had misconstrued instructions for obtaining customers' addresses for the store's mailing list.

At least two recent issues of *Sports Illustrated* magazine have had entire sections missing. Explanation? Somebody goofed at the printing plant.

A college student of my acquaintance not long ago took a telephone message for me from a gentleman calling from the world-famous metropolis of St. Louis, Missouri. She informed me, by hand-written note, that the call came from *San Luis.* The young woman is not herself a Latino.

In March 1983, one of the most important organized crime trials in U.S. history was under way in the notoriously crime-ridden city of Chicago. For the reader not particularly knowledgeable about the issue, Chicago is a city where organized crime not only exists, but has exerted enormous political influence for more than half a century. Nevertheless, U.S. District Judge Prentice H. Marshall, who presided over the trial, publicly announced that he was ignorant on the subject. "My one and only exposure to organized crime," His Honor stated for the public record, "was to watch Marlon Brando in *The Godfather.*"

In November 1988 the *Los Angeles Times* reported that 57 percent of the police officers working at the 172 Veterans Administration hospitals had criminal records, lacked adequate experience, or left previous jobs under a cloud, according to an internal audit. The VA inspector general's office reported that most agency medical centers and clinics had not performed proper background checks on police applicants before hiring them. Ten percent of the 1,742 VA police officers had previously been arrested for such crimes as murder, rape, armed robbery, assault, and embezzlement, and were convicted on related charges, the audit found. Dozens more were convicted of crimes after they began working at VA hospitals.

A telephone receptionist for a New York publishing company, responding to a request to speak to an executive, said, "He don't work here no more."

Not long ago I entertained at a National Association of Broadcasters' convention in Dallas. As is usually the case when I am in another city for any one primary purpose, I agreed to kill a number of other birds with the same stone. In that connection I was told that interviews had been arranged for me at Dallas radio stations.

My typed instructions for the date in question started out with the phrase, "Taxi or walk to the Communications Center." Since no address for the Center was given I assumed—strikingly incorrectly, as it turned out—that it was some sort of Dallas landmark comparable, for instance, to the Empire State Building or the Golden Gate Bridge, and that every local resident would be familiar with its location. As it happens, however, when I sought information about it at one of Dallas's best new hotels, the Anatole, I discovered that neither the concierge nor the doorman had any idea where it was. They had, in fact, never heard of a Communications Center. The foreign-accented cab driver I next consulted could hardly repeat the name of the place and had no idea what I was talking about. A consultation in the lobby of the hotel at last produced the address of the Center and I was taken there.

It is within the realm of possibility to walk from the Anatole Hotel to the Communications Center. For that matter it is possible to walk from Los Angeles to Cleveland. But in both cases one would be walking for a very long time.

The next phrase in my instructions was simply "KERA," the name of a Dallas television station. I was instructed to ask there for a Mr. Scott Carrico. Needless to say, neither of the two charming and efficient women behind the reception desk at the Communications Center had ever heard of him, nor should they have since he had no connection with the Center.

"Is this the location of KERA?" I asked.

"No, it isn't," they explained. "That would be Channel 13, which is at another location."

I was finally able to reach Mr. Carrico by telephone to explain that I was at the wrong place because I had been given erroneous information. Mr. Carrico himself, as it turned out, had no idea of the location of the Communications Center.

Coincidentally, while I was dictating these notes in a second cab while en route to Channel 13, I happened to hear, on the driver's radio hook-up, the voice of the cab company's dispatcher, a woman with a vaguely rural accent so thick as to approach incomprehensibility. She was handling a request for information about the location of something that was either the "Century" or "Sentry" building. It was not possible to tell which word she was attempting to communicate.

None of her drivers was able to help her.

A factor connected to the confusion emerged when I finally arrived at KERA. A small building in which the station is housed is identified as the *Rogers Communications Center.*

In 1983, sixteen doctors out of every one hundred were hit with malpractice suits. How many others had been professionally inept but not perceived as such, there is perhaps no way to determine, partly because most sick people recover from most illnesses anyway, whether a doctor does anything specifically helpful to them or not. What is significant about this, in the context of my larger argument, is that the number of malpractice suits has risen sharply in recent years. Some part of this may be attributable to the combined greed and dishonesty of certain patients and their lawyers, but the dominant reason may be that the number of mistakes by doctors is increasing.

One of the nation's leading jazz critics, in a column published in the *Los Angeles Times,* wrote that singer Tony Bennett "could care less." This particular error is now encountered at least as often as the correct "couldn't care less."

Here's a classic instance of dumbth, infamous in television circles:
   An NBC television official in charge of the network's film-storage facility in New Jersey noticed, one day in the late 1950s, that he was running short of shelf space. His "solution" to the problem was a cultural atrocity that almost ranks with the destruction by angry Christians of the ancient library at Alexandria. He actually burned almost everything he could get his hands on. Films from the early days of television—including its truly Golden Age of comedy and drama, whose films are now recognized as invaluable social documentation—this executive burned them right and left until wiser heads found out what he was doing and put a stop to it. Among the lost items were my three and a half years of the "Tonight" show.
   There are a few of those nights I might have consigned to the flames myself. But scores of now-famous individuals had made their professional debuts or early appearances on that series. Important writers,

political figures, artists, and other celebrities had been guests. Among the programs destroyed was a delightful show in which poet Carl Sandburg was the only guest. He told little-known stories about Abraham Lincoln, discussed his own life, told jokes, played the ukelele, and sang.

Also burned were newscasts showing presidents, statesmen, popes, kings, prime ministers, and other important world figures who made news in that decade.

Every employer with whom I have ever discussed this general problem has his or her own horror stories to tell. Bob Hope, the richest man in show business and one, therefore, able to afford the best office help, had one secretary who solved the problem of backlogged mail by putting a stack of correspondence into a cabinet, where it was not found until two years later. In the pile were letters from President Ford and Governor Nelson Rockefeller, among other important individuals.

There is no shortage of such evidence in my own production company. One of the most important kinescope films in my files was that of the second program of my 1950s NBC comedy series on which Elvis Presley, Andy Griffith, and Imogene Coca appeared as guests. This was before Presley appeared on the Ed Sullivan show. One of my employees loaned the film out, neglected to make a written record of the transaction, and then "just forgot" where it had been sent. It had cost more than $100,000 to produce the show. Needless to say, it could not be recreated at any price.

In another instance, a record album was taped of the score I had composed for a musical written by the late Rod Serling and me. Someone in my office simply lost half of it, thus rendering the other half almost valueless.

Ellis Weiner, in the September 1988 issue of *Spy,* tells of a conversation with an ABC television development executive in which Weiner explained that he was working on a novel that would, if all went well, be funny. "Oh," the network official actually said. "I thought novels were supposed to be serious."

In the same column Weiner describes appearing on a television charades-type game show with a successful television writer who had recently been working as story editor on the situation comedy "One

Day at a Time." The pair failed to agree on the book title Weiner had been trying to transmit. After their time ran out, Weiner gave the title, which was *Tristram Shandy,* Laurence Sterne's classic novel. Said the television editor, in all seriousness, "What's that?"

Not long ago I was in conversation with an otherwise seemingly bright young woman, active in social and political affairs in Los Angeles. When she asked my wife what kind of lectures she had recently been doing we explained that she discussed the lives of important women in history and referred, in that connection, to the famous birth-control advocate Margaret Sanger. The young woman had literally never heard of Sanger.

As inured as I am to instances of the sort here related, I was nevertheless startled not long ago by a conversation I had with a woman who was at the time employed as my personal secretary. She was, in many ways, a bright, quick-minded type, a college graduate, and professionally ambitious. It was those very factors, in fact, which led to my astonishment when seated at my desk one day I began to wonder whether a message I had earlier dictated for Sylvia Fine Kaye, widow of the comedian Danny Kaye, had been relayed. Sylvia had invited me to attend a special ceremony at the United Nations honoring her late husband, who had devoted years to working for the children of the world through the UNICEF project. The first thing I do when I receive an invitation is to check my appointment book to see if the date in question is already blocked out by some other obligation.

In this case it developed that I could not attend the U.N. commemorative services for Danny because on that date I would be working in Los Angeles. But because I couldn't recall whether I had shared this information with Sylvia, I mentioned the matter to my secretary.

"Did you explain to Mrs. Kaye that I won't be able to accept her kind invitation?"

"No," she said. "I didn't."

"That *is* a date on which I'll be working in Los Angeles, isn't it?"

"Yes," the young woman said, "but I thought you could also go to the event honoring Mr. Kaye because it's taking place in the middle of the day."

At that point I again assumed that I was in error and that the original letter might have referred to an event which, though sponsored by the United Nations, was nevertheless taking place in California rather than New York. But when I asked to see the letter and reread it, I saw that it was absolutely clear that the ceremonies were taking place "at the United Nations."

"Well," I said, somewhat puzzled, "when you knew that I was working in L.A. on that date, but that the ceremonies in honor of Mr. Kaye would be taking place at the U.N., didn't you—"

"I didn't know what to tell Mrs. Kaye," she interrupted, "because I don't know where the U.N. is."

Since not knowing where, in the geographical sense, the U.N. is located is like not knowing where the Empire State Building, the Eiffel Tower, or the White House are, I thought for just a moment that the young woman might be joking. She was not. But an even more startling surprise awaited me.

"Oh, I see," I said. "You had never heard that the headquarters of the United Nations is located in New York?"

"No," she said. "I don't know what the United Nations *is*."

"You never heard of it?"

"That's right," she said.

At that point, so as not to further embarrass the woman, I simply gave up on the conversation. To this day I do not understand how it is possible for a generally bright, college-educated young American never to have even heard of one of the most important institutions in human history and one, moreover, that is almost daily referred to on radio and television newscasts and in newspapers, magazines, and books.

My wife reported to me not long ago a conversation she had with a young college student who had recently become engaged. Knowing from the young woman's constant references to religion that she was a fundamentalist Christian, Jayne said, "What religion your fiancé?"

"Catholic," the young woman said, and then added, "Let's see, Catholics are Protestants, aren't they?"

Jayne spent the next several minutes providing the young student with a capsule history of the record of Christianity over the past two thousand years, including references to Martin Luther and other

Protestant reformers. At one point it occurred to her to say, "Do you know what the word *Protestant* means?"

"No, not really," the young woman said, although she was a regular churchgoer and a frequent Bible-reader.

"It's related to the word *protest,*" Jayne explained.

"Is that right?" the young woman said. It developed that she had indeed assumed that Catholics were simply members of one of the hundreds of Protestant sects.

When, in 1956, the motion picture *Moby Dick,* based on the literary classic by Herman Melville, was released, studio publicists announced that the "title role" was being played by actor Gregory Peck. Perhaps they thought that the word "moby" was some sort of obscure adjective.

A recent popular joke following one of the international Olympic athletic competitions went as follows. "Did you hear all those foreign athletes on the Olympics telecast recently? They spoke English so poorly they sounded like American athletes."

Humor often points the way to truth and this witticism, sad to say, assuredly does. One aspect of the general collapse of what was once considered simple diction in American speech is that we have slipped back at least as far as the 1920s so far as the American ability to correctly pronounce the sound of a simple "t" plus "h" combination is concerned, as in such words as *the, there,* and *this.* During my childhood in the 1920s and 1930s, I occasionally encountered people, some with foreign accents, who had trouble with the "th" combination, as a result of which they pronounced such words as *de, dere,* or *dis.*

America's urban blacks practically never mispronounced such words, although poorly educated blacks from rural communities in the South did. In show business during that period, on radio programs, and in plays or films, when a character was supposed to be tough and of the lower economic classes, he was deliberately given, in scripts, such mispronunciations as a way of establishing his ignorance of standard American English. Then during the forties and fifties there was much improvement so that relatively few people had difficulty with the "th" combination. Things on this line remained relatively constant during the 1960s. But at some time during the 1970s the standards began to slip back, so much so that even on television one frequently encounters the earlier mangling of the words. One prominent sportscaster, for example, is occasionally guilty of doing this.

I recently met a young woman—bright enough, personable—who was apparently so habituated to the utterly unnecessary use of the word *like* that she appeared almost unable to complete a sentence without using it at least once. She spoke as follows:

"Well, like, I mean, uh, I sometimes ride like the bus, you know? And like it freaks me out because like every other person, uh, uh, on the bus is, uh, like crazy, uh, or whatever. Like it freaks me out just because I think like, wow, are these people really like crazy or what? Like I think they may be carrying a knife and be like really dangerous, you know? Like I mean what kind of a way is that to live? Like it's the worst."

Although there is some amusement—involving the laughter of superiority, I suppose—in contemplating such language-mangling, there is a tragically serious aspect to the matter. Apparently it has never occurred to the young woman that her speaking mannerisms alone will make it almost impossible for her to secure certain kinds of employment. Many corporations, or even relatively small businesses, simply will not hire individuals who speak in this Valley Girl teenage goofola manner. This particular use of the word *like* of course, comes from jazz-musicians' lingo of the 1930s and 1940s and reached the present young generation by being incorporated into the hippie culture of the 1960s. But I've never met a jazz musician who overused the word in the way that many of today's young people do. There was a legitimate use of the word at its point of origin; employed sparingly it adds a certain loose color and interest to conversation. But this is to be sharply distinguished from the apparently compulsive and mindless degree to which the word is now employed. If you were an officer of a bank or a real estate agent, would you hire someone who would address a potential customer by saying: "Like, wow, you wanna take out a loan at this like bank? Like, hey, that's neat. I'll go see if Mr. Simpkins can like come out and like talk to you about that, okay?"

Conversation at Newark Airport:

S.A.: (*Approaching limousine desk*) Do limousine drivers meet arriving passengers here?

DISPATCHER: Yes. Where do you want to go?

S.A.: I'm looking for a driver to take me to Brickman's Hotel.

DISPATCHER: What hotel?

S.A.: Brickman's.

DISPATCHER: Ah, yes, that's in midtown Manhattan.

Thank God I knew where the hotel was or my informant could have sent me to a destination some 125 miles wide of the mark.

I've discovered that invariably, when the subject of creeping inefficiency comes up at social gatherings, guests vie for attention to exchange horror stories. New York journalist Jane Wollman recently told me one so sadly typical that I asked her to give me a typed account of it.

> Last February, my optometrist prescribed stronger reading glasses for me. I had an extra pair of frames, so all the lab had to do was make up the new lenses and insert them in the frames. So far, the glasses have been returned to the lab nine times because the lenses do not fit correctly within the frames. The lens bevel extends outside the frame, obscuring my vision.
>
> The optician in my optometrist's office says the problem is not that the prescription is too strong or that the frames are wrong for the prescription; it is simply poor workmanship. In some instances, one lens fits properly and the other doesn't. Obviously, if they can do one right, they can do the other right, too.
>
> Six weeks ago I spent time with my optometrist going over the problem. He said he would personally instruct the optician to direct the lab to be sure to put the bevel inside the frame. Six weeks passed and I received no word. A few days after writing

to the doctor about the situation, I received a call that my glasses were ready. When I went to get them, I was told that they had been returned to the lab "a few times" within this six-week period, but were still unacceptable. . . . This time, I sat in the optometrist's office and wrote out exactly what had to be done: "Hold the glasses with the temples toward you. Note that the lower bevel of the left lens extends beyond the frame. See that the lower bevel of the right lens fits perfectly within the frame. This is the way the left lens should fit, too," etc., etc.

My optometrist says, "Today they have machinelike people doing this job, whereas in previous years a craftsman performed such work and cared about what he was doing." The optician says, "The lab probably thinks it's doing the job correctly."

A bright young professional woman of my acquaintance wholeheartedly agreed with the thesis of this book when I discussed it with her recently. "More and more," she said, "I'm finding that people have a very strange attitude about their jobs and it's something I hadn't noticed until recent years. They seem to feel that the basic reason they receive their salary checks is because they are physically present on the job the required number of hours. The idea that the check is given to them because of the *work* they do doesn't even seem to occur to them. They feel no guilt at all about the high number of mistakes they make, and no matter how badly they foul up certain details of their work—in some instances costing their employers large amounts of money—they feel that that has no relevance at all to the work situation and they are still perfectly entitled to the payments they receive."

The point of such observation is not that employees should be penalized, say $4.00 every time they made a mistake, although in some sort of Utopian context it would be an interesting experiment to make. The point is rather that the conscious wish to do a good job seems not nearly so common in the workplace as it once was.

An often unappreciated but dismaying aspect of the larger problem has been perceived by one of our wiser social critics, Gene Lees. In his *Jazzletter* of June 1984, in commenting on the brilliant song lyrics of Dave Frishberg, Lees observed:

The art of the lyric has fallen on sad times. Just how sad is seen in the fact that the music department of Oberlin College offers a course on the songs of the Beatles. It does not offer courses on Kern, Gershwin, Arlen, Youmans, Schwartz, Dietz, Harburg, Porter, or Mercer. And indeed, if some of the deciding powers there are in their forties, it is possible that they have never even heard of these people. We have been hearing for some time the lament that our young are uneducated—so long, indeed, that we have begun to realize that the uneducated young have moved up into positions of authority, not only in government and journalism but in the sacred halls of academe. In other words, a great many of our educators are themselves uneducated.

Another factor in the decline of American intelligence may be that, increasingly, women who speak little or no English are caring for babies and young children—full-time. Apart from the fact that they cannot properly serve as language-models to emulate, they sometimes do little to stimulate the youngsters intellectually—they seldom encourage questions, engage in conversation, teach poetry, sing songs, develop the power of observation. This is distressing.

Typically it is because the mothers are working outside the home that women who are recent immigrants are looking after their children.

One sees these caretakers, governesses, and/or nannies with their charges on the buses of New York City. They generally are simply "minding" the children, not interacting with them on any sort of intellectual level. It's a pity because there's a lot that might be learned riding on a Manhattan bus—looking at the advertisements, the people, the mayhem on the street.

Again, given the general condition of American society as we move into the last decade of this century, the majority of this book's readers could supply similar stories of their own, since all of us now daily encounter the most incredible displays of ignorance, inefficiency, and—only slightly less often—stupidity. We have considered some of the causes, the factors that brought about the present stage of social disarray. Now let us proceed to the question of what might be done to improve the situation.

The Solution

Suggestions

To begin our leisurely if occasionally impassioned consideration of human thought, I have good news and bad news.

First the bad news.

This modest and incomplete outline by itself obviously cannot undo the harm resulting from hundreds of thousands of years of behavior-pattern formation directed largely by the needs of the human animal to survive in a frequently hostile environment. There is a blind will in nature that "cares" about the survival of the species, but the survival of individuals within the species is evidently of slight concern. *Within the cosmic "plan" the creatures of the natural world live chiefly by devouring one another.* It is no surprise, therefore, that human beings—as mammals—respond aggressively to certain kinds of challenges and threats. It is in their capacity as something-more-than-animals that they have slowly and painfully developed those higher abilities that distinguish them from the beasts. That the transition has not been totally achieved is something of which we see daily evidence.

Perhaps if one had two brains—one for emotion and the other for reason—the reasoning brain could turn off the emotional brain when the individual was faced with a situation requiring the application of dispassionate logic. In reality, however, the component parts of the human computer are intricately intertwined so that even the most reasonable among us can be driven to fury or depression by a seemingly infinite variety of troublesome factors.

The good news is that the bad news is not really terribly important.

As noted in the Introduction, there is no such thing as an all-purpose, universally agreed-upon definition of thinking.

I have, therefore, deliberately avoided submitting such a definition, since this is a book for the general reader. A definition, in any case, would be difficult simply because there are so many kinds of mental activities commonly referred to by the word *thinking*. Some thinking is primarily verbal, some is more visual. Some concerns simple arithmetic, other forms involve more complex geometric factors. Then there is *creative* thinking. Even "simple" logical thinking is intricate enough; creative thinking is more complex.

It is sometimes said that there are two kinds of thinking: one characterized by reverie, intuition, dreaming (awake or asleep), constructing beliefs from raw material drawn from the storehouse of wish, hope, love, fear, anger, and so on; and the other consisting of mental activity of the sort we call science—that is, thinking to practical effect, thinking out of respect for the virtues of evidence and consistency. But while a separation of the mental process into two such categories has its usefulness, thinking occurs in far more than two molds. When I—which is to say, my brain—create a melody never before heard through all the millions of years of universal experience, I am certainly thinking, but am neither daydreaming nor reasoning logically. I am simply thinking of assorted sounds and their hopefully congenial relationship. If a sculptor imagines, and then proceeds to produce an either abstract or realistic image, he, too, is thinking neither by reverie nor word-logic but on a separate plane, that of third-dimensional construction, which somehow achieves a level of beauty.

Such purely physical action-patterns as are susceptible to at least a degree of control by the consciousness—sexual and digestive activities, for example—may also be said to involve modes of thinking, or mental activity, that need not necessarily be either logical or intuitive. There is a certain animal practicality to achieving the objects of our desires for food or sexual expression. These, as I say, may call forth separate ways of thinking.

I propose, nevertheless, to concern myself with the two time-honored categories, since so much of what passes for mental process in human experience is a matter of the rationalization of bias, prejudice, fear, anger, desire, or hope, whereas pitiably little can be accurately described as disinterested reason.

Although the fact that you have started to read this book suggests that you are either optimistic or at least open-minded about the possibility of Americans, including yourself, becoming more intelligent, you may also have certain reservations. There is, after all, something roughly describable as *intelligence quotient,* I.Q. You may assume, as I do, that a good part of mental ability is a matter of genetic inheritance, although this does not mean that if one or both of a person's parents are not very intelligent—or, for that matter, are extremely intelligent—this will necessarily determine his or her own fate as a thinker. As Martin Gardner, in his delightful book *Aha! Insight,* reports, "Recent studies show that persons who possess a high aha! ability are all intelligent to a moderate level, *but beyond that level there seems to be no correlation between high intelligence and aha! thinking*" (italics added). Again, it is not necessary to have a remarkably high intelligence to reason well. If one's I.Q. is, for example, in the medium 100-125 range, one may have to spend a bit more time frowning and concentrating in reasoning one's way through problems. But the tools of reason are just that, and just as a hammer and chisel can be used by an amateur as well as a professional sculptor or woodworker, so we do not have to be near-geniuses to use the tools of reason.

Nor does one have to be brilliant in all respects to be a good and creative problem-solver. A classic instance, of course, is that of Albert Einstein, who was not especially competent at basic mathematics and whose school marks were far from distinguished. But despite the fact that he was average in some ways, Einstein was able to produce dazzlingly creative ideas in mathematics and physics.

More good news that Gardner and other experts share is that the creative, problem-solving function is by no means necessarily correlated with quickness of thought. So plodders can take heart. Thomas Aquinas, one of the ablest philosophers of the ages, was called a "dumb ox" during his early schooldays.

There is apparently no one on earth who is an expert at all kinds of thinking. For instance, I seem to have a modest degree of natural ability to reason well about certain kinds of things. But whenever I am presented with one of those problems that has a large number of factors to it, my thinking process tends to grind to a halt. I refer to problems that sound like this: (*a*) If it rains in Kansas only on Mondays, Wednesdays, and Fridays, and (*b*) Farmer Brown grows wheat on one-half of his acreage and rye on the other, and (*c*) wheat sells for $4.00 a bushel and rye for $3.00 a bushel, and (*d*) if Farmer Brown is a Republican—at about that point I tend to simply walk away from the problem because I have a sense of almost total incompetence even to understand the ultimate question, much less to answer it. Such problems, as the sophisticated reader may know, can be solved quite handily, by using symbolic logic. But the point is that I have no *natural* gifts whatever for addressing such complex puzzles.

But because of the absence of an all-embracing definition, we may still wonder: What *is* thinking? Let's approach an answer by the process of elimination. Each of us knows a million and one things that thinking is not.

Thinking is not, for example, apple pie.

Thinking is not singing a song written by U2.

Thinking is not swimming across the Yangtse River.

It may sound dumb to try to bring the concept of thinking into clear focus by first considering things that are not thinking, but such a method has its purpose.

No one of us could live long enough to enumerate all the things in the universe that are not thinking. But by merely considering a few of them, we do begin to narrow in on the general geographical area, so to speak, in which we might finally be able to run thinking to ground.

Thinking—we will quickly agree—has something to do with mental activity. But the two words *mental* and *activity,* in combination, do not encompass a small area but an enormously large one.

The Brain

One reason the area of mental activity is large is that its physical location is the brain. The brain itself is not one thing, in the sense that a kneecap or an eyeball is one thing (although even such unitary portions of the body are subdivided). We might get a better idea of the construction of the brain if we imagined a piece of paper toweling, or a long roll of computer paper, all loosely rolled up into a moist wad just large enough to fit inside a human skull.

Imagine that you can lift that wad of crumpled paper out of the skull, dry it off, and then open it up. If we decided to place it, all spread out, on the floor, we would need a very large auditorium indeed.

Another reason we may say that intellectual activity takes place in a large area is that the brain consists of billions of very tiny cells. It is individual cells, and groups of cells—working in combination— that take care of that part of thinking that is physical. We shall take a more leisurely look at the brain later.

The preceding paragraph, of course, carries the vague implication that there is some part of thinking that is *not* physical. This may well not be the case at all. But we need not spend much time on the question since the wisest philosophers of the ages have not yet been able to agree on it. In any event, all the thinking that we are confidently entitled to say we know about does take place by physical means. Whether there is any sort that is extra-physical, we simply do not know.

Even if it were to be argued that there is some actual entity called *the soul*—something, in other words, that has no necessary connection with the body—we have no evidence that it has ever done any actual thinking.

Millions of humans who believe that the soul exists after the death of the body for the most part assume that it goes to some perfect state, which may be called Heaven, or to some horrible state, which may be called Hell. But inasmuch as Heaven, by definition, involves a state of perfection, it would certainly be a place where thought—considered as problem-solving—would no longer be necessary. And if Hell were as advertised, it would be a place in which the ability to think clearly, to reason, to be logical, to be guided by evidence, to develop the ability to plan, would have no possible use.

We may, therefore, simply put all such theological and metaphysical speculations aside—as irrelevant to our present purposes—and concentrate on the earthly aspects of thinking, which are, in any event, troublesome enough.

Before we proceed, a brief but necessary digression. One of the "rules" for clear thinking you are about to read concerns evaluating ideas on their merits rather than accepting or rejecting them solely, even primarily, on the basis of their source. On that subject, I frequently hear it said that although my thoughts turn often to serious matters, it is not altogether proper that this should be so. "You are a comedian," runs the argument. "Therefore you have no business publicly discussing serious issues." The opinion is so clearly absurd that I rarely bother to refute it in conversation, realizing that the state of mind that caused the idea to be expressed in the first place would render the hearer impervious to counterarguments in the second. But perhaps a word on the subject would be in order here.

The basic mistake of such argument, of course, is that it treats comedians or entertainers generically instead of individually. Presumably we have learned the dangers of considering larger ethnic or social groups in this way. When we say, for example, that "Italians are musical," we do not really mean it. Most Italians are not in the least especially musical. What we mean is that although the proportion of musical people in any society is small, the Italians seem to have a higher percentage than other nationalities. So, too, it is unfair to assume that because some entertainers may be scatterbrained, narcissistic, or poorly educated, all entertainers may be tarred with the same brush.

Every citizen, actor or not, ought to be concerned with crucial social questions. Our society is in danger when there is a lack of interest in democratic processes, not when there is a great deal of it. In recent years, the involvement of Americans in public affairs—even to the modest extent of voting—has been dwindling. This represents a serious problem for our nation. Consider the observation of diplomat George F. Kennan, an expert on Soviet affairs:

> If you ask me—as a historian, let us say—whether a country in the state this country is in today, with no highly developed sense of national purpose, with the overwhelming accent of life on personal comfort and amusement, with a dearth of public services and a surfeit of privately sold gadgetry, . . . with an educational system where quality has been extensively sacrificed to quantity, and with insufficient social discipline even to keep its major industries functioning without grievous interruptions—if you ask me whether such a country has, over the long run, good chances of competing

with a purposeful, serious and disciplined society such as that of the Soviet Union, I must say that the answer is "no."

In light of this, is there any citizen who can go on feeling that the business of our world must be left entirely to the "experts"? We all know that, although there are brilliant and dedicated men and women in public service, there are also some venal and ignorant individuals so employed. I am therefore entitled to make the area of my concern the universe rather than just the little world of television. We all should.

What Is the Solution?

The many Americans who are consciously aware of, and given to speculation about, the depressingly long list of serious problems that trouble our society seem not to have either asked or adequately answered the simple question: "What is it that can, perhaps, bring us out of our present predicament?" But now that we are forced to consider the question, we might begin by listing the factors that will not achieve such a happy end.

It will certainly not be technology per se, for despite its dazzling achievements, it is both part of the problem and part of the solution. And it will not be military superiority or parity, since, given present conditions, the human race is as likely to be destroyed as to be preserved by the use of modern weapons.

It will certainly not be leaders of government who will save us, for we are more likely to elect charming or good-looking intellectual lightweights than philosophers; and the governments of the world, despite the efforts of international lawyers, the United Nations, the World Federalist Movement, and other groups, seem to agree on little and disagree on much.

It would be comforting to think that religion might be our salvation. Perhaps, if there were only one faith in the world, and a wise and compassionate one at that, such a dream might be realized—for if our conduct were effectively guided by edifying moral codes, the world would quickly become a far more civilized place. But all such happy speculations are fantasy. As for the reality of religious practice, much of it is all too depressing. Far from one sensible faith, we have literally thousands, almost all of which consider themselves vastly superior to the others. We would be fortunate if our problems with religion went no further, but from both the long record of history and the testimony of last night's newscasts, we see that the religions of the world are now, as they have ever been, literally at one another's throats, contributing at some times to peace and sanity but at others to bloodshed and fanaticism.

In this connection, a brief word on the concept of separation of church and state. There are sound, sensible reasons for such a separation being part of American policy, and even the casual student of history is perfectly aware of them. But there is a far more important reason that state and religion must never become one, or even enter into a particularly close relationship, and that is that states are, by the very nature of their tasks, either amoral or immoral institutions. A nation will condone mass murder, attacks on its own citizens, organized campaigns of deceit, thievery, pillage—indeed, it is difficult to think of a single crime that has not been committed under the justification of national defense or putting the enemy in his place. As we have seen, not all religions are especially virtuous either. But at least they have the chance to be. Millions of their followers sincerely wish they were. The achievement of this lovely ambition is obviously notoriously difficult, but never more so than when church and state are part of the same tightly woven social structure. For in every such case, not only will the state corrupt the church, but the state itself will become even more corrupt because its violent sins will seemingly be justified by the blessing of morally blind prelates.

The churches, then, can now play a remedial role in improving American education, but chiefly from the sidelines. One reason that Catholic parochial schools are more effective than public schools is that the parents involved are much more active and concerned. The children of such parents are very fortunate.

Another hopeful avenue to explore concerns the findings of groups specializing in infant-education. I refer, for example, to the Institutes for the Achievement of Human Potential in Philadelphia. Read one of their books, *How to Teach Your Baby to Read* by Glenn Doman.

Note that the title is not "How to Teach Your *Child* to Read." A number of specialists have suggested that inasmuch as we start learning to speak languages in the crib, just so we can learn to read those languages at the same early stage.

Recent studies, in fact, suggest that the human learning process starts before birth. The senses do not suddenly turn on—as would a light bulb—at the moment the new individual emerges from the mother's body. The only serious debate, I would think, can concern the question of how long before birth the baby is able to hear, smell, see, feel, and taste.

Whatever can be learned at so early a stage will naturally be nonverbal. Nothing the least bit complex could be communicated, but it may be that by exposing the infant's impressionable mind to certain simple messages, the result could be encouragement of the early learning process. Babies, during their first few months, do not actually understand the words being spoken to them, but they nevertheless profit greatly by the touching, the laughing, smiling, bathing, caressing, and feeding, in that certain simple emotional and physical lessons are learned. Their minds, we now know, are stimulated if they are spoken to a good deal as well as introduced to colors, closely positioned objects, sound-making toys, or soft, comforting music. The field of child psychology teaches us that, while children can learn early, they are not competent to absorb all sorts of messages at every stage. The brain seems conditioned by evolutionary processes to absorb certain kinds of information most effectively at certain chronological stages during which the individual improves gradually in the various practiced capabilities.

The one seeming exception to this rule concerns the ability to learn languages. This is more pronounced in very young children than it is among forty-year-old adults. A mature adult has considerable difficulty learning even one language, whereas a four- or five-year-old child quite casually acquires facility in even three or four languages if they are constantly spoken in his or her presence.

Susan Ludington, assistant professor of nursing at UCLA and researcher in fetology, was present during a birth at UCLA Hospital in which communication between a father and baby apparently took place. The baby's depressed heart rate might have necessitated a Caesarean section had not Ms. Ludington intervened. She suggested that the father speak loudly to the baby. He did so, with immediate results. The child's heart rate took a leap and remained lively throughout the normal birth process.

Although such studies are still in the experimental stages, Ludington and her colleagues believe that late in their development fetuses do perceive light, colors, and sound and can learn in utero by early conditioning.

Read also a book titled *Kindergarten Is Too Late!* by Masuru Ibuka, one of the founders of the Sony Company. Though there are still unresolved questions, children who start reading at the age of two or three have a significant head start over those who are not exposed to reading until they are five or six. The lead persists, right through to the university level. We must, of course, offer all early instruction in a loving, relaxed, and playful way, avoiding any sense of pressure.

According to David Elkind, child psychologist and chairman of the Eliot Pearson Department of Child Study at Tufts University, writing in *The Hurried Child: Growing Up Too Fast Too Soon,* some children in today's society are under "too much pressure to achieve, to succeed, to please . . . a new pressure to hurry and grow up. Unlike the spoiled children who remained children too long, hurried children grow up too fast, pushed in their early years toward many types of achievement, and exposed to experiences that tax their adaptive capacity."

According to Dr. Elkind, hurried children are driven by the fear of failure, "of not achieving fast enough or high enough." This group, he argues, includes many of the problem children seen by psychologists and social workers; often they are the ones who fail, become delinquent, and resort to drugs.

Pushing children to excel too quickly, too early in their development as human beings, often has the effect of producing apathy and withdrawal in later years. Says Dr. Elkind:

> In our own studies, and in those of others, we have found that *what is crucial to beginning to read is the child's attachment to an adult who spends time reading to or with a child.* The motivation for reading . . . is social. (Italics supplied.)

Dr. Elkind quotes the educational research of Henry M. Brickell, president of Policy Studies in Education (in a broad survey of educational research):

> The three most important ingredients in the school setting are the student, the teacher, and the length of time they are together. . . . given a particular student and a particular teacher, *the length of time they are together* influences student learning more than anything else. Once those three are established, researchers will discover little if any significant difference among various teaching methods.

Secondly, we must add a *fourth R* to our formal process of early education. The four will be reading, 'riting, 'rithmetic, and reasoning.

Aristotle defined humankind as "the rational animal," from which it follows that all other forms of life are nonrational. Impartial observers from other planets would consider ours an utterly bizarre enclave if it were populated by birds, defined as flying animals, that nevertheless rarely or never actually flew. They would also be perplexed if they encountered, in our seas, lakes, rivers, and ponds, creatures defined as swimmers that never did any swimming. But they would be even more surprised to encounter a species defined as a thinking animal if, in fact, the creature very rarely indulged in actual thinking.

Now it might be argued that you cannot introduce a six-year-old child to logical reasoning of a subtle and sophisticated nature. Indeed you cannot. By the same token you cannot successfully introduce a six-year-old child to calculus or geometry. No one, however, ever uses that fact to argue that we ought not introduce young children to basic arithmetic.

But we must do a number of things—and as quickly as possible—to encourage respect for reason in our society. We must teach, for example, what is really a simple lesson—although it seems to be rarely perceived on individual initiative—that there is a difference between consistent and conclusive evidence. This is dealt with in more detail in Rule 29.

We must inculcate a respect for wisdom and not put such heavy emphasis on material or financial accomplishment. Man was not put on this earth primarily to have hit record albums, to be utterly irresistible to the opposite sex, to get rich by any means, however unethical, or to wear the tightest possible jeans. Every other society in history that has accomplished anything of lasting importance has perceived such simple truths.

There is another reason—and a profoundly important one—that we should, as a society, inculcate greater respect for the rules of evidence, the ideal of truth, and the virtue of consistency. That reason is a moral one. We have seen the relative pointlessness of airy endorsements of freedom, democracy, and education by individuals and groups whose actual behavior sharply contradicts their professed ideals. At present we have hardly any commonly accepted intellectual standards in the light of which those guilty of such blatant contradictions can be called to account. As a result, the public dialogue on important issues consists in part of name-calling, exaggeration, ad hominem attacks, lies, one-sided propaganda, careless errors, threats, intimidation, and pressure-group tactics. None of this is consistent with the ideals of the Greek philosophers, with essential religious morality, or with American political philosophy as envisioned by the Founding Fathers, to mention only three standards we claim to respect.

Another thing we must do is initiate a broad campaign of public support for gifted children.

It would be a very peculiar state of affairs if our society took the position that children who are found to possess remarkable musical aptitude were, nevertheless, not to be given any special consideration or instruction. And it would be literally unthinkable if we argued that young people blessed with superior athletic ability should not be encouraged to develop their gifts. Indeed, so sensitive is our society to the commercial possibilities inherent in the exploitation of physical prowess, that college coaches and sometimes even officials of professional teams have their eyes on athletically superior high schoolers who may live hundreds of miles away.

But when it comes to students who are intellectually superior, we are remarkably careless, if not indifferent. There are, to be sure, individuals concerned with the special needs of gifted children, and some of their responses are organizational. But there is by no means a consensus concerning the necessity, or even the wisdom, of providing special nurture for those who, partly by the mysterious roll of the genetic dice, are intellectually superior.

As I dictate this part of my argument I happen to be sitting in a beautifully appointed sun-room in the private home of a man who was one of the most striking examples of a gifted child in our nation's history. Although he died in 1956, his name is firmly planted in the public consciousness for a number of reasons. Among these are New York's Sloan-Kettering Cancer Institute, the Kettering Hospital complex in Dayton, Ohio, and the scores of important inventions created and developed by the brilliantly inventive Charles Kettering.

Born on August 29, 1876, on a farm near Loudenville, a small town in central Ohio, Kettering came from a hard-working but otherwise undistinguished family. As his later accomplishments would show, Kettering was genetically programmed for genius, but he might not have enjoyed such a happy fate had he not had the good fortune, as a child, to come to the attention of John Row and Neil McLaughlin, teachers at the simple one-room, country schoolhouse near the Kettering farm. A few years later C. E. Budd, a young physics instructor, becoming aware of Kettering's potential, also gave him special attention. Because of these happy social accidents, Kettering went on to become America's most important inventor and engineer after Thomas Edison. His pioneer work included achievement in such fields as cash registers, automated inventory control systems, the electric self-starter for automobiles, Duco paint, leaded gasoline, guided missiles, freon refrigerants, and the diesel locomotive.

Obviously not every gifted child, even if offered support and encouragement, will be as productive as Charles Kettering, but it is still clear that we are terribly short-sighted if we continue to do so little for our intellectually superior children.

Does this mean we care more about athletic than intellectual achievement? I'm afraid it does, insofar as we can be judged by our actions. The national ego seems somehow involved with athletic competition, although there is some humor, I suppose, in the spectacle of good-ol'-boy, beer-drinking rednecks feeling better about themselves when the USA wins a gold medal in Olympic competition, considering that many of the American winners have been the descendants of former slaves.

Is there any way, then, that we could be made to even begin to imagine that the mind and spirit are more important than the bicep or the hamstring? The trick might be turned if we could plug this particular computer program, so to speak, into the national ego circuits. There would certainly be justification for such a connection, because in the long run it is a damned sight more important, and dangerous, that we are mentally inferior than that, in some instances, we are physically inferior.

To approach the problem from another angle, we must all somehow be made aware—to restate my thesis—that in the past thirty years or so, the American people have been getting demonstrably dumber.

We were shocked, some years ago, to be told that "Johnny can't read." Indeed he can't, at least not as well as he should; nor can he write, do simple arithmetic or, as noted above, even think very well. The steady erosion of intelligence in the American population is having painful results in the marketplace; I have not met an employer in the past two decades who did not complain about the difficulty in hiring good help, since such once taken-for-granted abilities as spelling, typing, punctuating, and communicating coherently are part of the large and lamentable crumbling.

In the face of such negative factors there is a depressing stupidity to our refusal to offer proper encouragement and nurture to the small percentage of our children who are *not* getting dumber.

Obviously, a number of superbright young people do somehow contrive to get a reasonably good education and to enjoy professional success. But a good many others of equal early competence are falling through the net because of public and official ignorance and neglect. That, I submit, we cannot afford.

The Japanese, to mention only one foreign people, score dramatically higher than Americans in certain kinds of tests. Japan cares about infant education, about special treatment for the gifted. The connection between this wisdom and recent Japanese industrial superiority is obvious.

Although there is an urgent need for an active program that responds to the needs of gifted children, it obviously does not follow that any and all such efforts will be properly conducted. Indeed, even well-intentioned parents can be counterproductive if what they intend as special attention is construed by the child—perhaps accurately—as the high-pressure message, "You'd better succeed, or else." There is a sharp difference between pushing students, gifted or not, to the point where they resist or rebel, on the one hand, and offering them sensible, affectionate nurturing on the other. This is so self-evident that we do not need to wait for evidence to support it; but even if we did, the evidence is abundant and available. Children who feel pressured may either drop out of the competitive race or develop bitter resentments they carry with them throughout their lives.

Concerned parents, therefore, must assess their own motives. Otherwise, they may become as destructive as the notorious stage-mothers, who sometimes do permanent damage to their children's hearts and souls because of the intense critical pressures they put on them to succeed as actors or performers.

The most successful programs of encouragement for superior children strike a reasonable balance between special instruction on the one hand, and warm, friendly encouragement on the other. I recall from my own somewhat chaotic educational experience that if I liked the teacher I tended to do well in the class. If the teacher was cold, insulting, sarcastic, or impatient, I learned little.

Anyone seriously concerned with this issue soon becomes aware that it exists within the context of a larger and unresolved philosophical debate concerning suitable relationships between what might loosely be described as the haves and have-nots of society. This is generally perceived in economic terms (the poor and the rich, or in Marxist analysis or Liberation Theology, the poor versus the rich). Regarding superior intelligence, the issue would at least be simpler to understand if all the strikingly bright boys and girls lived on the "right side of the tracks," and all the below-average children on the other side. God help the unbright ones if that were the case, since perhaps no society in history has morally distinguished itself by its treatment of the poor or otherwise disadvantaged. But, as in the case of Charles Kettering, remarkable intelligence can spring up in a rural shack or a ghetto apartment. If, as I assume, the primary factors are physical and genetic, it then becomes a matter of the most crucial importance that the unusually bright ones in poor neighborhoods be identified as early as possible. Otherwise it not only can happen, but does, that the initial natural gifts are wasted, swamped by the harsh realities of being brought up in conditions characterized by poverty, crime, inadequate diet, and parents who may be either absent, tragically ignorant and uneducated, or socially unstable, if not criminal. It is, then, all the more necessary that efforts be made to identify gifted children in the below-the-poverty-line segment of our society.

It would be an exaggeration to say that initiating a large-scale continuing and strikingly successful program of identifying all gifted children and offering them proper nurture could in itself resolve our larger problems. But not doing so will certainly make those problems more severe.

Consider the old saying that the rich get richer and the poor get poorer. Sometimes it is true and sometimes it is not, but it is at least as dangerous that in certain circumstances the bright get brighter and the dumb get dumber. Even if we cannot perceive that such injustice is tragic, we had better become aware, and fast, that it is dangerous. I consider it no exaggeration to say that if it were the case that an appreciable and ever-growing segment of our society were, in fact, becoming less well educated, less prepared for life in the marketplace, and less socially responsible generally, this would constitute a grave and growing threat to the stability of our nation.

Indeed, it is already painfully clear—in the rising statistics concerning violent crime—that the poor will not forever supinely accept their fate. If they cannot legally secure the benefits of life in the world's richest country, then some of them will simply break and enter, grab and run, even assault and kill, to get what they want.

As noted earlier, the serious problems of our society do not exist as a series of more or less separate issues. They are all part of a large, ugly machine, the parts of which are interconnected. It is the height of social stupidity for the white, affluent descendants of former peasants and menial laborers to say, "If they want something, let them work for it," when there are no jobs for 8 percent of America's workers, of any color, and when our poverty-stricken neighborhoods, rural and urban, are producing millions of young people largely unqualified to accept even the lowest-paying jobs that are available. Education is obviously important as a means of uplifting the human mind and spirit. But it also has a profound importance in the context of social and economic considerations.

So formidable is the larger difficulty, I repeat, that nothing short of adding formal instruction in "How to Think" to our educational process, starting at the kindergarten level, will fill the bill. It has been by no means established that even doing that much will civilize us in time to check our self-destructive tendencies, but we must go as far as possible in making the experimental attempt.

By seeming to contrast reason and emotion, I do not mean to suggest that there is necessarily a hopeless state of war between these two human faculties. What one wants is to achieve a balance. Life would be dreary indeed among a race of logical but emotionless beings. (Courses should also be designed in "How to Feel," since our emotionality is too often a thing of blind instinctual or impulsive response—in the case of both pleasant and unpleasant emotions—which most of us go to our graves never really understanding. On some separate level, then, our children may receive formal instruction in "How to Feel," or "How to Love," but at the moment we are closer, perhaps, to being able to teach them how to think.)

The rules for reasonable thinking here set forth are by no means the only rules, nor even necessarily the best. They may help, however, to interest children and concerned adults in the fascinating workings of the human mind.

If you stop to think of it, it's incredible that most of us reason so poorly, because it is, again, our reasoning powers that distinguish us from all other creatures.

But perhaps we have been guilty of what is said to be the first sin—pride—in regard to this dazzlingly important ability, restricted to humankind alone. Human beings are also the only animals that can play the piano, but that fact would not entitle us to ignore the formal development of music theory and instruction. Rather, we start with a modest innate aptitude and, by applying ourselves, develop our powers.

Just so, we are going to have to focus on the fact that, except for a few geniuses, we have no more striking natural gifts for reasoning than we have for playing the piano, performing sophisticated mathematical procedures, or painting the Mona Lisa. Instruction is always required. And is it not remarkable that we are offered instruction in every important human art except that of thinking?

So, all right. You now are convinced of the seriousness of the problem and want to do something about it.

The following suggestions will show you how.

81 Ways to Think Better

The following eighty-one "rules"—suggestions, commandments, tips, whatever one wants to call them—if acted upon, will without question greatly improve the ability to reason.

There is no way of stating these recommendations in an order or priority that is inevitable or proper. Individuals will vary in their judgments as to which are of major or minor importance. Fortunately, that doesn't matter very much. Every item will be helpful. The question of how helpful depends, to a considerable extent, on the present state of one's reasoning powers, just as a book on dieting would have different effects on its readers depending on their personal eating habits, or a book on exercising would be used differently depending on the health, strength, and age of its readers.

Rule No. 1

Decide that in the future you will reason more effectively

Believe it or not, this simple step, by itself, will produce positive results, however modest. It alone obviously cannot achieve the desired effect, but it is a necessary beginning. The conscious act of will it requires narrows our concentration on the particular task. As anyone knows who has ever attempted to learn chess, table tennis, roller skating, to play the piano, or any other activity requiring special concentration and coordination, the simple decision, the will to master the ability, is always a necessary part of the process.

But let's for a moment take a closer look at the business of *deciding*—deciding anything. Are we totally free to make virtuous decisions and stick to them?

The answer is: Yes and no.

Yes, we do have free will, but the will is by no means totally free. Our decisions may be influenced by desires, appetites, addictions, fears, anger, greed, and more admirable emotions as well. Loyalty—to our nation, church, ethnic group, or school—will influence our conduct. Or one may have an unfortunate behavior-pattern caused by poor thinking.

Some individuals, for example, become specialists in motive-attribution. People with paranoid tendencies are sometimes quite creative about it. They become quickly convinced that any act that works to their disadvantage was performed as part of a deliberate plan to harm them. I've received hundreds of letters from paranoids over the past forty years or so. Alas, a book like this is unlikely to help them. But I suspect that all of us have moments of partial paranoia. The present

126

argument can discourage such tendencies.

If you suspect yourself of fits of paranoia, keep the thought in mind that most of what you think the world is doing to you, you are actually doing to yourself.

I know, for example, a brilliant woman in New York who suffers from a behavior-pattern that makes her late to more than 90 percent of her appointments. Most of her longtime friends are perfectly aware that if she says she will see them at ten o'clock, she is likely to show up twenty or thirty minutes thereafter. The woman is an admirable person in many other particulars, but the significant fact is that she seems unable to recognize, and hence to concede, that she *has* the problem of habitual tardiness. She has "an excuse" for every instance of lateness. The phone rang just as she was leaving. A delivery man came and she had to talk to him. The maid didn't prepare her breakfast on time. Somebody had turned the clock in the kitchen back. A button was missing on the blouse she wanted to wear, and so on.

That such frustrations and obstructions are daily encountered, on all our paths, is clear enough. But the woman in question honestly believes that such factors, as a group, are the reason for her lateness. The obvious solution that she start her preparations for all departures about twenty minutes earlier is shrugged off with annoyance. Psychiatrists feel that those who suffer from habitual lateness have unconscious motivations growing out of early experience. Perhaps such people are reacting against a parent who was overly strict about punctuality. Or they may be repeating a pattern learned from parents who were also as careless about time. Or they may have a "need" to arrive late and make dramatic entrances. Human beings are, after all, incredibly complex creatures. That is why no book—even one far more wise and reasonable than this one—can possibly have precisely the same effect on all those who read it.

We must, in the end, settle for improvement rather than perfection.

Not everyone, the reader should be advised, shares my combined optimism and enthusiasm for the sort of program of public instruction that I recommend. Certain determinists and behaviorists are skeptical about some self-help books, though usually the kind dealing with the emotions. Certainly the troubled reader is unlikely to be reformed by nothing more than the act of reading the kind of get-better books one hears discussed on television talk-shows. Even long-continued psychoanalysis at the hands of the most highly competent and experienced therapists is not always successful. The behaviorists are right, too, insofar as they keep us on guard against romantic or naive approaches to campaigns of reform. And they are certainly right in arguing that anyone who imagines the human will is *entirely* free is very much mistaken. They are right, too, in feeling that it is a general constellation of physical factors—the conditions of our lives—that lead to much of our behavior, the good and the bad. Very well, but let us acknowledge that among the environmental factors involved are such things as schools, books, philosophical arguments, record albums, tapes, videocassettes, speeches, sermons, and exhortations to virtue. With that part of the human will, however small, that *is* free, let us determine to manipulate the conditions of our environment so as to produce more desirable results.

It would be an unseemly digression to say very much about the subject here, but what lies at the heart of such speculation is the ancient theological debate about the degree to which the will is free. Traditional religious believers have, for centuries, assumed that the will was almost totally free. They acknowledged the more or less contrary argument that because of a "natural" human tendency to do wrong—sometimes referred to (incorrectly) as *original sin*—humans would often act sinfully and/or negatively, but they also felt that if they were really determined to do so, they could—at specific moments—overcome such weakness.

Opposing this hard, clear line, another school of theological belief held that man could *not,* simply by an exercise of the will, become largely virtuous. Individual cases that seemed to contradict such a gloomy theory, such as the behavior of saints and other heroes, they said resulted not from the will of such fortunate individuals, but simply from the *grace* of God. Oddly enough, they argued that such grace was in no sense a reward for earlier virtuous behavior, but that it was simply dispensed—alas, to very few—by the personal decision of God in a process that, from the human point-of-view, seemed like that of random chance.

Another aspect of the long debate on this question concerns the theory of *predestination*. We can say about this dour hypothesis that it has seemed utterly nonsensical to 99 percent of the members of the human race who ever thought of it, but nevertheless it had many theological defenders. The theory, in essence, holds that, for reasons beyond human understanding, God has seen fit to send most of the human race into the realm of life absolutely fated to eternal damnation, despite whatever intermittent or long-continued efforts they might make to avert such a fate by behaving virtuously.

I suppose that such a bizarre opinion was constructed out of two prior views, one being the simple observation that most humans do fall into sin depressingly often, and the other that if God is indeed *all*-knowing, it is logically inescapable that he knows the future.

As I say, there would be no point—in the present work—for further presentation of the particulars of this ancient dialogue.

But most informed people of the present day, including millions within the churches, believe that we *can* improve ourselves by willing to do so. We can be quite certain that any clergyman who announced to his flock next Sunday morning that, despite what 95 percent of them did, they were going to end up in hell anyway, would soon find himself looking for work elsewhere.

So we should make a decision to think better. It's a good start.

Rule No. 2

Do some casual studying about the brain,
the mind, memory, the whole field of psychology

For those who are still in school, this should be easy. Others can visit a used-book store and pick up a couple of good, recent college-level psychology texts. Engineers read about engineering, musicians read about music, athletes about sports, etc.; anyone who decides to become something of a thinker should read about thinking.

All of us, except the severely handicapped, do a certain amount of thinking "by ear," in much the same sense that millions acquire a bit of musical knowledge or expertise without formal instruction. The latter may be a matter of having innate tendencies and/or it may be the result of exposure to environmental musical influences. But just as the formally instructed and much-practiced musician will be better— all other factors being equal—than someone who has not had such learning opportunities, so will we be better thinkers if we continue our studies on the subject.

A few words about the brain

What do you suppose is the most important part of your body? You might think the heart is, since its beating shows that we are alive. Or the lungs. Some might say the eyes, because seeing is so necessary. Some might even say the feet, since walking is so essential. And it would be difficult to get along without the hands. All of these obviously are important. But the most important is the brain.

It is the part of the body that makes the other parts work. It's something like a big switchboard from which orders go out to the rest of the human machine.

Years ago there was an actor in the movies named Mantan Moreland. I remember a scene in which he thought he was seeing a ghost. He naturally wanted to run away, so he said, "Feet, get movin'." It made everyone laugh, but actually the brain sends out messages of that sort all day long, although it does not have to transmit actual words to the various parts of the body.

To help it decide what the body ought to do, the brain takes in messages from parts of the anatomy. The senses—of sight, touch, hearing, smell, taste—gather this information for the brain.

How does the brain receive and send out messages?

When a light is turned on, electric current flows through a thin wire until it gets to a light bulb. It makes the light bulb shine. There are very tiny wires, *nerves,* that run from the brain to all parts of the body and back again. The central switchboard, the brain—which weighs about three pounds—has about ten billion nerve cells, all of which are constantly receiving and sending out messages by means of electrical impulses that travel from two to two hundred miles an hour.

The brain, which because it rests comfortably inside the skull is well protected, is not really just one large organ, but has separate sections that take care of different kinds of tasks.

One section is the *medulla.* It is the part of the brain directly above the spinal cord. It controls such reflexive functions as breathing, swallowing, sneezing, and coughing. You don't often *decide* to do any of these things, although the will can exert a degree of influence on them.

Just above the medulla is the *cerebellum.* It, too, is connected to the brain stem, or spinal cord. The cerebellum mostly takes care of information coming from the muscles, and helps send messages back to the muscles so that we can move around, walk, jump, run, climb, throw things, do the bugaloo, and so forth.

Above the cerebellum—but inside the brain—is a section called the *thalamus.* The thalamus has a pleasant job; it receives all those interesting messages from the eyes, ears, nose, and skin. When we say that we are hearing Barbra Streisand, seeing a sunset, smelling a rose, or feeling the cool water when we go swimming, it's the thalamus that actually enjoys all these lovely sensations. The thalamus also is connected with the state of being awake or asleep.

One of the most interesting parts of the brain lies just above the thalamus. It's called the *limbic system*. It's the place where emotions come from. Feeling happy, angry, sad, romantic, all involve the limbic system. If you didn't have a limbic system, you wouldn't ever feel anger, no matter what was done to you. In the case of such unpleasant emotions you might think that wouldn't be such a bad idea. Unfortunately you wouldn't feel the nice emotions either.

A fourth part of the brain—the *cortex* or *cerebral* cortex—is the one we are most interested in right now. The brain-functions we've been talking about are much the same for animals. Dogs, cats, monkeys, and giraffes can all see and hear and smell and run and jump and play and be frightened or have a good time. But the cortex is something special to human beings. It's just a thin, gray covering that fits over the top of the brain. It's the part we think with, decide with, and remember with (aided by the *hippocampus,* which is connected to the limbic system).

The cortex is a fantastically complicated computer with billions of cells capable of storing and sorting out a tremendous amount of information. The electrical activity in the cerebral cortex uses up a great deal of energy. That is why we sometimes feel tired after doing a lot of hard thinking or intellectual work, just as we feel tired after doing strenuous muscular work. Another amazing thing about the cortex is that different parts of it take care of different activities of the body. One part, for example, controls the ability to speak; another has to do with thinking about things one has experienced in the past.

Obviously, in a book about thinking, we cannot devote a great deal of space to an explanation of brain function. Nevertheless, a few observations are in order. The brain has two separate halves. At first this might seem a fact no more noteworthy than that the nose has two separate nostrils or the face two separate eyes. But while left eyes and right eyes—and left nostrils and right nostrils—do very much the same thing, there are startling differences between what the two halves of the brain do.

(The theological implications of this, by the way, are intriguing. Perhaps church scholars are already considering how present knowledge of the brain affects traditional assumptions about individual identity, the soul, free will, etc.)

What are the differences between the two hemispheres? Well, it has been known for quite a long time that the *left* hemisphere governs movement on the right side of the body and that the *right* half of the brain controls movement on the left side. But that is perhaps the least interesting fact about the hemispheric divisions. Far more intriguing is the discovery that in the brains of most people, *logical* thinking is somehow controlled by the *left* half. This half of the brain takes in countless millions of bits of sensory input and "files" them in an orderly way. As regards information received in the form of *verbal* communication—the speech or writing of others—it is the *left* brain that largely controls the process.

The *right* half of the brain, by way of contrast, perhaps has had longer evolutionary experience because it is concerned with visual images, which it interprets and organizes at remarkable speed. Emotions, too, seem to be primarily associated with the right hemisphere. (See: *limbic system*). This theory comes from the discovery that stroke victims afflicted on the right sides of their brains often calmly accept their fate, whereas those who suffer strokes on the left hemisphere are much more markedly saddened.

There are cases—some involving surgery, others accidents—where the two halves of the brain have been physically separated, so that the usual degree of intercommunication between them does not occur. The results sound at first like science fiction. They are based on observed fact.

There is a group of patients whose cerebral hemispheres were surgically disconnected in an effort to control their epileptic seizures, which had been intractable to medical (pharmacological) treatment. In order to evaluate the specific capabilities of each hemisphere, the researchers developed special equipment with which they could show certain pictures to one half of the brain at a time.

In one study, a picture of a nude woman was flashed to the right hemisphere of one of these patients. Because the patient's left (speaking) hemisphere had been disconnected from the right (almost mute) hemisphere, her left hemisphere had no knowledge of what her right hemisphere had seen. She could not verbally acknowledge seeing the picture because the right hemisphere has virtually no speech capability, but her emotional reaction showed that her right hemisphere did perceive the nude.

Again, it is perfectly reasonable to ask how simply increasing one's knowledge of the brain—its construction, development, and function— will, in itself, increase the intelligence. The answer is that it will not, except to the degree that acquiring a good deal of knowledge about any important subject will, in one way, increase intelligence. All other things being equal, a person who knows a lot about, for instance, history, science, or philosophy, will be perceived as more intelligent than someone who knows little or nothing about such fields.

But even though a study of brain tissue is obviously separate from a study of the methods of reason, I suggest that if we are going to make the attempt to become smarter, it is consistent with that ideal for us to familiarize ourselves with the organ of the body created, either by God or Nature, for the organization of intelligence itself.

The brain, in any event, is the only thing in the universe that can regard itself. Stones cannot consider stones, elbows cannot consider elbows, flowers can consider neither themselves nor each other. But the brain can observe itself. Not only do human relationships make possible an incredible pooling of knowledge, but something like this felicitous process takes place within the brain itself, so that even if one lived in isolation, one part of the brain could inform another. The brain not only perceives but—wonder of wonders—remembers. But there is a third level of magic to this incredible organ in that it perceives relationships.

One can learn to be a soldier without being taught the intricacies of the rifle. But all the armies of the world give instruction, nevertheless, on the construction and function of the weapon. One can learn to drive an automobile without having any knowledge whatever about the noisy part of it that lies under the hood, but the person who knows something of the mechanical details by means of which the vehicle moves will be a better driver than a twelve-year-old who might have been taught about nothing more than the ignition key, steering wheel, accelerator, and brake.

To sum up: We all want to think better. What we will think with is the brain. But for the brain to do its work, it must be fed, or—to use a word from the world of computers—programmed. It must receive, and sort out, information.

Receiving Information

The first sort of mental activity you engaged in, even before you had been expelled from the womb, involved receiving information. As explained earlier, an incredibly intricate system of nerves exists purely for this purpose. At first—in the womb—your information came from your skin; the data received was quite simple. You were able to sense the ideas of wetness and temperature. Eventually, as ears and eyes formed, you were able to hear and see. Certain portions of the nose prepared you to smell.

For all the rest of your life—unless you become physically handicapped—you never stop taking in information, not even when asleep.

Even if you had been genetically programmed to be the most intelligent genius of all time you would, in fact, never become any more than a subhuman vegetable if your information-receiving mechanism did not function.

Even those unusual abilities and sensitivities that are sometimes referred to as "God-given"—your conscience, for example—could not possibly have come into operation unless you had received information about how things felt, smelled, looked, tasted, and sounded.

Let us again take up the question: What does the brain do with the astronomical amount of information it receives? It does an almost miraculous thing: It stores it.

We have no way of knowing if it stores every single bit of it, although it may well do so.

We do know that the mind *consciously forgets* more than 99 percent of the data it receives, probably for the reason that it is generally busy concentrating on matters at hand. Even when we try very hard to recall a particular acquired fact or impression, we may not be able to do so, though the information is definitely in one of our mental filing cabinets and may, in fact, pop up into consciousness at a later time when we are not looking for it.

Now that we've been introduced to our brains, so to speak, we should resolve to do what we can—it will, alas, be all too little—to control the sort of raw data that is fed into our great, mysterious, moist computers. We should read better books; listen to better music; see better films, plays, and television shows.

And by no means accept only this sketchy introductory information about the brain. Good bookstores and libraries can supply the wealth of information that thousands of scholars and scientists have labored for centuries to unearth.

Rule No. 3

Beware of rushing to judgment

I do not mean to imply by this warning that we can never make up our minds, but it is extremely unwise to rush to a judgment about any issue characterized by even the slightest complexity. The danger, obviously, is that we will come down on the wrong side of the question and then defend our error, perhaps very vigorously and creatively, simply because we have made a personal ego-investment in it.

There's nothing whatever wrong about feeling quickly or "instinctively" that one side of an issue or the other may be the right one, or at least the best of the limited alternatives available. But we should entertain the possibility that in some such instances, and perhaps in many, we will be mistaken. Indeed, the sense of comfort and certainty we often feel at such moments is not necessarily due to any essential righteousness in our position; far more often it derives from the fact that the "conclusion" we have adopted harmonizes with our already firmly cemented prejudices or natural dispositions.

Incidentally, not all prejudices are evil in themselves. The reader and I, let us assume, are both loyal Americans. We are therefore full of all sorts of pro-American prejudices. For the most part, this works out well enough. But not always. Many Americans, for example, feel that it was an atrocity to have dropped atomic bombs on the Japanese cities of Hiroshima and Nagasaki. Even more might agree with that view were it not for the feeling that it is somehow un-American to adopt any position that implies a criticism of our nation.

There are circumstances, usually associated with war, in which it may be sensed that one's nation is on the wrong side of a particular issue or confrontation but in which nevertheless, out of loyalty, self-protection, or other considerations, one is obliged to act in defense of one's own side. But it is still possible—and morally necessary—to reserve judgment in such instances.

As G. K. Chesterton once suggested, the purpose of having an open mind is the same as having an open mouth, the object being eventually to close it on something solid. But one should close neither the mind nor the mouth until the general circumstances of the moment make it reasonable to do so.

Rule No. 4

Beware of falling in love with your first answer

All day long, and every day of our lives, we have to make guesses, assumptions, decisions, and conclusions. But it is not necessary to do so in every situation. We do have the option of reserving judgment. Suppose, for example, that you are sitting at a table helping a three-year-old girl eat her lunch. Suddenly, as you are watching her, she reaches out, tips over a glass. The milk that was inside of it spills out across the table and begins to drip over the edge onto the floor. Since you were a witness to the incident, you know exactly how the milk happened to be spilled.

But now assume that a moment later another member of the family walks into the room. He, too, notices the spilled milk and the look of annoyance on your face. He has absolutely no way of knowing that the milk was, in fact, spilled by the little girl. If he is intelligent, he will probably *assume* that this is so, but he will not pretend to be certain about the matter. After all, *you* might have spilled the milk, or the family cat might have jumped up on the table and tipped the glass over. Perhaps some other member of the family—or a neighbor or a friend—passed through the room a moment earlier and tipped the glass accidentally.

Or on purpose.

From this simple example we can see that there are often many possible explanations for the things that happen around us.

Since this is the case, it is more reasonable and intelligent to recognize our guesses and assumptions as merely that and not treat them as if they were firmly established until they have been verified by the evidence.

Since we have considered the steps of this argument one by one, we can perceive its common sense. But when it comes to real-life cases, something rather odd often happens. People may do what is called "leaping to a conclusion." That is to say, we make a quick guess, assume some sort of explanation of the events we observe, and then—precisely at this point in the transaction—our explanation, which may or may not be valid, gets locked in. As mentioned earlier, we make an ego-investment in the explanation.

At the next stage when our explanation—or our hypothesis—is questioned, challenged, or flatly contradicted, those of us who took a firm, no-doubts-allowed position on it feel personally attacked. In reality we are not being attacked. At this stage of communication about the incident, the challenger very probably has no interest at all in the fact that we, or Tom or Bob or Sally, offered a certain explanation for the events described. The questioner is simply concentrating on the assertion itself, which, to him or her, may seem only one of several possible explanations, or may seem completely erroneous. It is at this point that people sometimes become red in the face, raise their voices, get their feelings hurt, and in certain cases actually are foolish enough to permit the argument to escalate to a physical contest. In cases where the arguers are armed with knives or guns—or have access to such weapons—serious physical injury or even death may occur. It happens every day.

In many such cases there would have been no possibility of such tragic consequences if the people had known even a little about the methods of thinking clearly. If they had, either the argument would not have taken place at all or, if there was a difference of opinion, the arguers would have stated their positions in reasonable terms, rather than emotionally and combatively.

Consider the old saying "Circumstances alter cases."

They do indeed, although many people wish it were not so. This desire for simplicity sometimes appears in the ancient and always-to-be-continued debate about crime and punishment. It would be very convenient, would it not, if society could simply agree on certain quite specific forms of punishment for certain crimes? Let us say, for example, that all murderers should be sentenced to fifty years in prison, all rapists to twenty-five years, all bank robbers to twenty years, all burglars to ten years, and so on. And such prescriptions do, at first thought, seem to make sense. They would certainly save considerable time, and therefore money, in the courts. They would relieve judges of a great deal of responsibility. Unfortunately for such wishful thinking, not only the testimony of legal experts but simple common sense demonstrates the unworkability of the idea. In murder case A, the guilty party may be a longtime, cold-blooded professional killer. In murder case B, the perpetrator may be an individual with no prior criminal record who killed in the process of a drunken brawl after a football game or in a fit of passionate revenge.

But now let us take the principle we have just examined and apply it to the less dramatic circumstances of everyday life. At once we can see that here, too, we must not only reserve judgment until it is reasonable to take a formal position on a case, but even then must be willing to revise our verdict if additional evidence requires it.

Suppose you heard a man say, "I have tears in my ears." Perhaps you would assume that, to the extent that he made the statement with serious intent, he was speaking nonsense. Why? Well, everyone knows that tears, like all other objects in the universe, are affected by gravity and gravity pulls tears downward below our eyes, and does not move them laterally across our faces so that they end up in our ears.

But despite the reasonableness we are demonstrating in so thinking, we are wrong, because we have overlooked one possibility or been ignorant of one factor, as the case may be. The phrase comes from the old country-and-western song, "I've Got Tears in My Ears/From Lying On My Back/In My Bed While I Cry Over You."

Again, circumstances alter cases, and this is one more reason that it is wise to reserve judgment, or—if we have been forced to make at least a temporary judgment—to be willing to revise it when new information comes to our attention.

Another vitally important reason for resisting the temptation to fall in love with our first hypothesis is that, when we do, it chokes off the very sort of creativity we are attempting to encourage. When we approach a problem, it is a good idea to give our mind free rein. When we do that, we may, in time, think of several possible solutions.

It is the very obviousness of the value of having several choices that is part of the rationale of the process of groupthink sometimes called *brainstorming*. Several people go off together into one room, perhaps at one table, and are instructed to discuss the problem, to make notes, to see what possible answers to the puzzle of the moment they might be able to come up with. Part of the instruction may go something like this: "Now, whatever you do, *don't* try to play it safe here. There is nothing competitive in this situation; no one is going to be criticized for coming up with an occasional kooky or unworkable idea. What we want to promote here, at the moment, is the free flow of creativity. So let's just start to kick the subject around and see how many ideas we can come up with."

That sort of instruction goes a long way to free some or all of the participants from what would otherwise be a self-inhibiting fear of advancing ideas that the others might laugh at or that would "just seem too crazy."

A good many of the most important ideas in the history of thought have seemed crazy indeed to those with whom they were first shared. Some of them seemed so crazy, in fact, that they got the original thinkers into serious trouble, not only with the societies in which they lived but even with other experts in their narrow fields. There is, then, something in our heads, something rather mysterious, that will work on problems for us—or even help us in freer creative expression—but we must first *get ourselves out of the way* of that creative center.

I had no conscious awareness that this thought itself had occurred to me until some years ago when I began to notice that, in responding to questions from journalists about such modest creativity as I am capable of, I was, from time to time, using the phrase, "getting out of my own way." The phrase occurred spontaneously and was not the result of any continuing speculation, but some center of wisdom within me realized intuitively that for my own creative juices to flow it really was necessary that I get out of my own way, which is to say, step around factors of ego, fear, and inhibition. Sometimes it was just a matter of clearing other work off my desk and out of my head, so to speak. Again—one method for getting out of your own way is to avoid falling in love with your first hypothesis.

Rule No. 5

Beware of the erroneous assumption

It is important to understand the distinction between an erroneous assumption and a stupid mistake. Simply being wrong by no means necessarily involves an affront to sound reason. If a four-year-old child is taught that the first president of the United States was Charlton Heston, he or she will thereafter make a number of erroneous statements about that particular question. But this will *not* be because he or she has *reasoned* poorly. It will be simply because the child has relied on poor authority. Stupidity, of course, can eventually enter into the process if individuals so unfortunately conditioned persist in their mistaken opinions for the rest of their lives, despite the availability of mountains of evidence to the contrary.

But many an erroneous assumption involves good reasoning rather than bad. There is some protection in remembering that we are entitled to make almost any reasonable *assumption,* but should resist making *conclusions* until evidence requires that we do so.

An example: On a visit to the pleasant city of St. Louis, Missouri, not long ago, I stayed for three days at the Cheshire Inn. Since it is my custom to get a certain amount of exercise daily, I had brought along jogging attire and, one bitterly cold morning, went out to trot about the neighborhood. As I was returning to the hotel after my workout, I passed a series of three-story dwellings, some of them private homes, some apartments. In front of one building, on a low mound of grassy earth, I suddenly noticed two blood-soaked tissues. The bright red stains suggested that some injured animal—very probably human— had been in the area not much earlier. Dried blood would have been of a darker color.

143

As I paused momentarily to speculate on the evidence, I wondered what poor soul had been involved. Looking up at the building I noticed the sign "Dentist" in the first floor window. "Ah," I thought, "some unfortunate patient was still bleeding after leaving the doctor's office. Or perhaps bleeding on the way into the office."

Since I had other business to attend to at the moment I gave the matter no further thought just then. I proceeded to the hotel's restaurant, enjoyed a hearty breakfast, and then entered the lobby on the way to my room. As I passed the reception desk the manager said, "Oh, Mr. Allen, Mr. Honigberg, your publicity man, told me to tell you that he won't be able to go with you to the first appointment this morning because when he went out for a walk a while ago, he slipped on the ice."

"Oh, that's too bad," I said. "Was he injured?"

"Well," the man said, "he cut his lip pretty badly, I guess. He had to go to the hospital to have stitches taken in it."

The blood-stained tissues had been discarded by my friend. I had, therefore, been wrong when I assumed that the evidence had been left behind by a dental patient. This incident demonstrates that it is possible to take a reasonable approach to a problem and still be utterly mistaken in one's assumptions or conclusions about it.

It also reminds us that there are many questions that cannot be answered by reason alone. It is the combination of reason and evidence that has such impressive force.

A rural fellow sat on a fence on a backwoods Kentucky road. Next to him stood a ferocious-looking mastiff.

"Does your dog bite?" a stranger asked.

"Nope," said the farmer.

At that the dog bit the stranger, who cried out, "I thought you said your dog didn't bite!"

"That ain't my dog," the backwoodsman answered.

In a real-life situation, obviously, the farmer would have explained, after the stranger's first question, that the dog was not his. But the story nevertheless points out that all of us are in the habit of making unwarranted assumptions. Some of our assumptions are patently far-fetched. Others are at least understandable. We cannot do away with the assumption-making process altogether, since not every facet of daily life can be subjected to a lengthy question-and-answer analysis. But it is important to distinguish between what we actually know and what we only assume.

A woman who had an appointment with her doctor arrived at the physician's offices two minutes before the set time. As she happened to glance through the opened door of the inner office, she was surprised to see that the doctor was wearing quite heavy make-up, including an almost purplish lipstick.

Almost everyone, reading the preceding paragraph for the first time, will assume that either the doctor had a serious problem of sexual identity or was perhaps made up for some sort of theatrical production. In reality there is no problem at all; the doctor in the story is a woman. What her patient was surprised by was the heaviness of the make-up, since most women do not make themselves up so theatrically.

Author-editor Norman Cousins tells a story that—like many jokes—involves unwarranted assumptions. A seventy-nine-year-old man told his doctor that his father had suffered from the same disease that was troubling him.

"And of what disease did your father die?" the doctor asked.

"Did I say he died?" the man answered.

"Well, what did your grandfather die of?"

"Did I say he died?" the man repeated. "In fact, at the age of 117 he married a girl of 23."

"But," the doctor asked, "why would a man of 117 want to marry a girl of 23?"

"Did I say he *wanted* to marry her?" the patient replied.

In this instance, too, the doctor's assumptions were reasonable enough. They led, nevertheless, to error. We should beware, therefore, of absolute certainty about our assumptions.

And, we should not pretend to be certain about something when, in fact, we are not. If we are asked a question and do not know the answer, it is much better to say, "I don't really know," than to pretend that we do know and then possibly give a wrong answer.

The primary reason it is wrong to do so is that almost all of us are impressed by an attitude of certainty on the part of those providing information. The result is that each day millions of false statements are accepted as true, all over the world, because the people who hear the statements are impressed by the attitude of certainty on the part of the speakers. This is not, of course, an either/or proposition. Consider, for example, the statement "Los Angeles is the capital of the state of California."

Regarding your own possible responses to that assertion consider the following:

1. You are quite certain that the statement is *true*.
2. You are quite certain that the statement is *false*.
3. You simply do not know whether it is *true* or *false*.

Under the heading of number 3, however—and it is important to note this—there may be various degrees of uncertainty. You may, for example, have quite a strong feeling that the statement is true or you may have the vague suspicion that it is false. (Sacramento is the capital of California.)

To give another illustration that dramatizes the importance of this rule, I had occasion, not long ago, to fly from Portland, Oregon, to Honolulu, Hawaii. On the way to the airport it occurred to me that I might make a call to Los Angeles, to give some instructions to an employee. Because of having been on an extremely arduous work-schedule during the preceding three days, I had neglected to find out whether the Portland-to-Honolulu flight was nonstop or touched down in a California city before crossing the Pacific. On the way to the Portland airport I said to a local resident who was in the car with me, "Do you know if the plane I'm taking makes any stops before it gets to Honolulu?" "Oh, yes," he said with an air of absolute assurance, "it will stop in either San Francisco or Los Angeles."

"Are there no *non*stop flights between here and Honolulu?" I asked.

"No, there are not," he said.

I did not make the phone call at the local airport since I assumed there would be an opportunty to make it at our intermediate stop. Once aloft, I learned that there are indeed nonstop Portland-to-Honolulu flights and that I was on one of them. Of course I was partly to blame for the misunderstanding, which leads us to: Don't be too quick to accept information unless the source is authoritative. And even then realize that it is wise to seek supporting evidence before you consider the case closed.

The source I had trusted in this case was simply a resident of the city of Portland. That made his word on this specific question worth more than my own, but not nearly so authoritative as that of (*a*) the pilot of the plane, (*b*) any other representative of the airline, (*c*) a frequent air-traveler from Portland to Honolulu.

Facts may be considered to exist in isolation, but in reality they are rarely encountered in such a state. Let us say, for example, that two entertainers—Sid Caesar and Steve Allen—are booked at a given nightclub and that each of us ends the performance after a three-week run.

At first glance the three-week factor seems to be a constant and have the same general significance.

But Sid Caesar, let us say, had been booked for only two weeks and was held over for a third week, whereas Steve Allen may have been booked for six weeks and canceled after three, due to poor box office.

Look at facts in context, not in isolation.

Again, it is not unusual for even the simplest-sounding statement to have more than one possible meaning.

Consider the following sentence. "Jayne Meadows and Steve Allen have gotten divorced."

Sounds like a headline in the *National Enquirer,* doesn't it?

Well, it happens to be true. Jayne and I have gotten divorced.

But not from each other. Each of us was married once before.

Rule No. 6

Beware of making predictions
on the strength of insufficient evidence

Perhaps you've heard the story of a gentleman who greatly enjoyed the game of golf and habitually gambled with his friends about various players, comparative scores, and individual shots.

One day a man walked out to the first tee at the fellow's country club accompanied by an erect 400-pound gorilla.

"Fellows," he said to his friends, "you're not going to believe this, and I don't blame you, but I've been training this animal, in seclusion, for several years and I've finally achieved notable success. If you don't believe me, get a load of this."

At that, the man signaled the gorilla, which stepped up to the tee, looked down the fairway, and then thwacked the ball straight ahead for over 400 yards, something no human has ever been able to do.

"Why, that's incredible," one of the bystanders said. "As a matter of fact, since I'm a betting man, I'd like to place a bet right now on this magnificent beast against any and all comers."

Bets were hastily exchanged, after which the party, including the gorilla, trooped ahead to the hole, where it was discovered that the gorilla's ball lay a scant 15 inches from the cup.

When the inveterate gambler saw this, he said, "I'm so confident about this incredible animal that I'd like to double my bet right now."

After his bet was taken, he said to the beast's owner, "Tell him to go ahead."

The man signaled the gorilla, which looked intently at the ball for a moment, accepted a putter from the caddy, then thwacked the ball, as hard as he could, for another 400 yards.

Again—don't make up your mind too hastily. Don't be overly influenced by early returns.

Rule No. 7

Examine your superstitions

A separate book could be written on this particular category of dumbth. In fact, a good many such books have already been published. There is no evidence that they have diminished the amount of superstition in the world. On the front page of the *Los Angeles Times,* May 5, 1982—as I dictate these obvservations—there is a feature story about the city of Antananarivo, the capital of Madagascar, where, according to the *Times*'s staff writer Charles Powers, "Nine million people have discovered that Tuesday is unlucky. In fact, they have identified 120 unlucky days in the year. People so finely-tuned for calamity are extremely careful. They almost always wear hats. They never kick the walls of their houses. They don't like the number 8. Before building a house, opening a new business, taking a job or getting married, they consult an astrologer."

There was a period, starting in the eighteenth century, when the newly enlightened European intellectuals assumed that increased opportunities for popular education would eventually do away with superstition. If such hopes were seriously entertained, they were obviously groundless. The absurdity of specific superstitions is always apparent— even to the dim-witted—so long as the observer is not party to the superstition in question. But once an individual has accepted a superstitious belief, it isn't likely that any amount of either simple common sense or formally logical argument, including reference to relevant scientific data, will suffice to demonstrate the combined error and foolishness of the belief. The only thing, therefore, that might be able to greatly diminish the amount of superstition in the world is the very means this book proposes: introduction to the methods of sensible

149

reasoning in early childhood. The time factor is crucial since my argument is based on the premise that, because superstitious belief is exceedingly difficult to eradicate, the thing to do is create a state of mind that will make it much less likely that absurd beliefs will be accepted in the first place.

Rule No. 8

Recognize that you have personal prejudices

There is in the American philosophical tradition—if not always in our behavior—a long-held antipathy toward prejudice. We quite rightly regard the prejudiced individual as inferior to the unprejudiced, and this is no less so even in instances when we ourselves are guilty of prejudice, just as we regard the virtuous individual as superior to the evil even if we ourselves from time to time break the a law. But there is something faulty, limiting, in the perhaps generally unexamined definition of prejudice; for we apply it almost exclusively to relationships with people having religious, racial, ethnic, or political backgrounds different from our own. It is important to give analytical consideration to the phenomenon in such a context, but in doing so we miss the basic point about prejudice—that it violates common sense, whether construed as what Christian theologians have called "right reason" or what secularists might regard as the scientific method.

To speak plainly, to be guilty of prejudice is to act stupidly. The stupidity may, of course, take a variety of forms. In one form we simply adopt an attitude or belief from our parents, friends, neighborhood acquaintances, religion, or economic class without ever subjecting it to even the most casual critical analysis. In another form, we may imagine that we have reasoned out our biased view on the basis of empirical experience, whereas we may actually have committed the common error of formulating a principle on the basis of insufficient evidence.

We may, for example, after having actually been cheated in business dealings by, let us say, three Armenians, assume that either all or most Armenians are less trustworthy than the rest of the human race in the conduct of business affairs; or, having encountered a few individual Irish-

151

men who, let us assume, were less intelligent than normal, we have assumed that the Irish, as a categorical class, are less intelligent than the norm.

Turning from such purely hypothetical instances to those from the context of actual social prejudice, consider the hypothesis that members of the black race are "naturally lazy." It does not fly in the face of purely rational—as distinguished from empirical—considerations to assume that one race might, in fact, be inferior in terms of natural physical energy. But if blacks actually were deficient in this way, it would hardly be the case that *in those categories in which physical energy is actually measurable*—in the context of athletics—members of this supposedly inferior group should daily distinguish themselves by running faster, jumping farther, punching harder, and playing football, basketball, and baseball better—in other words, giving ample evidence not of inferiority but of superiority.

If, in the face of this information, the bigot nevertheless persists in pointing to specific blacks he has known who have, let us assume, actually appeared to be lazy, it would usually be discovered that the tasks society had assigned them were such that a lack of enthusiasm was a perfectly reasonable response. In my youth I held certain jobs that were (*a*) physically exhausting, (*b*) very poor paying, and (*c*) boring. I'm afraid that in the performance of such tasks I acted in such a manner that an unprejudiced observer would have described me as lazy, whereas once I was fortunate enough to secure employment that challenged my capabilities and paid well, I was willing to work industriously, for very long hours, and with unflagging gusto.

There are probably thousands of homes in the United States in which white women who perform little or no physical labor employ black women to do a great deal of it, and yet the white women may consider some of the black women lazy. No doubt if the roles were reversed, the same adjective would be employed.

But again, to return to the root of the matter, it is the faultiness of the reasoning process that is basically wrong with prejudice. Its unfortunate social effects stem from that central error.

Because of their unedifying record, bias and prejudice have unattractive connotations. We tend to think that only rather terrible people are biased and prejudiced. In fact, everybody is biased and prejudiced. It is not even possible to grow up on Planet Earth without having to accept a good many ideas as true before we can possibly be mature enough to know if, in fact, they are true. There is no way to get around this. After all, we cannot give four-year-old children long philosophical explanations and documentation about things. We generally simply share with them such knowledge or opinion as we ourselves have already accumulated. If, let us say, 17 percent of what we believe is one form of nonsense or another, then we are passing this degree of error on to our children. They absorb additional errors from other sources.

Another complicating factor is that it seems necessary to humankind to develop some sort of overall philosophy of life. In the case of many of us, that philosophy is quite hazy around the edges, even though we may consciously think of ourselves as Christians, Jews, Rotarians, chess players, Communists, or whatever. But as soon as we carry even one such card of identity, it means that we have an overall way of looking at a great deal, if not all, of our experience. It is at least theoretically possible, I suppose, to grow to maturity without having any such cohesive world-view or philosophy at all, but most of us do absorb both what is good and what is bad from our social environment.

It is important for us to grasp that whatever our personal philosophy might be, it will inevitably affect our way of perceiving reality and, therefore, our way of reasoning. Whether we personally, for example, believe there is a God, whether we believe or disbelieve in democracy, whether we believe or disbelieve that capitalism is the best economic system, whether we believe men are superior, or inferior, to women— such separate beliefs will profoundly influence our reactions, attitudes, and views about a thousand and one separate questions.

Reasoning itself is, in part, a painstaking and sometimes painful process of attempting to use the logical parts of the brain in a disinterested fashion, deliberately casting off—to the greatest possible extent—the restraints imposed by social conditioning. Some people seem to be able to do this rather well; some never seem able to do it.

Imagine a classroom inhabited by one hundred students. They are hearing a lecture by one of the world's leading geologists. Ninety-seven of them will have no problem at all accepting the expert's casual statement that Planet Earth is billions of years old. The geologist will, in support of this statement, refer to fossils found in rock formations known to be of particular ages because of carbon dating. But three of the students in the class—who may, so far as native intelligence is concerned, be every bit the equal of the others—nevertheless will be shocked by such assertions because, as fundamentalist Christians who believe that the Bible is the literal word of God, they will be unable to see how the world can possibly be more than a few thousand years old.

It is not my point here to say which side of the issue is wise and which is foolish, because doing so would be irrelevant to our purpose of the moment. The point is simply that once the few students in question have accepted the fundamentalist philosophy they are, in a certain sense, literally unable to agree with a statement which, to all others present, will be no more remarkable than the assertion that grass is green or ice is cold.

In just the same way, a convinced Marxist will have great difficulty accepting the reality of details about Soviet prison camps—barbed wire, machine guns, slave labor, and so on. Catholics may be made extremely uncomfortable, both physically and emotionally, by being forced to consider the full story of their church's Inquisition, the hounding of heretics, burnings at the stake, boilings in oil, and other montrous tortures and atrocities.

One of the reasons for the predicament of the American Indian is that few U.S. citizens are emotionally able to get into clear focus the ugly reality of the treatment of the native inhabitants of the North American continent during the past four centuries. All of us have grown up seeing *ourselves* as the "good guys." We have identified with heroic figures in motion pictures—Clark Gable, Gary Cooper, John Wayne, Alan Ladd, Clint Eastwood, Robert Redford. It is this tendency of each of the world's peoples to see themselves in complimentary terms, and to see others as either inferior or as the "enemy," that makes it so shocking when one travels overseas and for the first time learns about attitudes of the world's various peoples. Again it is reason, and reason alone, that attempts to pick its way across the minefields and potholes of bias, prejudice, superstition, selfish rationalization, fear, and ignorance. Many people have little interest in truth for truth's sake. What they are interested in is being right, in winning. The majority of the world's population who believe in a God of truth, however, must conclude that while individual religions may sometimes be enemies of truth, the source of all truth cannot possibly be such.

Rule No. 9

Beware of prefabricated answers

There is nothing wrong, per se, with "wise sayings," proverbs, or fortune-cookie aphorisms. But their chief use seems to be to support decisions already arrived at. It would usually be unwise to base your course of action on an old saying, whatever its content. Laurence J. Peter, creator of the famed Peter Principle, which holds that people tend to rise to their level of incompetence, has collected pairs of "wise sayings" that cancel each other out:

1. Look before you leap.
   He who hesitates is lost.

2. You can't teach an old dog new tricks.
   It's never too late to learn.

3. Where there's a will, there's a way.
   Time and tide wait for no man.

4. Out of sight, out of mind.
   Absence makes the heart grow fonder.

5. Two heads are better than one.
   If you want something done right, do it yourself.

6. Never look a gift horse in the mouth.
   All that glitters is not gold.

7. You can't tell a book by its cover.
   Clothes make the man.

8. Many hands make light work.
   Too many cooks spoil the broth.

9. Better safe than sorry.
   Nothing ventured, nothing gained.

The point here is certainly not that because some pairs of old sayings are mutually exclusive you should therefore never give the slightest consideration to any of them. "A stitch in time saves nine" came into common use all over the world simply because it is observably the case that we ought not to wait till things fall totally apart to begin the process of making repairs. But the underlying point is that such prefabricated thoughts really ought to be used to stimulate your own creative abilities rather than replace them.

Some old sayings, of course, are of very doubtful value indeed, for example, "All's fair in love and war." Really? No civilized society has ever thought so, even though unspeakable atrocities and savagery are all too characteristic of the behavior of humans engaged in war. As for love, there is no moral code in the world that sanctions the commission of any act—rape, adultery, incest, kidnapping, child abandonment, and so forth—simply because the committer is, or perceives himself to be, seized by the emotion of passionate love.

Rule No. 10

Beware of arguments by slogans or epigrams

This is not to say that such forms of expression have no rightful place in human communication. Indeed they do. They are often colorful, pithy, and may make a perfectly valid point. But in the context of reasonable argumentation they should serve as no more than attention-getters. Consider, for example, the expression common among professional anti-Communists, "Better dead than red." It is a waste of time to walk into the trap suggested by such a limited choice of alternatives. Instead one should consult the relevant contextual realities. Doing so immediately brings to our attention the fact that the large dilemma of nuclear war is inherently tremendously complex, regardless of what one's biases may be, or even wherever the center of gravity of justice might lie. The factors to be considered number literally in the hundreds. To limit oneself to a consideration of only two of them, therefore—deadness and redness (the latter taken to mean living under a Communist government)—is to short-circuit, at the outset, any hope of thinking rationally about so perplexing an issue.

Incidentally, when we consult the reality of the unfortunate hundreds of millions who do live in states controlled by Marxist governments, we at once perceive that every one of those individuals has the utmost freedom to choose between deadness and redness. The striking fact is that none of them choose deadness.

A good many of them would no doubt not choose redness, either, if they had the power to make such a choice. But that is beside the central point.

In any event, the sensible way to approach the larger problem is to study and work very hard to avoid both deadness and redness.

The point applies to all inherently complex issues.

Rule No. 11

Be aware that your opinions, assumptions, and beliefs are often affected by peer-group pressure

Some time back, on a television program, I asked our studio audience to indicate by applause its verdict on three famous Supreme Court cases. We did not use a mechanical device for measuring the volume of applause. In each case, I simply made a guess that the number applauding constituted 10 percent, 40 percent, or some other portion of the 400 individuals present. So, on that basis, our sampling could not be said to be scientific.

Another factor also detracts from the scientific objectivity of such experiments: Individuals frequently permit their opinions to be swayed, or even reversed, because of the influence of group pressure.

A Dr. Richard Crutchfield, at Berkeley, California, has demonstrated this by an ingenious test. Using 600 subjects, he first divided them into 120 groups of five, and then sent the five individuals in each group into five separate closed booths.

Once inside, *each* subject observed that the cubicle was marked by the letter "E." At this point, each erroneously assumed that the booths of his or her four colleagues were marked A, B, C, and D.

A simple question was flashed on the wall of the booth. Before answering, the individual was able to *see* the answers apparently given by those in booths "A" to "D." In reality, however, the first four answers—all the same—were supplied by the operator; each was *incorrect*. In most cases, the individual knew the correct answer but was led to believe that his four associates had given an answer that disagreed with his own.

What would you do in this instance? Human nature being what

it is, you will now insist that if you knew the right answer, you would simply give it and not be in the least affected by the ignorance of your four colleagues. What actually happened, however, was that up to 45 percent of those tested immediately mistrusted their own judgment and decided to go along with the majority.

When another factor was introduced—the complimentary suggestion that the four other subjects were doing fine—it was found that adherence to majority opinion would go as high as 90 percent!

The questions involved were all reasonably simple. It was not a lack of knowledge that weakened the confidence of the subjects in their answers. Mathematicians, it was discovered, would surrender their judgments on questions involving grade school arithmetic.

You may think this is nothing but an interesting psychological experiment and that it has no personal application to you. If so, you have missed the point.

Anyone with the power to control channels of public communication can bring to bear the force of the pressure toward conformity that this test reveals. Authoritarian governments, obviously, exert a massive amount of such pressure. But such things can happen even in relatively free societies when citizens of a community are subjected to one-sided interpretations of important issues and events.

William Randolph Hearst was, perhaps more than any other individual, responsible for the Spanish-American War. Because of the hysteria his newspapers created, honorable men were regarded as unpatriotic if they presumed to question the wisdom of our war with Spain.

You may take a bemused or contemptuous attitude toward this obvious stupidity because it happened so long ago. If so, re-read the preceding paragraph, but this time substitute the phrase "our war with North Vietnam." During much of the sixties and seventies distinguished citizens were accused of unpatriotic behavior or secret sympathy with communism if they publicly expressed doubts about our course in Vietnam. Even such lifelong dedicated anti-Communists as the late Bishop Fulton J. Sheen were subjected to bitter criticism for pointing to the folly and immorality of the Vietnam war.

Only very gradually, after the loss of 58,000 American lives, was it realized that the majority of the American population had serious reservations about our course in Southeast Asia.

Americans must be aware of this danger. Our Founding Fathers understood it. They knew that the independent thinker must be permitted to think, regardless of majority disapproval. The tyranny of the majority can, under certain circumstances, be as harmful as the tyranny of the despot.

Rule No. 12

Do not make an exclusive commitment
to either optimism or pessimism

It is absurd to be consistently either an optimist or a pessimist. We may—indeed, we usually will—oscillate between moods at one extreme or the other, in an ongoing process that is often determined by factors having no direct connection with the main question at issue. A lack of sleep, a missed meal, a throbbing headache, the puzzling loss of some valued object, thousands of such happenstances can incline us toward a gloomy view at any given moment. A sunny day after a storm, the return of spring after a painful winter, hearing good news, a raise in salary, the warmth of a friendly hand, a smile from a stranger— such pleasant experiences can lift our mood and make almost everything we consider seem more likely to turn out well.

There is a degree of reasonableness to this. But to adopt a consistently optimistic or pessimistic policy is unreasonable. The wiser course is to do what, fortunately, most of us do by nature, which is to constantly assess our prospects and, on the basis of available evidence, however haphazardly perceived, make a loose calculation of the chances of our predicament getting better or worse within a limited amount of time.

Rule No. 13

Beware of giving children only factual answers

When children ask you a question, it is better to help them reason their way toward the answer rather than simply providing it. This is possible, of course, only in the context of certain kinds of questions. If a child asks, "Who was the first president of the United States?" it is extremely unlikely that you can assist him to reason his way toward the correct answer, particularly if he is too young to have heard of George Washington. To provide an example in which the alternative is possible, I cite an instance in which my then-seven-year-old grand-daughter, Stephanie, who with her mother and father and two younger brothers was visiting me in a Spokane hotel, did the right thing when encouraged to do so. Standing inside the central door of our three-room suite, she asked, "What is the number of this door?"

"Why?" I said.

"Well," she said, "when we go out to get ice I want to make sure I know what door to come back in."

"There's a very easy way for you to tell what the number of the door is," I said. "Think about it for a moment and see if you can tell me how to do that."

Almost immediately she said, "You look on the *outside* of the door."

Not a great deal of reasoning was required in this case, but it was still better for Stephanie to exercise her own mental powers rather than simply have me provide the answer, at no intellectual cost to herself.

As regards the matter of enabling children to think better, it is obvious that a great majority of the rules and suggestions provided in this book can be taught to children, although not by simply handing them a copy of these instructions. "How to Think," originally published in record album form, was designed specifically for children. The recording, in fact, is still available and is presently distributed by the *Gifted Children Monthly* (Gifted and Talented Productions, Inc., 213 Hollydell Drive, Sewell, New Jersey, 08080). But because of the time limitation imposed by that form, only a sketchy outline of a method of thinking improvement could be given. All the suggestions included in the record album, in any event, are included here, and a great many others besides.

It is easier, when dealing with young children, to provide both factual information and a method for reasoning with such data, but we must still not expect a ten-year-old to reason as competently as an adult, all other elements being equal.

There are two separate qualities or factors involved during the early learning period: (*a*) the simple acquisition of knowledge, and (*b*) the development of that mental power generally denoted by the word *judgment,* which implies the faculty of reason. Driving an automobile is such a simple procedure that there is no normal six-year-old child in the world who cannot be taught its essentials in just a few minutes, a fact I know since I taught my youngest son, Bill, to drive when he was that age. (Indeed, there came a crisis situation, when he was about ten, when his ability to drive one of our cars, which had been stalled in a torrential downpour, moved both the car and himself out of danger after I had had to leave it for a few minutes to try to reach a telephone.) But despite the ease with which young children can manipulate automobiles, we do not permit them to drive until many years later. At the age of six their eyesight, hearing, and quickness of physical response are superior to those of millions of middle-aged or older adults; but for all their physical superiority, *they lack the ability to make sound judgments.* For precisely this reason we control their lives at the dinner table, at school, in making purchases, and in many other situations.

The part of judgment that involves problem-solving can be taught. Morality also can be taught, and teaching it encourages the faculty of judgment. At least it does unless we are foolish enough to preach morality as a simple matter of strict-orders-and-no-backtalk, a collection of rules handed down from on high that, without such divine sanction, might not always be demonstrably wise. Fortunately for the purposes of civilization, the greater part of social and personal morality involves simple common sense. There are perfectly good reasons, after all, why we should not lie, cheat, steal, kill, assault, or rape. In inculcating moral instruction, therefore, care should be taken to emphasize the sweet reasonableness of moral behavior. One reason this is a wise course is that millions of people, as adults, have either consciously abandoned or casually drifted away from their original spiritual homes. If they believed in certain moral rules simply because, say, the Mormon or the Catholic church insisted on them, they are likely to lose part of their respect for such rules if, for whatever reasons, they abandon Mormonism or Catholicism. But if they have been shown the simple common sense of a moral code, it is likely to persist as part of their mind-set.

Rule No. 14

Beware of thinking that because you are bright and quick-minded, you therefore reason well

It is commonly assumed that an innately high intelligence, in and of itself, is a reliable protection against irrationality. Since this is not the case, it ought not to be believed. There is a degree of truth in the belief, for it is probable that notably intelligent people are less inclined to clumsy reasoning than are those who are less gifted. But there is a wealth of evidence, both contemporary and historical, to show that literate and articulate individuals have cleverly—sometimes brilliantly— defended utterly preposterous assertions. In a school for gifted children that I had the pleasure of visiting some time ago, a teacher asked members of her class—in the ten- to eleven-year-old range—to tell me what individual projects they were working on. One girl shared the information that she was writing a report on strange creatures, such as the Loch Ness monster, Bigfoot, and the Abominable Snowman.

"Are you starting with the assumption that such creatures actually exist?" I asked.

"Yes, I am," she said.

If so intelligent and charming a young person had been given even a few days instruction in the proper methods of thought, she would not have begun by committing herself to a position and then simply looking for evidence consistent with her assumption.

This is not to say that it would be impossible for a researcher to end up constructing an argument in favor of the existence of creatures that scientists and scholars believe to be nonexistent. What I take exception to is not the child's position, but the method—or lack of method—by which she arrived at it.

165

Rule No. 15

Beware of reacting to labels rather
than to specific individuals

In California, an investigative journalist, whom I met in 1979 in connection with a conference on organized crime, told me that before our
first meeting he had been discussing my participation in the campaign
against the Mafia and other professional criminals with a friend who
worked in law enforcement. The government man, the journalist
explained, seemed perplexed by my involvement in such an issue. "Steve
Allen?" he said. "Wasn't he against the war in Vietnam?"

"So was Bishop Sheen," I said to the reporter, and I then explained
that I planned to use the lawman's question as an illustration of a common
sort of breakdown in logical reasoning.

The clumsiness of the man's thought process is so apparent that
it does not require analysis, but the man's question is more than merely
poorly thought out. It is actually stupid. I in turn would not be justified
in assuming that the speaker was *habitually* guilty of such ineptness,
but that he was guilty of it in this instance is clear. Mafia criminals
and their non-Italian allies, as it happens, are characteristically highly
patriotic Americans, generally take conservative positions on social
questions, and decidedly supported the Vietnam war. Liberals,
progressives, socialists, and most other leftists are strongly critical of
organized crime, which has no necessary connection with their position
on the war in Vietnam, the value of mother's milk, or any other important but irrelevant question.

A daily edition of almost any newspaper, particularly in the letter-
to-the-editor section, provides depressing examples of fallacious reasoning concerning our society's response to crime. Consider, for example,

the common question, "Why are liberals so concerned with the rights of criminals but not concerned at all about the rights of victims?"

Such a question, first of all, is a classic instance of the either/or fallacy, concerning which I shall have more to say later. But the most remarkable thing about such a question—often rendered as a flat statement or conclusion—is that it simply does not conform to any observable reality. There are, in fact, no liberals—or, for that matter, illiberals, married men, or kangaroos—who are concerned *only* with the rights of criminals and not concerned with the rights of victims. Even the most monstrously cruel criminals themselves become sensitively concerned with the rights of victims if they, or members of their family or circle of friends, are victimized by other criminals.

If we want to assist our conservative friends to do something constructive about the debate on the general dilemma of the American legal system, we should first encourage them to isolate the two constituent factors of their question. If they do so, they are then perfectly entitled to ask, "Why are liberals, among others, so concerned with the rights of criminals?" This, as I say, is a perfectly legitimate question. In fact, it is a question that ought to be asked a good deal more than it is, since presumably those who express curiosity on the issue will want to have their curiosity satisfied. The reason that not only liberals, but almost all professionals who hold positions in the American system of criminal justice (as well as their counterparts in many other parts of the world), are concerned with the rights of criminals is that we see— from the record of history, not to mention the examples of the behavior of despotic governments of the right and left in today's world—what happens when governments and peoples are not concerned with such rights.

But there is a danger in the use of even such a legitimate question, and that is that those who ask it will assume that a criminal is anyone who has been arrested. It would be fortunate if only criminals were arrested. But innocent people are often wrongly accused of crimes. Indeed, it is precisely this fact that requires the burdensome and expensive legal machinery our system has erected in the first place. For long centuries, even in the most civilized states and nations of Europe, *all* who were apprehended by the police were assumed to be guilty unless they could prove their innocence. Since this was in a great many cases impossible, the actual fact of the accused's innocence had no legal relevance. Unlucky detainees were simply tortured or executed, despite their perfectly truthful protestations of innocence.

I draw the reader's attention again to the phenomenon of torture. It was not the case that torture was suffered only at the hands of individual sadists and bullies in uniform. It was—God help us—the norm, part of the system consciously ratified not only by the powers of the state (in those days monarchic) but by the church. All of Europe, during such periods of history, was full of dungeons, torture chambers, and fiendish devices designed to induce such hideous pain that even the most virtuous among the innocent would gladly confess to any crime, however atrocious, if only to put a momentary end to their sufferings.

It is this monstrous historic background that accounts for the civilized, compassionate desire that, rather than vicious cruelty or revenge, *justice* be served by the machinery of the law and its courts. To return to the root point, beware of assuming that because some individuals are liberal, conservative, Communist, anti-Communist, or of some other political persuasion, it is therefore possible to say that we know *all* or even a great deal about them.

Labels, even when properly applied, may serve only to narrow our focus. They do not conclude our study; they merely help us to properly begin it.

Rule No. 16

Study the subject of sensory preception

We should not be inhibited, at the outset, by the fear that the ideal of a largely rational society can never be achieved. Of course it cannot. Ideals as a class can never be permanently realized, but nevertheless serve as magnetic points on the spiritual compass, orienting us in the direction of virtue and wisdom, however often we may deviate from a desired path. Our goal is to make our thinking conform to reality. It is no proper objection to this to observe that it is notoriously difficult to perceive reality. It is indeed, and all the more reason for a lifelong conscious effort to apprehend what is real.

I do not use the word *real* here to mean simply valuable but to refer to that which *exists*. In addition to observing phenomena—hopefully accurately—or at least adequately perceiving it, we should become generally familiar with our senses.

This will require reading books, attending lectures or seminars, listening to audiotapes or radio programs, and viewing films or television programs on the subject of sensory perception. At first thought, the common enough acts of seeing, smelling, tasting, etc., may seem simple. Actually they are remarkably complex physical achievements. On the one hand, there is that great, theoretically infinite collection of physical objects "out there." On the other hand, there is our *perception* of this physical evidence. The evidence of our senses will sometimes be misleading. What we think we see, hear, smell, etc., can be affected, to a large extent, by our previous conditioning, social prejudices, fears, resentments, and so on. Any good college-level psychology text can introduce you to the fascinating world of the perception of physical reality.

169

Rule No. 17

Learn how to learn

There are many kinds of learning, but for our present purposes we will consider just two. There is learning from books, teachers, tapes, computers—involving the sort of instruction given in schools; then there is learning from experience.

Despite the ancient adage "Experience is the best teacher," it is pointless to argue about which form of learning is superior, since we should avail ourselves of all possible forms and to the fullest possible extent. We can, of course, say that for countless ages before it occurred to humankind to construct schools and to elect certain individuals as specialists in teaching, humans learned almost everything they knew from experience. This is not to say that an adult might not teach a child how to make a fish-hook, kindle a fire, or lift a heavy weight. But we can still say that learning by experience was dominant.

Considering ourselves as learners from experience, it may be instructive to examine the various steps in the process:

1. We have some sort of actual, concrete *experience*.

2. We *observe ourselves* having that experience.

3. We *reflect* on the experience.

4. Some sort of *theory* or working hypothesis about the experience—whether hazy or distinct—begins to form in our minds.

5. Whether the original experience was dangerous or productive, pleasurable or painful, the working hypothesis now becomes useful *insofar as it may be applied to the future.*

6. The preceding point means that we can now begin, simply by an act of will, to *control* our future, though obviously never completely.

If, let us say, while wandering through a jungle you have happened upon a bright red berry, tasted it, and found the taste pleasurable, it may then occur to you that you will want to repeat so delightful an experience. It may strike you that it would be a good idea to examine the plant on which the berry was growing. At a later point in time—perhaps just a few seconds thereafter—you may consider digging the plant up and transporting it to an area adjacent to your hut. You may even consider sharing information about the plant with other members of your family and tribe, by way of inducing them to scout the surrounding terrain to see if they can find more such plants so that you might cultivate a small field of them.

At a later stage it may occur to you—or another member of your group—that digging-up and transplanting are unnecessarily laborious ways of creating the desired patch of berry bushes. If your tribe has advanced on the scale of civilization to the point where it realizes that plants grow not by spontaneous generation, or by the will of the gods, but from a combination of seeds, earth, water, and sunlight, you may thereafter go into the wild to gather not complete plants but berries and seeds.

At this stage some bright member of your group may say, "It makes no sense to forage through the jungle for seeds, since the ones we find so far afield are apparently exactly the same as those growing on our own bushes. Let us, therefore, simply save, and plant, our seeds from now on, instead of throwing them away as we formerly did."

As your group's sophistication in solving simple problems grows, plans may be developed to provide a sufficient supply of berries for the winter or for the nongrowing season. Later, if you have an excess of berries, and some nearby tribe has none, you may consider using your surplus as an item of trade.

What we have outlined here is a simple enough process, but the model sketched is perfectly valid. One thing we see is that learning is by no means something we are supposed to do only from the ages of five to twenty-one, in buildings called schools, but rather that it is a lifelong process, the proper conduct of which is not only absolutely necessary for the physical survival of individuals but for the survival of entire societies.

Rule No. 18

Develop the old-fashioned virtue of humility

The virtue of humility has important relevance in the context of any serious attempt to improve our intelligence. The reason for this is that many of the things upon which we most fervently insist involve only probabilities, not certainties. And, of course, regarding some of our beliefs and opinions, we are simply mistaken. Therefore, we must be less opinionated, less dogmatic, more willing to "listen to reason" and the dictates of evidence.

The opposite of humility, of course, is pride. For long centuries pride was not considered merely an insignificant failing, but the very first among the serious sins. (Christian theology listed the seven deadly sins as *pride, covetousness, lust, anger, gluttony, envy* and *sloth*).

Are you right about absolutely everything?

Only an insane person would answer yes to such a question.

Our present study, then, will enable us to recognize at least a few, and perhaps a great many, of the particulars concerning which we hold erroneous or doubtful views.

Being proud and stiff-necked will impede the search for such wisdom and truth.

Being humble will greatly facilitate it.

As part of the search, we will, it is hoped, develop a new degree of respect for the words *no* and *not*. Even quite aside from questions of rightness or wrongness—in the context of either reason or morality— we must grasp that the words *no* and *not* have a function much like that of the minus sign in mathematics. To an extent this is obvious, but I suspect it is rarely considered.

The concept of *is not,* in any event, is as valuable to the process of rational thinking as the concept *is*.

We should not be so rigid about our *is*'s.

We should be willing to concede our *is-not*'s.

Part of my thesis is that just as theologians, prophets, and moralists have, for thousands of years, been quite rightly telling us that mankind has a natural tendency to do evil, it is also true that there is a certain naturalness to stupidity and ignorance.

I am painfully aware of such tendencies within myself; perhaps the reader is prepared to make the same concession. But, if so, the two of us are members of a very small club. The majority of our fellow humans are evidently quite unaware that they suffer from this natural combination of ignorance and stupidity—*dumbth*.

One of the chief purposes of this book, therefore, is to "raise the consciousness" of the average citizen to the point where he will have the ego strength to concede that his larger consciousness stands very much in need of raising.

Rule No. 19

Concede ignorance when you are ignorant

Let's begin to apply the word *not*.

It may strike you as odd, even comic, but the truth is that one of the wisest things we can say is, "I do not know." I have not the slightest doubt that the drama of history, and the unknown prehistoric ages, would have been somewhat more peaceful if the honest concession of ignorance had been more common.

But not all men and women have been equally to blame for their failure to admit specific gaps in their personal knowledge. No, it is the failure of those in power to behave so felicitously that has done much of the damage. I refer not just to supreme rulers, for it is by no means only chieftains, kings, prime ministers, presidents, poets, and other authorities who are to blame, but rather anyone, anywhere, in a position of power.

That every authority figure who has ever lived has had vast blanks in his supply of factual information is clear enough. The question we must ask is, Why, in the face of such palpable ignorance, was it ever thought necessary to deny the obvious, to suggest instead that the ruler, general, administrator, bureaucrat, was, at least approximately, all-wise?

We shall find half the explanation, in my opinion, in the human ego, so feeble, even among the strongest of us, that at certain times the concession of any imperfection is simply too painful an act.

To repeat a fundamental point: All of us are ignorant. Some of the world's most serious troubles grow out of the fact that people "know" so much that is simply not so. This is constantly being brought to my attention in regard to one particular subject about which I know more than anyone else: myself.

It is perfectly acceptable to me that a given individual would not know one fact or another about my life and professional activities. There is no problem about that at all. Nevertheless problems do arise when individuals speaking to me—sometimes interviewing me on television or radio—phrase questions in a way that is rationally unacceptable. Many of the questions put to me are written by members of my audiences, since when I do comedy concerts question-cards are passed out to almost everyone present. Recently I received the following note from a woman in the Midwest: "I read and enjoyed your book *Funny People*. What was the reason you never wrote a follow-up to it?"

There could not be any such reason because there *was* a follow-up to it, titled *More Funny People*.

Again, there's no problem at all about the woman not knowing of the existence of the second book. The great majority of the inhabitants of the human race have no information at all about my various professional pursuits. But the woman's question should have been phrased as follows: "I read and enjoyed your book *Funny People*. Did you ever write a follow-up to it?"

In another incident that occurred during the same week, a woman called in to a radio show on which I was being interviewed and said, "I remember one night, back in the early 1960s, hearing you perform some songs from a musical you were writing at the time. Why didn't that show ever make it to Broadway?"

The fact was that the show—*Sophie,* based on the life of entertainer Sophie Tucker—did make it to Broadway. The form of the woman's question should simply have asked if the production ever reached New York. But the objection might be raised, "Well, aren't you just nit-picking? The woman merely assumed that your musical did not last long enough to reach a Broadway theater."

Indeed she did. But she could not possibly have *known* something that was not, in fact, the case; which leads to just my point. All of us know very much less than we *assume* we do. That's a given fact that we ought to be able to accept. Nor is there anything basically wrong with making assumptions, guesses, about things, as long as we do not mistake our assumptions for facts.

Another relevant factor is partisan bias. The reader is perhaps familiar with the true story about a political leader who spoke in confidence to one of his allies. "I'm afraid," he said, "that our esteemed leader, Mr. _____, has turned out to be a true son-of-a-bitch."

"You're absolutely right," said his companion, "but he's *our* son-of-a-bitch."

Just so, in cases where a leader, even an American president, is privately, and perhaps to a degree even publicly, known to be either a general ignoramus or at least woefully uninformed about vitally important matters, it is sometimes privately conceded that he is, in effect, something of a dunce, "but *our* dunce."

Well, while it would be too much to expect honest public concessions by party officials in such contexts, at least we can personally benefit by the awareness of the ignorance or other weaknesses of such leaders as are nominated or elected.

And it will help us think better, too, if we can concede that—in some situations—we are the ignorant ones.

Rule No. 20

Use words wisely

We should try to be as careful with our words as scientists are with their test-tubes, chemicals, currents of electricity, and other things they work with. The reason is that we do most of our thinking with words; and most of our communicating with other people is done with words, too. So we should always try to use the right words to express our thoughts.

It's not that words themselves paint an exact picture of things. As a matter of fact, they don't. Words often have fuzzy or vague meanings rather than clear, sharp ones. But that's all the more reason to be as careful as possible in using them.

It's partly because words are often vague in meaning that we must be tolerant in reasoning with others. You see, the meaning of a word may actually change depending on who says it, when it is said, and where or how it is said. Take the word *lazy,* for instance. Someone might say, "The weather is so beautiful and warm today that it gives me a wonderfully lazy feeling."

Someone else might say, "Tom Jordan is a very lazy man." The first lazy meant something relaxing and pleasant. The second lazy was a harsh, critical term. It meant something unpleasant.

The same is true of many words. So when we try to understand what someone else is thinking, or saying, we should remember that his meaning for a word might not be the same as ours. And perhaps his meaning is just as good as ours. Or better! So we should be tolerant. We should keep our minds open. We should not jump to conclusions.

There is often a difference between the literal meaning of a question or statement on the one hand and its intended meaning or probable implication on the other.

Suppose a man is asked, "Since the day of your wedding, have you ever kissed a woman other than your wife?"

The answer, "Yes, my mother," might be perfectly reasonable but would be beyond the scope the question was presumably intended to cover.

If, therefore, we desire to limit the territory of our statements or questions, it will sometimes be necessary to add qualifying clauses to them. In the example given, the question could have been amended to, "Other than your mother, sister, or other relative, have you ever, since the day of your wedding, kissed a woman other than your wife?"

Communication is one of those human activities that in essence seems simple but is actually complex. On one level it is as natural to human beings as flying is to birds, but it is a far more intricate process than flying is for winged creatures. At birth we are scarcely able to do it at all except insofar as our pitiful cries or probably accidental smiles may be said to communicate something.

Those who, for the first time in their lives, are asked consciously to consider the process of communication almost invariably do so by constructing a one-to-one model in their minds. They envision a child talking to a parent, two men speaking, two women, a man and a woman, and so on. But the list of social contexts in which communication takes place is much longer than that. And, in all situations in which more than two people are involved, the chances of something going wrong in the commmunication are considerably increased.

In some cases, we think better than we speak. One of the brightest people I have ever met is a woman who has remarkable intuition, sensitivity, and general intelligence. As regards personal communication, however, her mind works so fast that she often simply forgets to articulate certain parts of messages, with the result that there are frequent breakdowns in communication.

I find I do something of this sort when I am dictating, the method by which I do all my writing. Sometimes, when I see the typed manuscripts made from dictation tapes, I am surprised that a connective idea I clearly recall having thought was never actually spoken.

Effectiveness at communication obviously requires a degree of proficiency at thinking itself, but the two activities are nevertheless distinct. Many people, in fact, are such polished speakers that the illusion of their intelligence is sustained. Ronald Reagan is a classic instance. Since he worked for a good part of his life as a radio announcer and actor, and inasmuch as he is gifted by nature with a clear, forceful speaking voice, he is well practiced at communicating such ideas or information as he has acquired. In any event, though it is perfectly possible to think well but communicate poorly, so far as communication is concerned, one should be proficient at both activities.

In his dissertation on Plato, Emerson says:

> The first period of a nation, as of an individual, is the period of unconscious strength. Children cry, scream, and stamp with fury, unable to express their desires. As soon as they can speak and tell their want and the reason of it, they become gentle. In adult life, while the perceptions are obtuse, men and women talk vehemently . . . blunder and quarrel; their manners are full of desperation; their speech is full of boasts. As soon as, with culture, things have cleared up a little, and they see them no longer in lumps and masses but accurately distributed, they desist from that weak vehemence and explain their meaning in detail. *If the tongue had not been trained for articulation, man would still be a beast in the forest.* (Italics supplied.)

In today's world, an ever-enlarging percentage of young Americans are passing through their difficult years and arriving at maturity with precious little true culture and a tragically weak ability to express the thoughts and emotions they may feel.

Recently, after listening to a young athlete on a radio program, I wrote a satire on his manner of speech and, because of its relevance, I quote it here.

> Well, you know—I knew I had to give it my best shot—so I waited for a chance and I took a shot and—you know—gave it my best shot and that shot was my best shot.
>
> So—it was just a matter of giving it—my *shot,* I mean, and he gave it *his* best shot, too, so we was *both* giving our best shot and *my* best shot was better than *his* best shot.
>
> So everybody's got to have a shot and I shot my best shot and that was one of them shot-giving situations where you want to shoot your best shot.

The sad thing about this comedy is that the speech is only slightly exaggerated.

Quite aside from selecting words with precision and using them with respect, I wish there were some way everyone could be induced to fall in love with words themselves. Many of the other living creatures of our planet have primitive languages of some kind, comprised of clicks, hums, buzzes, drones, pops, whistles, moans, howls, thumpings, and God-knows-what else. But only humans can claim the glorious possession of words.

Since almost all readers of this book can speak English, they should be aware of their good fortune in that it is a language close to ideal for the expression of subtle, complex variations of meaning.

I recommend, in this connection, James Lipton's delightful modern classic *An Exaltation of Larks* (Viking, 1968). Lipton is one of those lucky individuals seized by the beauty of language, as others might be seized by the beauty of music, paint on canvas, natural vistas, or women's faces. Consider his account of the historical factors that contributed to the present richness of the English tongue.

> With each new wave of traders or invaders came new semantic blood, new ideas, and new ways of expressing them. The narrow, languid brook of the Celtic tongue suddenly acquired a powerful tributary as the splendid geometry of the Latin language burst into it, bringing such lofty sounds and concepts as *intellect, fortune, philosophy, education, victory, gratitude.* From 449 on, the blunt, intensely expressive monosyllables of the Anglo-Saxons joined the swelling stream, giving us the names of the strong, central elements of our lives: *God, earth, sun, sea, win, lose, live, love,* and *die.* Then, in the eleventh century, with the Norman Conquest, a great warm gush of French sonorities—*emotion, pity, peace, devotion, romance*—swelled the torrent to a flood-tide that burst its banks, spreading out in broad, loamy deltas black with the rich silt of WORDS.
>
> It was in precisely this word-hungry, language-mad England that the terms you will encounter in this book were born. They are prime examples both of the infinite subtlety of our language and the wild imagination and verbal skill of our forebears.

Rule No. 21

Understand that your perceptions, opinions, and beliefs are, to a remarkable degree, determined by your point of view

The common phrase "point of view" is frequently misused. People say, "Well, that's your point of view," when they might better say, "That's your opinion." Your opinion may be determined by your point of view. The phrase is easy to understand because it means something specific. It suggests that your image of something—a mountain, a man, a horse, a political party, almost anything—is what it is partly *because of your actual point in space at the moment of viewing*.

Consider a mountain. If you are standing at the peak of it, it will have one sort of image for you. If you are standing on a flat plain twenty miles from the base of the mountain, it will look very different indeed.

But it is not only your position in *space* that determines your interpretation of things about you. Your position in *time* is also important. If you have the same sort of experience twice in your life—let us say once when you are ten years old and the second time when you are forty-five—you may be certain that the two events will seem very different.

But the term "point of view" also refers to a third sort of circumstance, which is that just about everything that has happened to you in the past affects your perceptions of reality in the present.

Assume that you and a friend are exactly the same age and, standing very close together in space, have the same experience at 10:30 in the morning next April 17. Despite the similarity of factors of time and space there is little likelihood that you will form identical images of the thing or experience to which you are exposed. Your friend may have been born in a different city, his parents will certainly have been different from yours and therefore have treated him differently from the way you were treated by your mother and father. He may be of another race or religion. His family may have different attitudes about important social questions like what to do about pollution, poverty, nuclear radiation, and so on.

Perhaps you now have a better understanding of how difficult it is to arrive at the Truth about anything. I do not say that it is literally impossible to do so; merely that recognizing the truth is often a difficult feat rather than the easy one that most of us imagine it to be.

We will automatically become better people, philosophically and morally, if we develop the ability to appreciate other points of view and the opinions to which they inevitably give rise.

Rule No. 22

Know that reason need not be the enemy of emotion

When some people hear reason being endorsed they assume that, if the amount of rationality in the world is increased, it must inevitably follow that certain increments of sensation and emotion will decrease. The supposition—or fearful concern—is, of course, groundless. Certain things will indeed be decreased if the domain of reason is enlarged, but they are such things as foolishness, fanaticism, brawling, fear, ignorance, bigotry, and racial, ethnic, and religious prejudice.

As for the enjoyments of the senses, as for the warm, beautiful, endearing emotions, two things are possible: Either they will be unaffected by an increase in the reasoning faculty or—as seems more likely—they will be enhanced since the increased exercise of reason will to a certain extent decrease those negative emotional factors that now limit the sensible joys of life.

Almost by way of underlining these observations, as I sit dictating them on the breeze-washed patio of the open-air dining room of the Outrigger Canoe Club on Waikiki Beach in Honolulu, I perceive in the distant background enormous white clouds, blue sky, low mountains; off to the right the tall waterfront hotels of the area curving around the long beach; in the middle distance sailboats, catamarans, curling white waves on turquoise-blue water, surfers, and bathers; and, in the immediate foreground, palm trees, bright green shrubbery, a remarkably beautiful Hawaiian woman seated at a nearby table, and a kingfisher-like bird, with a lipstick-red head and brown body, that flits among the tables looking for fallen crumbs. In a moment—it is hoped—I shall enjoy the equally pleasant prospect of my wife, for whom I am waiting. All such wonders of physical nature, and the appreciative emotions to which they give rise, need not at all be dulled by an improvement in the powers of reasoning.

183

Rule No. 23

Familiarize yourself with at least
the basic elements of logical reasoning

Logic is a very easy word to understand. It refers to good, straight thinking and reasoning. It means, in part, that we can't believe two statements, if one of them disagrees with the other.

For example, let's suppose someone says two things about the moon.

(*a*) The moon is made entirely of dried cheese.

(*b*) The moon is made of various kinds of sands and rocks.

Can you accept both of those statements? Of course not, because one automatically rules out the other. They might both be wrong. But it's impossible that both could be correct.

When we understand that simple point, we understand one of the basic ideas of logic.

Next, here's an example that's slightly more complicated. Consider not just two statements, but *three*.

(*a*) All Chinese have somewhat yellowish skin.

(*b*) Kim Lee has somewhat yellowish skin.

(*c*) Therefore, Kim Lee is Chinese.

Let's assume that the first and second statements are correct, that all Chinese do indeed have yellowish skin, and that Kim Lee has yellowish skin. The question is, Are we correct when we say that Kim Lee is Chinese?

Well, no; in this particular case we are mistaken. Kim Lee happens to be Korean. Koreans, too, have yellowish skin, and so do Japanese and Vietnamese and Cambodians and other peoples as well. Therefore, it would have been wrong to jump to the conclusion that Lee was Chinese. He might have been, but we did not have enough evidence to decide.

Suppose that 57 percent of the yellowish-skinned people on our planet are Chinese. If we knew that, then we could have said, "There is a 57 percent chance, or probability, that Kim Lee is Chinese." At least we would have put it into proper words. We would have done the right kind of thinking, or reasoning. And we would never have been foolish enough to *argue* that Kim Lee was Chinese, with someone who said that he was not.

But many people do argue—some of them almost every day of their lives—about things they cannot possibly be sure of. Again, what these people often do is make a guess about something, or just accept what somebody else tells them, and then, once they have formed an opinion or belief, they become very fond of that opinion, mostly because it is their own. And they will defend it vigorously. If you contradict their opinion, they may feel that you are attacking them personally. And because they reason so poorly, they get themselves into all sorts of trouble. We should avoid making the same mistake.

A key word in the reasoning process is *argument.*

When the average person thinks of argument, he tends to think of raised voices, red faces, and bitter feelings. Such factors, however, do not point to the heart of argument. They are merely the result of certain arguments, particularly those in which the subject matter may give rise to strong emotions. But an argument, in essence, is nothing more than a series of statements strung together in support of a particular assertion.

Let us, for the sake of example, ad-lib an assertion here and then develop an argument to defend it.

Consider the assertion: *All Chinese are stupid.*

It will be immediately evident that the assertion is absurd, which is to say that it cannot possibly be true. But its truth or falsity have no relevance to our point at the moment, which is simply to clarify the distinction between (*a*) assertions and (*b*) arguments to defend them.

Here is my argument:

1. My former laundryman, Hong Chi, was stupid.

2. I have only met nine Chinese people in my life and all of them have been—in my opinion—stupid.

3. Therefore, *all* Chinese are stupid.

The sentences numbered 1 and 2 are called *premises*. Sentence number 3 is the *conclusion* of the argument.

Even if we assume that sentences No. 1 and No. 2 are literally true, it should be apparent that their combined truth nevertheless could *not* possibly establish the truth of sentence No. 3. The reason for the weakness of the argument is that inasmuch as there are more than a billion Chinese on the earth, not to mention the billions who have lived in the past, reference to the extremely small sample of nine simply does not entitle us to draw conclusions about so enormous a group.

Some readers will perhaps feel emotionally moved to respond to the assertion by observing that the Chinese are, in fact, one of the world's superior peoples and will refer to the five thousand years of Chinese history, the remarkable cultural, scientific, and social achievements of the Chinese, and so on. But, again, we are not concerned here with disproving the *substance* of the argument. *All we need to show is that the method of supporting the conclusion is structurally faulty.* It does not matter whether we are talking about Chinese, Italians, hockey pucks, false teeth, Republicans, or bull-frogs. Whatever the objects of discussion, and whatever properties the speaker might attribute to them, such methods of reasoning are instances of dumbth.

Since we have acknowledged that the sample appealed to was too small to be used in making judgments about so large a group as the Chinese population of our planet, we can see that the implication is that *reliable probability increases as the size of the sample increases.*

Ideally, theories are supposed to cover all relevant cases. The whole point of scientifically testing a large sample is to find out if, in fact, the theory is borne out when it comes up against actual experience. If it does *not*, if even *one* clear-cut counterexample appears, then the theory does not hold water and must be either abandoned or greatly modified.

Suppose, for example, that someone advances the theory that *all Jews have dark hair.* Saying as much is neither to praise nor criticize Jews, since there is nothing wrong with having dark hair. One simply refers to reality to find out if the assertion is valid or not. Obviously, as soon as we begin to examine actual members of the Jewish population of the United States or of the world, we find a good many of them who do *not* have dark hair. Some have blond hair, some red, some white, some grey, some no hair at all, and a few in punk rock have lavender, green, or orange hair. But we do not have to proceed to find a good many of them. All we have to find is one Jew with red or blond hair and the theory collapses.

To say that the theory collapses, however, does not necessarily mean that it is of no use whatever. Some theories are pure nonsense and must be totally discarded. But it might turn out—let us estimate—that 77 percent of the world's Jews do have dark hair. Accordingly, then, we would be justified in restating our theory by incorporating the figure of 77 percent into it.

Even those who know very little about formal logic generally sense that, in certain kinds of arguments, if the *premises* are true then the *conclusions* must also be true. These are what are called *deductive* arguments.

For example:

1. Among humans only men have male sex organs.

2. Jackie Gleason had male sex organs.

3. Therefore, Jackie was a man.

Again: *If* the first two premises are valid—in other words, if they state the truth—then statement No. 3, the *conclusion* of the argument, is logically inescapable; it is just as valid as the premises.

As for *inductive* argument, it has importance and usefulness, but is more likely to point the way to a high degree of probability than to certainty.

1. So far, my brother-in-law has lied to me more than he has spoken the truth.

2. Whatever he says to me next will be a lie.

If statement No. 1—the premise—is accepted, then the conclusion—statement No. 2—*may,* in fact, turn out to have been correct. But all we can say, in advance of the actual event, is that it refers only to a probability, not certainty, since even the worst liars make many truthful statements.

Some arguments might be referred to as "if/then" arguments. Or we might call them "if something, then something else" arguments. For example:

1. If it rains all this week, then the corn will grow.

2. It *will* rain all this week.

3. Therefore, the corn will grow.

Note that in this case the argument hangs together quite neatly, partly because, all other things being equal, plants do grow when they are watered. In constructing such arguments, therefore, it is important that the first assertion be valid.

For example, if we said:

1. If it rains all week, then new Toyotas will lose a lot of their paint.

We might proceed to say that:

2. It will rain all week.

3. Therefore, new Toyotas will lose a lot of their paint.

But we know, by referring to reality, that Toyotas are as well painted as other new cars and that rain has no noticeable effect on modern automobile paint. Therefore, even though the *structure* of the argument is valid, the *conclusion* is total nonsense, simply because the original assertion—statement No. 1—was not true.

You will recall my mentioning earlier that among the most important words in the entire process of reasoning are *no* and *not*. Notice that you can add negative factors to the form of the argument just explained, as follows:

1. If A, then B.

2. Not B.

3. Therefore, not A.

To give the form substance we might say:

1. If football players have whiter teeth than non-football-players, then dental examination should establish the fact.

2. Dental examination shows nothing of the sort.

3. Therefore, football players do *not* have whiter teeth than non-football players.

The following joke makes the point very well. Two men are sitting on a park bench on Chicago's lake front. Suddenly, one reaches into his pocket, takes out a small can, and begins to sprinkle its contents all about him.

"What are you doing?" the other says.

"Oh," the sprinkler explains, "this is anti-tiger powder. All you have to do is spread a little of it on the ground all around you and no tiger can get closer than a hundred yards."

"But that's ridiculous," his companion said. "There are no tigers in Chicago."

"Of course," says his friend. "This is really powerful stuff."

The absence of tigers in Chicago was, of course, evidence perfectly consistent with the deluded gentleman's theory. His mistake was in taking it as conclusive evidence.

There is obviously a great deal more to the study and practice of logic than limitations of space permit here. An extremely useful book on the subject is *The Art of Deception,* by Nicholas Capaldi (Prometheus Books, 1987).

Rule No. 24

Always feel at least a twinge of shame
when you employ an ad hominem argument

The Latin phrase *ad hominem* means that your thrusts are directed, not at details of the opponent's argument itself, but at the individual (*hominem* = to the man) opposed. Ad hominem, of course, has a long history among specialists in debate, although it is essentially premised on the bias, stupidity, or gullibility of the audience. Negative emotions can be brought into play easily enough by speakers who suggest that their opponents are guilty of anything of which a given audience disapproves. If a particular audience is, for example, anti-Catholic, and one speaker is a member of that faith, then it would be a rare debater who would not contrive to make at least a passing reference to the Catholicism of his or her opponent.

It does not follow from this, however, that it is always inappropriate to refer to an opponent's points of vulnerability. It would be perfectly legitimate, for example, to refer to the Catholicism of the spaker if he were arguing in defense of the expenditure of federal monies for Catholic schools.

But in most cases there is nothing so reasonable in the ad hominem attack. Like a physical blow, it is usually indulged in by debaters who, because of the relative weakness of their own position, resort to unedifying methods by way of deliberately confusing the issue.

The use of the word *deliberately,* of course, implies that the offending debater is intelligent and cynical. In most social contexts, stupidity and pettiness are motivators; the speaker may literally be unaware that he is stepping beyond the rules of rational argumentation. A male motorist,

191

for example, whose car has run into one driven by a female, may say, "What would you expect of a woman driver?"

When factors of life and death are at stake—as in a war, for example—the ad hominem attack is often deliberately employed by the propaganda or public misinformation department of governments. But whatever the justification, there is never any inherent moral dignity in such practices, any more than there is in a good many other wartime practices, such as bombing civilian areas, setting fire to human beings with napalm, torturing prisoners, and using poison gas.

The better course of argumentation—even simply *understanding* statements made by others, whether they are opponents or allies—is that your attention should be concentrated on the statements and arguments rather than those who express them.

My wife and I happen to be personal friends of George and Barbara Bush. George, in my view, is a good fellow, with decent intentions. Unfortunately, either because of personal insecurity during his campaign against Governor Dukakis of Massachusetts, or because he permitted himself to be swayed by another personal friend, Roger Ailes, Bush's chief media advisor during the election campaign (and one-time producer of my television show), he resorted to unedifying methods of debate and was, of course, widely called to account by the nation's news media as well as millions of concerned citizens. One thing we might conclude from this is that, although there will usually be something ethically unsavory about the *ad hominem* argument, it is nevertheless quite effective.

Rule No. 25

Be realistically skeptical—even of leaders

We have already seen that, for a series of separate statements to stand as a valid argument, it is important that the basic premises be related to reality. But it will occur to the thoughtful reader that no one of us—however intelligent—has the time to investigate personally the truthfulness of very many of the statements we hear. That is so, and there is not a great deal to be done about it.

Still it is necessary to do a certain minimum of things: First, we should be as careful as we can about accepting information. One of the reasons we all believe a certain amount of nonsense is simply that it has been taught to us. We have picked it up over the course of many years from parents, friends, teachers, newspapers, magazines, radio and television programs, films, record albums, books, and social institutions. Every one of these, no doubt, would prefer to communicate the truth and nothing but the truth, but the ideal is never reached. Nevertheless, we can at least protect ourselves against such a daily mass of mixed good and bad information by developing a reasonable degree of skepticism. It does not take a great deal of intelligence to perceive that among several newspapers, one or another might be the most believable. Is there anyone not intelligent enough to observe that the *New York Times* is a more reliable source of information than a supermarket tabloid?

It also does not take a great deal of intelligence to observe that some sources of information are more likely to be reliable simply because it is in their interest to be so. In other cases we must be on guard against information dispensed by those who are motivated by self-interest. They may be trying to sell us something. They may be trying to influence our religious or political thinking. There's nothing wrong with such attempts per se but we must keep our guard up.

As Daniel S. Greenberg has advised, "Don't ask the barber whether

193

you need a haircut."

As for leaders, there is a somewhat pathetic need, in all of us, to place our trust in them. When in God's name will humanity recognize that leaders are *never* what they seem? In rare cases they may be even better than is apparent. More often they are worse than our perception of them. But their power, even on low levels of authority, carries a certain glamour; and it is this magic dust, which we insist on throwing into our own eyes, that blinds us.

The reasoning behind the old saying that no man is a hero to his own valet is not that valets are any wiser than the rest of us. It is simply that long-continued close proximity to the exalted personage makes it clear enough that he is merely human, that his excretory functions are the same as everyone else's, and that he is subject to the same lapses of memory, inconsistencies, contradictions, mistakes, embarrassments, and stupidities as everyone else. The leader cannot long hide this from those in the rooms across the hall, but he has little difficulty keeping it from the general population, for the two reasons given here.

There would be little point in such speculation if it represented merely an interesting digression from our theme. It is, in fact, central because it points to the source of a great deal of the suffering, warfare, atrocity, and other tragedy with which every page of history is stained. For, because the leaders cannot concede their ignorance, and because we ourselves do not want them to, it has therefore been common for countless ages for leaders—both political and religious—to make the most preposterous assertions, to issue the most absurd ultimatums and commandments, simply because if they told the truth at a moment of crisis they would have had to say to their followers, "You know, actually I haven't the slightest idea how we're going to handle this problem, but I'll have a meeting with some of my advisors and see if we can come up with something helpful by Thursday."

To have communicated with the masses in so sensible and truthful a fashion, however, would have scared them to death. So, to repeat, the combined ego-needs of the leaders and the self-inflicted gullibility of the people have led to the incredible collection of nonsense, misinformation, myth, superstition, and evil that has almost crushed humanity during the long epochs of its chronological advance.

I argue that this simple perception ought now to be as widely broadcast as possible and that the banners under which it can most legitimately be propagated are those of reason and truth.

There have been two conflicting currents of social and political development throughout human experience: the authoritarian and the democratic. For not very mysterious reasons the totalitarian impulse has generally ruled the day, partly because it is, at least when it is considered under the rubric of systems analysis, a simpler matter than any form of democracy. The functioning of a democratic society requires a great deal of bother. There are endless meetings, writings, lectures, arguments, conventions, votes, party rivalries, and appeals for funds. It is all quite troublesome. The rule of one strong man or party, whatever its other merits or horrors, is usually a tidier matter.

Actually both systems can work well given that certain additional factors are added to the equation. A totalitarian form, for example, would work as well as anything human ever could if the leader were a philosopher-king, a person remarkably wise, compassionate, fair-minded, and personally decent. Such a leader might at times have to be firm with unruly individuals or factions, but by definition he could not resort to the atrocities and other outrages characteristic of the rules of Stalin, Hitler, and other tyrants too numerous to mention.

But, on the other side of the scale, what is required for the fair, rational functioning of a democratic society, of whatever specific form, is an intelligent population. This is not to say that every citizen must be a scholar. But once the general level of intelligence falls below a certain minimum requirement, social chaos will result and the system itself will be likely to swing toward an usually hideous alternative. This then brings us to the point of my seeming digression: It is a matter of our society's survival that we begin to train our children, and ourselves, to think.

Leaders, in any event, will always emerge, despite the fact that in recent years we have had a tendency to elect charming dummies to high office. But even the best leadership will have sharply limited powers if those they seek to lead do not understand what they are talking about, just as the greatest military tacticians and generals would achieve a sorry war record if they were given only poorly trained, ignorant, and apathetic troops to command.

Rule No. 26

While you must always look for evidence, do not be bowled over simply because it exists

One afternoon recently, while leaving my office building in Van Nuys, California, I detected the odor of something burning. Los Angeles had just been suffering a severe hot spell. There was also a nationwide strike of telephone company employees. At that moment I happened to be standing next to a telephone connection-box in the parking lot behind our building. The problem-solving part of my brain immediately brought these three factors together and suggested that they might have something to do with the disturbing odor I had become aware of only a moment before.

To see if the smell was emanating from the telephone-equipment cabinet, I put my nose close to it and took a deep sniff. The smell became even stronger. I stood for a moment trying to decide whether I should go back upstairs and have my secretary alert either a maintenance man, the telephone company, or the fire department.

When thinking about things, oddly enough, we often look up slightly and off into the distance. Doing that in this instance made me see that on the second floor porch of the next building a barbecue was producing flames and smoke as one of my neighbors prepared his dinner. That was the source of the burning smell.

Again, the incident suggests that while seemingly relevant evidence must always be carefully considered, we are unwise if we become inordinately fond of the first explanation that such evidence seems to suggest. Innocent men have been sent to the electric chair, and a far greater number have been imprisoned over the centuries, because police officials have developed an ego-investment in their first hypothesis, particularly in situations where either a heinous crime has been committed or the police have taken a long time to produce a suspect.

196

Rule No. 27

Understand the process of rationalization

As an example of a context in which rationalization occurs, consider the ongoing debate on capital punishment.

Those who favor the death penalty fall, generally speaking, into two classifications. The first group, an extremely small minority, consists of those who have taken the trouble to examine the pros and cons of the argument and who have concluded that the electric chair, the gallows, and the gas chamber have some deterrent value and that therefore, however brutal, they ought to be retained for the protection of society.

The second classification, which apparently includes more than 95 percent of the death-penalty advocates, consists of those who know little or nothing of the particulars of formal conjecture or debate on the issue and who therefore did not arrive at their position by rational means. One can often identify these individuals by the heat with which they present their arguments.

It is certainly possible to make out a respectable case *for* capital punishment, but the individuals to whom I now refer seem incapable of manufacturing, or even repeating, such an argument. Their statements, letters to the press, and public diatribes are overemotional and not infrequently manifest exactly the sort of venomous hatred we associate with murderers themselves.

It ought to be more commonly realized that all of us harbor within us paralyzing fear, murderous rage, and animal lusts, without which, of course, the Ten Commandments and numerous civil laws would be unnecessary. Science tells us, and most theologians now readily concede, that human beings have walked the face of our planet for at least hundreds of thousands, probably millions, of years. For much of that time they have lived as sometimes murderous savages; it is only during the past tiny fraction of their long history, so to speak, that they have become relatively civilized. But in the process of acquiring the veneer of civilization they have by no means altered their inner nature. Every human born in the modern age starts out life as a willful animal and must be lovingly taught, during his childhood years, such essential social wisdom as the race has accumulated. It is this very fact that inclines many to pessimism regarding the possibility of the outbreak of nuclear war. The forces of fear and rage do exist, they are currently being fanned to dangerously high temperatures by international conflict, and therefore now seriously threaten not just our individual lives and the lives of our neighbors but human life itself.

It is these generally repressed dark forces that explain the vehemence with which many in our society insist on the retention of the death penalty. It is a difficult thing, of course, for proponents of capital punishment to concede as much, even to themselves, and the difficulty is compounded by the ease with which man constructs cathedrals of rational argument *that have nothing whatever to do with the original formation of opinion.*

Psychologists are familiar with the phenomenon and can easily demonstrate it by use of hypnosis. For example, a man is hypnotized, told that in a moment he will be awakened and that five minutes thereafter he will walk to the window, lift a flower pot from the sill, take the pot to the sofa, and wrap a towel around it. He is then told that when he wakens he will remember none of the instructions he has received. After a moment the subject is returned to consciousness. When pertinent questions are put to him he replies that he has no recollection of what happened while he was hypnotized and adds that he merely feels that he has been asleep for a short time.

A period of small talk follows; the man engages in normal social conversation. After the passage of exactly five minutes, however, he suddenly walks to the window, picks up a flower pot that is on the sill, carries it to a nearby sofa, and wraps it in a towel. At that point the hypnotist and the others present ask the subject *why* he performed these peculiar actions. The man appears puzzled and replies that he does not know; he "just felt like it." So far this experiment, in terms of common knowledge about hypnosis, is in no way extraordinary.

But now comes the fascinating part. The others in the room refuse to let the man off with the explanation that he "just felt like" moving the flower pot to the sofa. They put additional questions to him in an effort to explain his peculiar behavior. Almost at once the man begins to give various *reasons* for what he has done. First, for example, he says that he recalled having noticed that the flower pot seemed in danger of falling from the window sill. At this point he had walked to the sill merely to position the pot more securely. On picking it up, however, it occurred to him that the plant might be cold because there was a noticeable draft coming through the window. Therefore he decided to move the plant to the sofa and give it the additional warmth the towel provided.

The subject was convinced that these were the good and logical reasons that explained his actions. In reality they had no connection with his behavior whatsoever.

You miss the point if you suppose that what happened is nothing more than a fascinating laboratory experiment. *Rationalization of precisely this sort is what you and I do every day of our lives.*

Now there is nothing inherently wrong with accumulating additional arguments to defend a cause we are convinced is just. The danger comes from misunderstanding our motivation; for if we come clearly to see that a particular motivation, in regard to a particular issue, was unedifying, it will be easier for us to evaluate our argument itself. Remember that almost all of the evil-doers the world has ever known have been able to explain their behavior. Communists are articulate philosophers. So were Nazis. Many professional criminals are adept at "justifying" their outrages. Those who are clever at debate can defend almost any position, however absurd, evil, or dangerous, and make it seem at least relatively plausible. Therefore we ought more often try to determine the *real* reasons for our acts and opinions.

The word *rationalization,* of course, is an extension of the word *rational.* What is involved in the process is self-deception, where the individual lies to himself—and usually to others—in attempting to make his behavior seem rational when it is actually caused by other factors.

When you rationalize, you might be compared to a defense attorney whose job it is not to determine all the facts of a case but to concentrate only on those that are favorable to his client, and—what is even worse so far as trying to recognize truth is concerned—deliberately to introduce into the argument theories, possibilities, and interpretations that cast doubt on the factual evidence the prosecuting attorney may bring forth.

It would be better if, instead of playing the defense attorney, you assumed the impartial role of judge, one whose only interest is in discovering what actually did happen, rather than in convicting or freeing the defendant.

It is of course expecting a great deal to imagine that a simple word of advice would lead us all to abandon self-interest in courts of law. But in the privacy of our own minds, it is by no means impossible for us to become aware of the process of rationalization and, secondly, to recognize those situations in which it is operative. Toward this happy end, we will have to remind ourselves—as often as necessary—that *rationalization is a natural enemy of truth.*

This is not to say that every fact that the process will suggest is a lie, or that every rationalized argument consists of nothing but invalid parts. Indeed, there is a remarkable cleverness to the process, which suggests what a powerful opponent of truth it is. It is almost consistent with the ancient Christian belief—once common, but now rare—that the body can be possessed by an evil spirit or spirits. *Something* takes possession of our reasoning powers and our powers of argumentation when we rationalize. That something converts us into sometimes remarkably clever defense attorneys. That something is, of course, in no sense an outside power, foreign unto ourselves. It is part of ourselves. That is why it is so utterly necessary to acknowledge its existence and to be wary of its power, for it is dangerous. It converts us into something very close to liars, which harms us morally. It produces dissension in our immediate world and sometimes in the world at large if we happen to have access to the press, radio, or television.

Much political argumentation, for example, is rationalizaton. An individual, or a segment of society, may do something because of envy, jealousy, anger, hatred, fear, selfishness, lack of compassion. But who could concede something so shameful? So the process of rationalization, like a lightning-quick computer, goes into action to clatter out intricately constructed arguments that supposedly explain and justify the sometimes destructive acts or policies we have undertaken or propose to enact.

If one is permitted to write the rules of the game one can "prove" anything. Consider, for example, the patently absurd assertion that the world began, not some five thousand years ago, as fundamentalist Christians believe, not almost four billion years ago, as modern science tells us, but last Wednesday morning. A debate on the question might be conducted as follows:

Believer: The world began last Wednesday morning.

Nonbeliever: Do you mean that as a statement of literal fact? That the entire physical universe, as we know it, did not exist in any sense until last Wednesday morning?

Believer: That is precisely what I mean.

Nonbeliever: How can you believe anything so preposterous?

Believer: Oh, I do not *believe.* I *know.*

Nonbeliever: How do you know? On what evidence or authority?

Believer: Because God has personally communicated the information to me.

Nonbeliever: Ah. But how do you account for massive physical evidence to the contrary?

Believer: Very simply. I know what sort of things you're talking about: the fact that there are coins stamped 1914, books that seem to have been published in 1822, rocks that geologists assert are hundreds of millions of years old. The answer is simply that Almighty God, in His infinite wisdom, can hardly have erected a universe in which everything appears to be brand new.

Nonbeliever: I don't know what you're talking about.

Believer: Of course you don't. You have not been enlightened by God's grace. Are you arrogant enough to pit your puny human mind against that of the Almighty? Don't you think that He has the power to create a universe only a few days old and yet to give it the *appearance* of age as a concession to the weakness of our minds?

It is obvious that no combination of science and logic, no exercise of pure, sweet reason, will be equal to the task of penetrating such invulnerable fanaticism.

It is a simple matter for the impartial observer to see that the Believer's position, and his method of defending it, are absurd. The problem is that there may be no way to convince the Believer of what, to the reader, is so obvious. Again, the medicine indicated is preventive. Children taught to respect the testimony of evidence will not grow up to be guilty of such stupidity.

Even for those of us who are past the point where we can learn to read in the crib, or learn to reason at the age of six, it is, of course, not too late at all to noticeably improve our intelligence.

But first—this is something so basic that I have almost neglected to mention it—we must be guided by the ancient instruction of moral theology regarding the predicament of the sinner, whose case is absolutely hopeless unless he concedes that he is a sinner. And just as, before he can begin to be cured, the alcoholic himself must first publicly state, "I am an alcoholic," everyone in the United States at this moment ought to get up, raise his hand to heaven, and say, "I am dumb."

But one could also add, "There is no reason why I must continue to be so ignorant. There is nothing that compels me to reason so poorly. There is no reason that I must continue to be guided only by factors of emotion or social bias. I am capable of reform."

Again, we must take that first step, the step of conceding our ignorance. Will Rogers once said, "We are all ignorant, only on different subjects." Just so, we all reason rather poorly, although in varying instances and situations.

Rule No. 28

Beware of the A-B fallacy

The letters A and B here represent events occurring at two separate points on the time-scale but with B following A rather closely.

Let's say that on January 1 you eat a nice, ripe persimmon. The eating of the persimmon is event A.

The following morning, January 2, you wake up with a rash across your abdomen, event B.

People vary widely in the ways they might consider such separate events. Some will view them as only that, two utterly unrelated occurrences. The possibility will never enter their minds that event B— the rash on the abdomen—might have been caused by event A, the eating of the persimmon.

Others will not only quickly consider the events as a connected pair but will confidently assume that event A caused event B.

Individuals in both of these groups—insofar as we may judge from this instance—are poor thinkers. The people in the first category—those to whom the possibility of a connection between the two events never even occurs—may be dull and unimaginative. We must use the word "may" here because it is also possible that some individuals in that group are quite brilliant but that their attention may be so concentrated on other matters that they simply do not have time to devote to a consideration of the two events. An individual in this subgroup, for example, might be working, during the early January period, on a cure for cancer. It is therefore reasonable to assume that a great many events and experiences will be largely disregarded because of concentration on more important matters.

But such cases will be the exception. Most of those who do not connect the two events in their minds will be rather inept at either analytical or creative thought.

The people in the second category—those who quickly assume that B was caused by A—are, as we have already said, thinking very poorly, so far as the factors of reason are concerned, but *they are at least thinking creatively*. Their minds have suggested to them the possibility of a connection between the events. To that point they have done nothing wrong. They have, in fact, done something right. The breakdown in their reasoning process occurred at the moment they mistook their perfectly reasonable *hypothesis* for a *conclusion*.

But, you may object, what if, in fact, the rash *was* caused by the eating of the persimmon? Doesn't that establish that those who thought there might be a connection were reasoning soundly?

No, it does not. And it is crucial to grasp why it does not. First of all, it is perfectly possible to arrive at a correct hypothesis by the most stupid process of thought.

Imagine that a murder has been committed in your community. Both the police and private investigators are totally at a loss to identify the murderer. Assume further that a dimwitted fellow in the neighborhood becomes convinced that "the butler did it." Assume next that the murderer was indeed a butler who worked in the house where the murder occurred. But, to continue our little fantasy, it turns out that the *reason* the dimwit felt quite confident that the butler was guilty was that he had never liked butlers, a social prejudice stemming from the fact that when he was three years old he had been beaten up by a larger boy named Jim Butler.

We can see from this incident—and such things do occur in reality— that although the dimwit did happen, by hook or crook, to come up with the right answer to the puzzle, he nevertheless reached the conclusion by a stupid route. We see from this example that simply being right about something, coming up with what happens to be the correct answer, does not at all, in and of itself, establish that one is reasoning well.

Now let us return to the matter of the persimmon and the rash. In this case I have arbitrarily suggested the story-factor that eating the persimmon did cause the rash. In reality, however, life rarely delivers to us such nuggets of truth in complex situations. It would be far more typical that you would (*a*) eat the persimmon and (*b*) have the rash, but then not know at all whether there was a cause-and-effect relationship between the two events.

If the question was important to you, you would, one hopes, quickly see that one reason it is difficult to establish such a relationship is that between the time you swallowed your last bite of persimmon and the time the rash broke out you would have had a great many other physical and psychological experiences, any one of which might have caused the rash. You might, for example, have eaten several other foods, and drunk a variety of liquids as well, and, moreover, done so *before* eating the persimmon. You might have had an unpleasant emotional experience—a violent argument, perhaps—and that might have produced the uncomfortable physical reaction. Or you might go to your grave with the question still undecided.

Suppose then that you decide to approach the question in a general sense rather than arbitrarily limiting yourself to the small amount of evidential material at hand.

One way of widening the scope of your investigation would be to call a skin specialist.

"Doctor," you might ask, "does eating persimmons ever lead to a rash?"

Let us assume that the doctor says, "Yes, sometimes it does." Let us assume that you then give a smile of satisfaction and dismiss the matter from your mind, having happily concluded that the mystery was solved.

If you do any such thing you have once more earned the dunce cap. Again, it is utterly irrelevant if in fact it turns out that eating the persimmon did indeed cause the rash. You would have been reasoning better if you had said: "Doctor, have you any idea *what percentage of people* who eat persimmons break out in rashes?"

Suppose he told you that this occurs—insofar as he has been able to learn—in 1.5 percent of such cases. Immediately you will perceive that the smallness of such a figure makes it extremely unlikely that your persimmon led to your rash. The failure to ask that one simple question could have led you to accept a very unlikely answer and therefore to abandon a search for alternative and more reasonable explanations.

It will be readily perceived, from such a casual sketch, that it is wise to suspend judgment until such time as there is enough evidence to render your hypothesis either valid or invalid.

Rule No. 29

Be aware of the distinction between
consistent evidence and conclusive evidence

It is important to make the distinction between consistent and conclusive evidence, even in cases where your creative intuition is apparently
borne out by the evidence. Even if, let us say, the skin specialist tells
you that 94 percent of those who eat persimmons get stomach rashes,
all that has been established is that there is now a *high* degree of probability that your theory that event B was caused by event A is legitimate.
You are by no means entitled to shout "Eureka," because you are still
faced with the difficulty of the other 6 percent, not to mention the
fact that there are causes for stomach rash other than persimmon-eating.

Now let us take up the question of what your position should be
if you were to discover that every single case of stomach rash known
to medical science had been occasioned by persimmon-eating. Surely
you would in that case be entitled to 100 percent certainty about your
case, would you not?

No, you would not. The reason is that the relevant statistics would
establish only what the statement obviously means, which is simply that
all past cases of stomach rash known to medical science have indeed
been caused by persimmon-eating. After all, we may be very certain
that the number of cases of stomach rash known to science is vastly
smaller than the number of cases that have actually occurred down
through the perhaps millions of years of human experience. There may
well have been cases of stomach rash for countless ages before botanical
evolution developed the persimmon, although there is now no way of
determining this. But even for those cases of stomach rash arbitrarily
limited to the past ten years, it is entirely possible that here and there

206

over the surface of the planet there have been cases of stomach rash that were *not* caused by persimmon-eating but which, for whatever reasons, did not come to the attention of skin specialists.

But now let us assume that it is possible to know about every single case of stomach rash since the occasion of the first one countless eons ago, and that in all such cases the cause-and-effect relationship has been borne out. Would we then be entitled to absolute confidence in the validity of our theory?

No, we still would not. Such knowledge would indeed drive the probability factor so high that it would be scarcely possible to see the distance between that degree and the 100-percent level, but there would still be that infinitesimal margin for possible future exceptions to our general rule. There are, after all, new chemical compounds, new substances introduced into the modern world almost every day. Some of these, sad to say, are discovered to be carcinogenic or harmful to our health in other ways. It is well within the realm of possibility that one of the unfortunate side effects of one or another of these newly introduced chemicals is stomach rash. Nor does this by any means exhaust the theoretical possibilities. While all of this may seem to be nothing more than hair-splitting, be assured that it is of vital importance that you do split such hairs.

We are certainly not entitled, however, to assume that because knowledge is less than perfectly certain it is therefore of little value. You would be well advised indeed to avoid eating persimmons if in every known instance of their eating a stomach rash had followed. We see from this that even in the absence of absolute certainty we may still mark our course through life on the basis of the knowledge that is available to us. But if we look at the harm wrought in this world by two separate attitudes of mind: (*a*) an ever-ready sense of absolute personal certitude, and (*b*) an open-minded, scientifically sound recognition of high degrees of probability, we see that the latter has done very little harm indeed, whereas the former has led to countless wars, pogroms, mass-slaughters, barroom brawls, family fights, social dissension, and tragedy of many kinds. People who are what Eric Hoffer called "true believers" may well believe a number of things that are, in fact, true, morally sound, and socially sensible. But they seem invariably to believe, in addition, a good many things that are not true at all but that their firm insistence upon may cause a good deal of serious harm. Torquemada, the Dominican monk who helped bring about the Inquisition in Europe, for example, deserved high marks indeed for faith and loyalty to principle. But his very insistence on holding to certain views led to countless unspeakable crimes and atrocities. His single-minded fanaticism not only seriously besmirched Christianity itself, but so tarred the good name of Catholicism that the church has never been able entirely to recover.

Rule No. 30

Beware of the search for the "right answer"

There *is* always just one right answer to a question, isn't there?

Answer: No.

A common error that people make when confronted with such a suggestion—assuming that they are willing to accept it—is to assume that if it *isn't* always the case that there is a right answer to a question then rightness be damned and one answer is as good as another. The latter is a hare-brained alternative and in any event does not follow from an acceptance of the earlier premise.

There are certain questions that do have one right answer, but there are other questions where this is not the case.

To the question, "Who was the first president of the United States of America?" there is only one correct answer: George Washington. But to the question, "Is it *ever* morally permissible to have an abortion?" different answers will seem reasonable to different people.

Some will argue, tidily enough, that the answer to the question is *no.* They believe that abortion is evil, that it is merely a form of murder, and of a particularly defenseless victim at that, and that so far as morality is concerned there is literally nothing more to say about the matter.

But others, perfectly intelligent and moral individuals, may argue that while abortion generally is an unfortunate and destructive practice, there are nevertheless cases—that, though statistically rare, number in the many thousands—in which an abortion is utterly necessary; for example, if it is the only means by which the life of the mother can be saved.

For a very long time in the history of Christian moral theory, it was the first of these two positions that was dominant. However many individual Christians might resort to abortions—which they have done, of course, by the millions—theologians steadfastly maintained that all those who performed such abortions were committing sinful acts and that, if a certain number of women died in the process of childbirth, such tragedies were nevertheless to be considered God's will, and no one had the right to interfere.

The minds of theologians do change over the centuries, of course, and gradually the second position—that *some* abortions are justified—came to dominate the moral debate on the question.

But these two alternatives by no means exhaust the theoretical possibilities. There are other perfectly law-abiding people who believe that, in addition to saving the mother's life, there are other factors that justify an abortion. In the case of pregnancy resulting from incest with the woman's father, they may argue, the pregnancy ought to be aborted. Others would add to the list pregnancies resulting from rape or pregnancies resulting from intercourse with a male suffering from certain mental or physical diseases likely to be transmitted to the child.

Others would add that an abortion is justified if the fetus is known to be hideously abnormal, or the mother is very young—say, twelve or thirteen—and a member of a family already demonstrably unstable or criminal.

It will be perceived at this point that the list of factors that might be added is theoretically infinite and in any event lengthy. Opinions on the issue may also be affected by other factors, such as the age of the fetus. Few people consider it just to end the life of a baby only a few days short of the time for normal birth. At the other end of the time-scale—when the newly created individual bears much more of a resemblance to a smear of tapioca pudding than to anything describable as human—millions of the same individuals can conceive of factors that would justify a resort to abortion.

My purpose in introducing such factors for the reader's consideration is certainly not to review the particulars of the centuries-long debate on this difficult social question, but merely to demonstrate that there are questions that, in view of the total human jury, are not susceptible to a clear-cut, once-and-for-all answer.

Rule No. 31

When it is possible to check facts
for yourself, do so

In many cases it is not possible to check the facts. We cannot personally lift ourselves out of our present time-context and, at will, saunter back through certain portions of the earth in the year 1492, in order to find out if the published details about Columbus's adventures are reliable. But we can do fact-checking about events in our own time and place.

That much is so self-evident it seems never to be contradicted, although some people take longer to realize it. Alfred Korzybski, in his important book *Science and Sanity,* placed great emphasis on comparing maps to actual territories rather than relying totally on the accuracy of the maps for use in the everyday process of decision-making.

But even after you have accurately observed a good deal and noted a number of undeniably clear facts about a given situation, you are still faced with a quite separate process of brain function: interpretation. There are facts and physical realities so simple that interpretation may be irrelevant. If somebody places a bright yellow lemon on a perfectly empty card-table—well, the lemon is just there and, unless separate questions arise, that is all there is to it.

It's perfectly possible, of course, that your senses can be deceived even in such a simple context. The lemon, for example, might be imitation, made of plastic. Or you might be in a state of hypnosis, staring at what everyone else in the room is perfectly aware is a bright red apple, and yet swearing—on your mother's honor—that the object before you is a lemon.

Most of the reality we encounter, however, is vastly more complex. Consider: A middle-aged man is seated at a restaurant table, from time to time sipping from a tall glass of iced tea. Two observers at a nearby table discuss the tea-drinker.

"Isn't it a shame what some people have to suffer?" says the first. "That man appears to be stricken with palsy."

"You're right," says the speaker's companion. "I had an aunt whose hands shook like that. My heart goes out to the poor fellow."

The tea-drinker, in fact, has not a trace of palsy. He does, however, have the habit of shaking any cold drink he holds when it is in a glass largely filled with ice cubes. He has the idea that somehow the shaking of the glass brings more liquid in contact with the cubes and consequently lowers the temperature of the drink. Also, something about the tinkle of the cubes as they bump against the inside of the glass is pleasant to his ears.

Another instance: In an Italian film of some years ago, a scene showed a Catholic priest, late at night, entering a house of prostitution. The audience at once assumes that something scandalous is taking place. The priest, in fact, has entered the building to administer the last rites of the Catholic faith to a repentant and dying whore.

The point of these episodes is not simply that we are occasionally wrong in our judgments and interpretations. Of course we are, and usually many times a day. The point is that *because* we are so frequently wrong, we must recognize our quick assumptions as merely assumptions and not insist on treating them as firm conclusions.

Do not suppose that your knowledge—about anything at all—is total. The foremost scientific authorities in the world—in other words, the people who really do know more about their specialties than anyone else—would never dream of assuming that they know everything. They are aware, to begin with, that they cannot possibly be in possession of all the facts that will be discovered from the present moment of time to the unimaginable reaches of eternity. But even in the context of all the information that has already been established in a given field, the very fact that there is an enormous volume of it precludes the possibility of any one individual absorbing 100 percent of such information. Needless to say, if true experts do not make such errors of thought, you and I have far less reason for doing so.

Rule No. 32

Be aware that reality is complex, not simple

By way of emphasizing to my own children and their friends the simple idea of the complexity of all aspects of existence, I developed a little theoretical game that goes as follows:

> Take the simple situation we are in at the moment. I am sitting here, in this large green chair, speaking to all of you. Now suppose I were to ask you to pick up a writing pad and pencil and just make whatever accurate statements you can about what you see before you. I suppose you might think that you would have difficulty in thinking of more than five or six factual statements about the moment. You might, for example, write entries of the following sort:
>
> 1. A middle-aged adult—named Steve Allen—is talking to four young boys.
> 2. He is seated in a large green chair.
> 3. He is speaking to us about reasoning, logic, straight thinking, and that sort of thing.
> 4. We are beginning to be bored by his remarks.

At this stage in the introduction I introduce a new factor, that of *reward* for good performance. Oddly enough, in several experiments of this sort over the years I've discovered that it does not make a great deal of difference whether the rewards are actual or imaginary. The simple possibility of being urged to do better produces the desired results.

I now say to the group:

213

Now let's suppose that we start the whole process of fact-listing again, but this time you will be given a *reward* for each fact you can specify. I have here a stack of quarters and I will give you a 25-cent piece for every item on your list.

As a result of this sort of direction, the list begins to look as follows:

1. There's a man speaking to us.
2. His name is Steve Allen.
3. He is wearing horn-rimmed glasses.
4. His hair is still dark but is beginning to turn gray.
5. He is sitting with his legs crossed most of the time.
6. Every few minutes one of his hands touches the other.
7. He does not seem to realize that he is doing this with his hands, since he is concentrating on what he is saying.
8. He is wearing a brown tweed jacket.

There's no point in adding to the list here, since the reader can at once see that it easily could be made to contain thousands of factors. Hundreds of observations could be made about such separate categories as one's wardrobe, the content of one's remarks, the chair on which one is seated, all the other furniture in the room, the room itself, its lighting, approximate temperature, and so on. All reality is complex.

Rule No. 33

Beware of the "mind-reading fallacy"

The "mind-reading fallacy" refers to the attribution of motives. It may—in some circumstances, at least—be easy to say what another person did. The facts of a given case may be strikingly clear. A man may have driven his car through your rose-bushes. He may have made a critical remark about you to your boss. He may have made a speech urging nuclear disarmament. He may have sent a one-hundred-dollar contribution to the American Civil Liberties Union. He may have done any of a thousand and one morally virtuous, neutral, or evil things.

Second, let us assume that everyone concerned is in perfect agreement about what was done. You should know, parenthetically, that this is far from common, since most of us are not especially reliable witnesses. If a hundred people witness an event, a certain percentage of them, and perhaps a very high percentage, will start the process of error at the moment of observation. Whether the act being witnessed takes only seven seconds from beginning to end—let us say an automobile running into a telephone pole—or takes an hour and forty-five minutes, it is very unlikely that all witnesses will agree about exactly what did take place.

Besides the errors made at the moment the action was performed, an entirely separate assortment of errors will take place during the process of recollection. Let us assume that the witnesses will not be called upon to give their testimony, whether formally or informally, until seven days after the event. Far from what you might expect—that the long period of time will be used to reinforce the original impressions, to cement them in the memory and thus render them even more reliable—what will in fact occur is that certain details will begin to slip away, at least insofar as their availability to the consciousness is concerned.

Please understand that I do not refer here either to imaginary or actual people who are characterized by a striking stupidity. I am talking about run-of-the-mill human beings, covering the whole range of I.Q. measurement. While those who are noticeably bright may make fewer errors, they will certainly, as a group, make some.

But now let us return to the assumption that no such process of error will take place and that all statements about what did occur will be factual.

To this point, let us assume whatever you as a witness say about the act performed is factually reliable. But it often happens that we are not content to stop at that point. We may, whether we approve or disapprove of the performed action, proceed to a second stage, in which we go beyond reportage to analysis or interpretation. We may decide to address the question of *why* the individual acted as he, or she, did. On this level the possibilities for error are greatly increased, and they were bad enough to start with.

For example: Starting in 1959 I addressed the eternally difficult problem of disarmament—nuclear or otherwise—in some of my lectures and writings. Almost immediately I became aware—through letters written directly to me, letters published in newspapers that subsequently came to my attention, personal conversations, newspaper and magazine articles, comments on the radio, and so on—that at least some of those who differed with me on the question wrongly assumed that what I was recommending was not simply nuclear disarmament per se, but *unilateral* nuclear disarmament, which is, of course, quite another matter.

Needless to say, all those who made this erroneous assumption proceeded at once to conclude that the *reason* for my imaginary recommendation was that, for whatever unexplained reasons, I wanted to aid the Marxist and/or Soviet campaign for world domination.

In responding to such unfounded accusations I sometimes simply provided the facts of the case and in other instances employed the device of wit to make my point. I said, for example, that in fact I *was* strongly in favor of unilateral disarmament, but only for the Russians, who were in any event as unlikely to take the proposal seriously as were we Americans.

The error in thinking of which my accusers were guilty is common.

It is called the "mind-reading fallacy," since those guilty of attributing nonexistent motives would have to claim that they were able to read the mind of the accused if they expected their judgment to be honored.

Do not conclude from this that it is never possible to attribute motives, and to do so accurately. If an individual is, let's say, a member of the Communist party, it would be perfectly reasonable to assume that his motives for preaching *American* nuclear disarmament grew out of his loyalty to communist principles. Unfortunately the bulk of such motive-attributing is just dumb, wrong-headed stuff. It is wrong so often partly because it overlooks an important point mentioned elsewhere in this book concerning the difference between consistent and conclusive evidence.

It is important to grasp that there is a difference between *motives* for performing an act and *reasons* for performing the act. Also note that both reasons and motives may be good or evil.

Let us suppose that two men, at separate times and places, performed the act of burning a cross on a stranger's lawn. One may have the motive of furthering the interests of the local branch of the Nazi party. The other may be an FBI anti-Nazi provocateur who burns the cross simply so that he can claim credit in a nearby saloon for having done so, in order to find out which habitués of the place will congratulate him for so disgraceful and un-American an act.

Or let us say two men are sexually propositioned by a woman. They both refuse her. One may have done so because such sexual contact would have been a violation of sincerely held religious and moral principles. The other may be a notorious libertine who refused the woman simply because he knew she had a venereal disease.

From such examples, you can see that *simply knowing what was done by no means makes clear what motivation lay behind an act.*

Rule No. 34

Decide to continue your education until death

Most of us think of education incorrectly. The word itself does not come properly into focus. We know readily enough, in a general sense, what it means, and we grasp the obvious, which is that education is a matter of acquiring knowledge. But when we think of the process, what comes to mind is a series of vague images of school buildings, books, teachers, classrooms, tests, data. All of these have their relevance, but we should pass through them to the heart of the matter. The central item in the process of education is the individual human being. To you, the most important player in the ongoing drama of education is yourself.

If you are eminently self-satisfied with your present state, then the process of education has ended for you, if indeed it ever properly began. But I assume that no one is fully satisfied with one's intellectual estate, nor should one be. In any event, the importance, the excitement of education, is that it will—beyond any question—change you. It will not change you in slight or inconsequential ways, for as Norman Cousins puts it, "Education represents a flying leap from the tenth to the twentieth century." Education is the process by means of which the startling discoveries of the greatest scholars, philosophers, and scientists are made available to you. It is a rare individual who, when he turns on a light that instantly converts a black room to one in which all objects are clearly visible, pauses for even a fleeting moment to feel gratitude to Volta, Edison, and the other pioneers in the field of electricity. Just so, it is a rare individual who, upon learning a fact, or being introduced to an idea, ever gives the slightest thought to the thousands of scholars who devoted lifetimes to unearthing such facts and developing such ideas.

But the great mysterious mountain of accumulated information is there nevertheless, and we are all privileged to march toward it, through whatever mists and over whatever obstructions, and to make its substance our own. For it is all, in a sense at least, free for the taking. The scholars of the world do not copyright their dazzling discoveries and dole them out only to the highest bidders. They publish, they share, they freely dispense their knowledge to the world. Would not a man be counted a great fool who passed through a field strewn with gold and diamonds but never paused to pick them up and convert them to his benefit and to that of the world? Would we not be equally foolish if, passing through a world in which dearly bought information lies about us at every hand, we disdained it and instead directed our concentration to the most inconsequential, trivial, and indeed harmful things?

Rule No. 35

Find out what's going on

What's going on in the world? It's not hard to find out because we are surrounded by sources of information—television and radio newcasts, newpapers, magazines, public lectures, high school and university courses, video and audio tape cassettes, record albums, cable television, computers, Buck Rogers–type satellite transmissions—all are technical wonders that would have dazzled thoughtful men and women of earlier centuries, though you and I take all such near-miracles for granted.

In the light of such achievements and services we no longer really have much excuse for being dumb.

For hundreds of thousands of years, ignorance, illiteracy, and superstition were the *norm*. They were characteristic of human life. Everywhere, about 1 percent of the population was educated, knowledgeable, informed. The other 99 percent lived out their lives in general ignorance, although some individuals might have known something of a trade or other narrow personal interest. It's all different now.

You don't have to be ignorant anymore.

Rule No. 36

Listen to newscasts on the radio
and watch them on television

To the average reader of a book like this, this recommendation will seem unnecessary, but we all have friends and acquaintances who rarely keep informed about significant events.

For the United States government to bring Oliver North to trial in 1989 it was necessary to find twelve jurors who apparently knew nothing at all of one of the most important news stories of the preceding few years, the Iran/Contra scandal. It had been referred to in a thousand and one newscasts as well as covered daily by radio and television networks.

Telling typical Americans that they should watch and listen to more news broadcasts, therefore, is analogous to telling those concerned about their health that they should get plenty of fresh air, physical exercise, and a balanced diet. Even such simple and "obvious" recommendations must be endlessly repeated.

Radio—as mentioned earlier—is one of the things that has made us dumber, although that is largely our own fault since, in addition to mindless music and chatter, radio also broadcasts a good deal of worthwhile material. It follows that we can use the medium to increase our general knowledge and awareness.

If we are fortunate enough to live in a city that has a radio station with an all-news policy, we can get into the habit of tuning to that station when we get into our cars.

The United States is such a mobile society that car-radio is big business. During the morning and evening rush-hour periods—from 7:00 to 10:00 A.M. and from 4:00 to 7:00 P.M.—millions of drivers across the country have their radios turned on. There's nothing wrong with occasionally listening to music, but if that's all we listen to we're losing a valuable resource for adding to our store of information and our general intelligence.

Most all-news stations have a policy that "gives you the world in twenty minutes." Public radio stations often provide even better information services. Their newscasts may run a full thirty or sixty minutes. They also often feature interviews with scholars, political leaders, authors, and others who have something important to say. Remember, we are not comparing these snippets of education with a full four years of formal instruction at Harvard. The proper and relevant comparison is between listening to such instructive material on the one hand, and listening to the usual rock-jock radio drivel on the other. If you are fortunate, you may be able to hear more than one public radio station in your community. They will be glad to send published lists of their programs. Perhaps you will be lucky enough to become newly introduced to such radio treasures as the "MacNeil-Lehrer Report" and "All Things Considered."

Rule No. 37

Watch less commercial television

Novelist Walker Percy, among millions of others, is concerned about the great amount of time people spend watching television. Its influence? "Nobody has any idea," he has said. "It's the greatest, most revolutionary change in our culture since print. It has even more influence on our lives. People average five to six hours daily watching television. You can't tell me that five or six hours a day of feeding the mind is not having a profound influence." Percy is right.

On May 4, 1982, the National Institute of Mental Health issued a report summarizing ten years of research on the behavioral effects of television-watching. The studies—one would hope, once and for all—disposed of the idea that television entertainment is merely innocuous and time-passing. The almost 2,500 research projects produced the following conclusions:

- Violence on television does lead to aggressive behavior in children and teenagers who watch the programs.

- Heavy viewers of television, of all ages, are more apt to think the world is violent . . . trust other people less, and believe that the world is a "mean and scary" place.

- Entertainment television has become an important sex educator, but by no means an edifying one. Extramarital sexual activity is referred to on television programs approximately five times as often as legal and moral sexual conduct by married couples.

- Both I.Q. and reading tests show an absolutely clear-cut pattern: *The more time spent watching television, the lower the scores.* In one town, students' reading scores fell significantly within two years of introducing television to the community.

While it would be a mistake to assume that television is the sole cause of the serious weakening of intelligence in the United States in recent years, it would be an equally serious error to assume that it is not among the causative factors. The debate on this question, as it happens, has nothing whatever to do with whether television has contributed to our present unhappy condition. The fact that it has seems to be universally taken for granted. What is at issue is simply the matter of degree. There would be no point in trying to determine, even if one could, whether television should be first, third, or seventh on a list of such factors. Let us proceed, then, to the more important questions.

My opinion is that even if no resident of the United States was permitted to watch television until he was twelve years old, years of habitual viewing after that age would still contribute to a dulling of the mind. This would not be the case if the process of selection—either imposed or self-initiated—were such as to concentrate on those elements of television fare that have a beneficial effect on the intelligence and the aesthetic sensibilities. In our haste to point the finger of blame at television, we must not overlook the fact that, if properly used, it could serve as almost the sole means of education. I am convinced that I could go into any university in the United States and, with nothing more than the twenty-four video-cassettes of the PBS television series "Meeting of Minds," contrive to teach a body of students, over the course of several weeks, a great deal more about history and philosophy than they would be likely to learn by conventional methods during the same time period.

Again, there is much on television that is worth the viewing time of any intelligent person. Network newscasts, "Washington Week in Review," "Face the Nation," and "Meet the Press"; "Masterpiece Theatre," telecasts of Shakespeare, and other examples of good theater, opera, ballet; "Sixty Minutes" and Bill Moyers's interviews with writers, artists, and scholars; some of Phil Donahue's or William F. Buckley's programs on important social questions; Ted Koppel's "Nightline,"

"Roots," "Shogun," and academic instruction provided by local public-service stations—these are only a few of hundreds of instances in which television fully lives up to its thrilling potential. When critics speak of the harm done by television, therefore, they are obviously not referring to such admirable fare. But the sad fact is that such material represents a minute fraction of the total.

I do not intend to be the least bit Calvinistic about this. I do not recommend that the government, or any other authority, assume control of television and limit it to nothing but informative and aesthetically uplifting material. There is certainly a place, for example, for the broadcast of football, basketball, baseball, golf, and other sports. Even scholars and artists may indulge in athletic pursuits as a means of mental relaxation or physical refreshment—as the ancient Greeks perceived—and there is a place for television material that one views just for fun and relaxation. Indeed, the bulk of my own contribution to the medium for some four decades has been precisely of this sort. And, too, a given program may be both entertaining and, on some level, instructive. A good many of the programs in the "All in the Family" series, for example, were not only well written, acted, and produced, but also taught a moral or social lesson. And some Americans would—God help us—never be exposed to certain leaders of thought at all if they had not from time to time seen them interviewed by Johnny Carson, Phil Donahue, Merv Griffin, and Dick Cavett.

To cite another example of how television can be used to inform and inspire, there is a television game show called "Know Your Heritage," the subject matter of which is African-American history. It features black high-schoolers responding to questions about people, places, events, and ideas associated with black history. For information, the reader may contact Donald Jackson, Central City Marketing, Inc., 1716 South Michigan Avenue, Chicago, IL 60616.

But when all such justly complimentary observations about television have been made, the depressing fact remains that the overwhelming majority of programs are, as I have earlier observed, light-weight.

The harm starts in childhood. It is truly depressing to learn that the majority of American children get their first lessons about the great, wondrous world outside their homes and immediate neighborhoods from television. Little of what they see is closely related to reality. A good percentage of it, for example, will be cartoons. Or it will be action-adventure, Captain Avenger, and cowboy or police shoot-'em-up fare.

But the children who watch such programs are doing far more than wasting time that might be better spent. They are absorbing ideas about society, human relationships, violence, and sex. They are acquiring impressions about *what sort of persons society admires and respects.* They are acquiring standards of taste about music, art, morals, vocabulary—almost everything.

It is particularly disheartening to recall that children's television was not always as atrocious as it is at present. In the 1950s children could, along with having fun, acquire a little information from programs like "Mr. I. Magination," "Ding Dong School," and "Mr. Wizard."

How, then, did the situation deteriorate? Simply because the bad money drove out the good. Violence, cartoons, and noisy nonsense not surprisingly attracted more four-, five-, and six-year-olds than did the sorts of things they should have been watching. Parents, by and large, abdicated their responsibility to guide or control the viewing habits of their children. The result was inevitable because of one of the more uncomfortable facts that Americans must come to grips with—there is never going to be any serious hope for marked improvement in the quality of commercial television, simply because television is primarily an advertising medium, which is to say that *it is plugged into the machinery of the marketplace.* Conservatives of America, be of good cheer, if only for the sake of your blood pressure. As a practicing capitalist, I am hardly about to recommend a totalitarian alternative.

If in some distant future we do come to a situation in which the American people—or some influential segment of them—will demand government intervention, if only to prevent further damage to the national mind and soul, we will have the excesses of the marketplace to thank for it. It is the same old process we have seen before in other subdivisions of the business world. Early in the century, America's meat-packers, not content with their customary large profits, began to sell disguised poisonous and rancid meat to the unsuspecting public in such quantities that reformers were able to stimulate a sense of public outrage and use its energy to create laws and regulations designed, not to hamper the meat industry in the honest pursuit of its aims, but only to prevent it from sickening and killing American citizens. Something like the same process has occurred in scores of our industries, not to mention those in other parts of the world. But the analogy—discouragingly enough— breaks down when it is applied to television, because here, perhaps for the first time, there is a situation in which the public is saying, in effect, "Please! Give us more, not less, garbage."

No individual viewer will admit any such thing, of course. The biggest klutz in town will insist that he wants better television. But whenever a high quality, edifying, instructive program is put on opposite something like "Beverly Hillbillies" or "Gilligan's Island," the victory almost always goes to the schlock. The process works particularly insidiously when viewers are at the tender ages between three and fifteen.

But children's television does not do harm only directly. Some destructive effects come indirectly. Most American children spend so much time watching television, in fact, that even if its effects were neutral there would still be a largely destructive result, because during the same three or four hours a day the children will *not* be doing things that are better for them—reading, for example.

It is remarkable that our nation's publishers continue to produce as much high-quality children's literature as they do. These books, of course, are purchased by parents, not children; but they are being given to at least a minority of fortunate young people. It eventually occurs to some of them that there are important differences between what they read and what they see on the glass screen. To start with, the act of reading itself is the one skill that opens the door to all others. It would be possible—and I'm sure it happens—for one to watch television and simply never learn to read. The same, obviously, is not true of exposure to books. Furthermore books make certain demands that television does not. The young readers may linger over certain passages, pause to reflect, experience the first stirrings of their own creativity. A book—even one with pictures—does address the mind. It does call into play the imagination. And, as critics have been pointing out for four decades, television is a spectator sport, so it tends to make us lazy.

Books teach us different things about human beings, too. They describe characters and motivations more fully than television can or will take the time to do. One may, after all, dawdle over a book for as long as one wishes. But on television the decisions about time are made for us. Things are supposed to be fast and snappy, even though real life seldom is.

Just as in the early days of television, there are current children's programs that run counter to the trend, at least in most respects. "Mr. Rogers' Neighborhood," "Sesame Street," and "Square One Television" are three. But *they are not seen on commercial television.* I wonder how many children in slums and ghettos—the very audience for whom some of this good programming is primarily intended—ever get to see them. For the reader who would like to make a separate study of the problem of children's television, I recommend *Saturday Morning TV,* by Gary H. Grossman (Dell, 1981).

Watching less television obviously doesn't mean giving up newscasts, presidential addresses, good-quality drama and comedy, documentaries on important issues, and other excellent fare that NBC, CBS, and ABC provide, if never in sufficient quantity. It does mean giving up much of the junk-food for the mind that is the basic staple of commercial television.

It also means turning the television set off altogether on certain nights and bestirring ourselves to go to the theater for the purpose of seeing a motion picture or a live drama. Here again, we should be selective. We will add little to our education if the films we see are simply more slickly produced versions of the froth already available on commercial television. But there are motion pictures that can culturally enrich as well as entertain us. Modern film-makers, especially the best of them, often meaningfully explore important social problems. *Kramer vs. Kramer* dealt with the painful subject of divorce. *The China Syndrome* alerted many of us to the dangers of our nation's growing dependence on nuclear energy. *The Verdict* and *And Justice for All* said something important about the American judicial system. *Gandhi* was wonderfully instructive. This is not, of course, a new development. Such classic motion pictures as *Gentlemen's Agreement,* which dealt with anti-Semitism, *Grapes of Wrath,* which revealed the tragic plight of the nation's poor farmers and farm workers, and *A Man For All Seasons,* which told the story of Sir Thomas More, are among hundreds of films that have informed and enlightened while entertaining.

In terms of making ourselves better informed, we have a somewhat wider choice in seeing plays, since a light comedy in the theater is generally a considerably more artistic production than its television equivalent.

Neil Simon, for example, is hardly producing dramatic literature for the ages, but he is a top-notch modern comic playwright nevertheless. Even more important, the theater itself is a cultural resource to be treasured. It is a subdivision of literature as well as a distinctive art form. We are not well-rounded persons if we never attend the theater.

What about the ballet, opera, and Shakespeare? It takes a bit longer to develop a taste for these forms of art, but the riches are there.

Your own socially imposed insensitivity may make it a bit difficult to unearth them, but the verdict of history is in. It's not up to you to decide whether the opera, Shakespeare, and serious dance are worthwhile. They are. Your job is to find out what all the excitement has been about these last few centuries.

Consider first the opera. You will hear glorious voices, excellent orchestras, and perhaps see some superior dancing and what is generally a good show. It will help to understand a given production if you prepare yourself before the curtain goes up. Consult an encyclopedia, a book on the opera, a knowledgeable friend—do something to tune yourself in to the proper wavelength.

When you get to the theater don't just sit there talking to your companion about baseball, food, or sex, and staring at the overhead chandeliers. *Read the program.* Familiarize yourself with the biographies of the singers, the conductor, the composer, the author of the book, and the plot of the show.

Later seek out friends and acquaintances who know more about the subject than you do. Engage them in conversation. Put questions to them.

The same applies to Shakespeare. He is the world's greatest dramatist, the world's greatest poet. In this case, too, prepare yourself for the experience of seeing one of his plays. Because the language may at first fall strangely on your ears, and because the plays were written centuries ago, it's a bit more difficult to follow the plot than it is while watching "Miami Vice." But there are great treasures on that stage and you don't have to work terribly hard to perceive them.

Lastly, relax. This book is giving you scores of suggestions. You're not under absolute obligation to be guided by every one of them. I'm a professional musician but I attend the opera rarely, largely because I never had the opportunity to see an opera until I was an adult, and our tastes about cultural matters are generally formed during our early years. But despite my early deprivation I enjoy an opera when I see one. You can, too.

Rule No. 38

Watch your local educational channels

Some people are so far gone on the road to dumbth that the very word "educational" has a negative effect on them. In reality the Public Broadcasting System's chain of more than two hundred television stations across the country presents some of the most exciting, stimulating, and enjoyable programs in the forty-year history of television.

This is not to say we need feel any obligation to watch every program our local cultural station transmits. I have done a series for public television myself—a talk-show with actors portraying historical figures, called "Meeting of Minds"—but I see only a modest percentage of the PBS shows. But to miss everything that this superb network broadcasts is to be deprived of some wonderful viewing fare.

On PBS, we see nothing less than the best acting in the world, almost all of it provided by the British casts of the dramatic programs produced by the BBC and other British production companies. And there is the "Nova" series, the Jacques Cousteau specials, the "McNeil-Lehrer Report," and much, much more.

Rule No. 39

If you have any problems with speech,
use the radio, television, films, and tape recorders
to help solve them

Speech problems, for the most part, have no direct connection with
our reasoning faculty. But in some cases, they do. In certain social spheres,
vocabularies consist of significantly fewer words than the norm. Some
segments of the population tend to mispronounce common words (*duh*
for "the," *aks* for "ask," *chirruns* for "children"). Listening to or watching
programs on which people of all races speak in a generally correct way
can help to correct such errors.

If you have difficulty speaking coherently, you might find some
use in an exercise I developed when I was twenty-one and first working
in radio, in Phoenix, Arizona. There was no problem in reading
commercials or other scripted materials, but even then, as a lowly local
announcer, I had to do a certain amount of ad-libbing, even if it was
just identifying the station, giving the correct time, suggesting that listeners stay tuned for the following program, and so on. And there were
occasional assignments—sports events, parades, interviews—where
scripts were not provided. The solution was to use my car as a rehearsal
studio. As I drove about the city, I would simply give a "play-by-play"
description of whatever I was watching. It sounded something like this:

> Here we go again, folks, as I continue my description of the things
> and people and places I see as I drive around good old Phoenix,
> Arizona. It's slightly rainy out this morning, which is pretty unusual
> for this time of year and—come to think of it—for this part of
> the country, which is essentially desert, as you know. But in any
> event, I now see, as I pass the corner of Fourth and Jefferson,

232

two elderly women about to cross the street, waiting for the light to change. One of them is walking a small poodle. At least I think it's a poodle, although I'm not sure it's pure-blooded. On my right now, as I proceed along, I see a hardware store, a bakery shop, and a place that sells Indian turquoise jewelry.

As you can see, there was nothing the least bit noteworthy about what I was saying. However, it was providing invaluable practice at communicating the impressions made on me.

You may choose to emulate my example by using your automobile as a private rehearsal studio, but there is no reason to limit yourself to that physical context. You can perform the same sort of simple exercise almost anywhere you find yourself. The next time you're at home alone, for example, make the "play-by-play" experiment by simply describing to an imaginary audience what you are doing or experiencing at the moment. A sample monologue might go as follows:

Good morning, ladies and gentlemen, I'm broadcasting to you from my house here at 314 West Simpson Street, and my purpose at the moment is just to tell you what's going on here in my kitchen. It's not the most fascinating thing in the world, I guess, but you might find it of moderate interest.

For example, in the background you might be able to detect the sound of our washing machine, inasmuch as my wife put a load in about fifteen minutes ago and I'm just hanging around at the moment waiting to turn the machine off for her, since she had to go visit her mother.

I'm also making my own breakfast just now, which consists of cornflakes with a little skimmed milk, a sliced banana, and honey instead of white sugar. Both my wife and I are, if not actually health-food nuts, at least people who eat a sensible and well-balanced diet.

That's more than enough to give you the idea. Don't be in the least concerned with making your account dramatic or "interesting." The purpose of the exercise is not to thrill or fascinate an audience (there is none) but simply to keep your own mouth working in as intelligible and coherent a manner as possible. Don't be put off by the fact that when you first start this sort of exercise you "feel dumb."

Of course you do; there is an inherently absurd element to the business of speaking aloud in an empty room. But that is not of the slightest importance in the context of your purpose. Needless to say, if during the simple description of what you're seeing in your immediate environment you also happen to have a profound thought or two—include it in your remarks. But nothing of the sort is at all necessary.

Later, tape record your remarks. Compare your speaking style with that of Ted Koppel, Bryant Gumble of the "Today" show, or Ed Bradley of "Sixty Minutes." They speak well. If you don't, learn from those who do.

Rule No. 40

Watch the best of the television talk-shows

Phil Donahue, Oprah Winfrey, and Geraldo Rivera book relatively few guests from the world of entertainment. Consequently, there are a minimum of blondes in low-cut dresses flirting with the male hosts, lightweight chatter about new rock albums, and X-rated movies. Almost every show features discussion of important social questions. For those who must get a daily fix of drama from television, there is considerably more drama on the average Donahue, Winfrey, or Geraldo show, and every bit of it is real, not imaginary. The same goes for Sally Jessy Raphael.

One must be realistic enough to recognize that for many Americans it is difficult to get excited about programs like Ted Koppel's "Nightline," "Meet the Press," and William F. Buckley's discussions. But because of the structure of the issues-oriented talk-shows—a wide-open forum in which members of the audience are permitted, even encouraged, not only to put questions to guests but to express their own opinions— no viewer will feel intellectually inadequate. The hosts and their guests use plain language and rarely indulge in philosophical abstractions. They talk about the reality of the human condition. And almost all their discussions are stimulating and informative, despite the tendency that became pronounced in 1989, to depend more and more on shocking and titillating subject-matter. The reason for this change of emphasis, of course, is not that Winfrey, Geraldo, Raphael, or Donahue have become somewhat strange in their personal interests, but that sensational subject-matter gets higher ratings.

This suggestion, however, does not involve watching such programs five days a week!

Rule No. 41

Make a point of visiting aquariums, museums of natural history, art museums, and planetaria—frequently

Before making a trip to the natural history museum, the art gallery, or the planetarium, we should prepare ourselves for the wonder and literal glory of such displays. We can stand in front of a particular exhibit and sometimes within sixty seconds absorb information that it may have taken centuries to accumulate, information for which thoughtful individuals of earlier ages would have paid almost any price.

Another way to appreciate the inherent merit of such wonders is to imagine oneself trying to construct such displays, or attempting to gather the information required to construct them. Imagine that you have been given $10 million, so that money is no object, ten years of time, and all the supplies of raw materials considered necessary. Even in the presence of such factors you would almost certainly find it impossible to equal what others have achieved and now place at your casual disposal.

And—when we go to museums—we should take the children.

Rule No 42

Take a speed-reading course

The ability to read faster will not, of itself, necessarily lead to a measurable improvement of our reasoning faculty. Nevertheless, it will enable us to absorb more information and philosophy than we otherwise could within given time-contexts. It will also exercise our ability to make decisions and choices since such programs are not solely a matter of picking up speed; they also help us discriminate among various sorts of reading matter and improve our comprehension.

I quote from the remarks of Jack Valenti, president of the Motion Picture Association of America, at the degree convocation of Boston University's College of Communication, delivered Sunday, May 21, 1989.

> Commencement speakers, like former presidential assistants or university economists, seldom say anything memorable. So, if I leave you with any single impression, I pray you will remember this: Get into your bones the essential structure of the ordinary English sentence which, as Mr. Churchill said, is a noble thing indeed. Read, read, read. When you are on an airplane, read. When you find yourself with an idle hour, read, and if you have no idle hour, create one. Read the best of writers who have passed the test of time, whose works are populated with ideas that have reach and whose rhythms stir both heart and brain. Read the best of the moderns even though their works have yet to be judged. Read Elmore Leonard and Edward Gibbon, John Steinbeck and Lord Macaulay, Anne Tyler and William Prescott, John Updike and Winston Churchill. Read and absorb.

A speed-reading course will enable you to increase the volume of your reading.

Rule No. 43

Take advantage of your local library

Imagine that you are idly poking about in an out-of-the-way antique shop in New England, in a section rarely visited by tourists. Your eye falls on an obviously quite old desk, of the sort with many drawers, large and small. You seat yourself and begin to look through the little compartments. In the back of one of them your prying hand feels some papers, which you draw out into the light. They are a group of letters. You open the first envelope and remove the folded pages it contains. The most incredible thing has happened. You are holding in your hand a letter actually written by the first president of the United States, in which he describes to his wife what he has been doing during his first days in office. Imagine the excitement you feel at being able actually to share Washington's thoughts on so important a subject.

The story outlined is, obviously, fiction. But we do not have to live through such an intriguing adventure to become aware of what Washington did, thought, and wrote about his participation in one of the most interesting adventures of history. We need not haunt obscure antique shops. We need only go to our neighborhood library. It can open up the world for us.

That familiarity breeds contempt is one of the sadder truths. There seems nothing so glorious, so beautiful, noble, true, necessary, productive, effective, inspiring that long-continued exposure to it does not dull our sense of appreciation. Men trapped in a disabled submarine would willingly barter ten years of their lives for a return to sweet, fresh air. Yet how many of us stop to appreciate the air we daily breathe?

Imagine how the once-blind appreciate the simple ability to see. Most of us give no thought to it at all until we begin to lose it. How many loved ones or conscientious fellow-citizens are largely unappreciated until, in a rush of grief and loss, we extol their virtues upon the occasion of their death?

As for reading, it represents an incredible achievement in the long, painful march toward civilization. First, speech itself had to be developed out of assorted grunts, groans, giggles, and growls. Then a few simple marks were made to stand for words representing things, people, animals, actions, and—eventually—ideas.

At much later stages came the separate abilities to reproduce copies of important documents. Humankind developed things to write on and to write with. Those who knew how taught others to read, and recognition of the preciousness and power of the ability spread throughout the civilized world.

Eventually the printing press brought the blessings of reading, and the knowledge it imparted, to all parts of the planet. As recently as a hundred years ago, in our own part of the world, there was enormous respect for the printed word. Almost any book was correctly perceived as the precious thing it is. Men and women would walk to another town simply to see a book, or to have the opportunity of spending even a few minutes reading its pages, absorbing its message. The poor, in those days, could look forward to very little education, if any. Most were illiterate but they wanted to know, which is to say, they wanted to be able to read.

Now survey the present. Less than 10 percent of the American people buy books! Millions who are able to read seem interested chiefly in comic strips, the sports pages, pornography, trashy novels, fan magazines, or check-out counter scandal-sheets notoriously careless with facts.

The love of reading is in part a compulsion. I am powerless to resist the temptation to read. I perceive the magic, wondrous power that reading brings, and wish that more people could share this simple insight. The great majority on our planet, which not very long ago we imagined was generally civilized, is still illiterate. These damnable polysyllabic words—like *illiterate*—serve as mental filing-devices but obscure the reality they were intended to convey. Think for a moment— really think—what it means to be unable to read. Of course we are all illiterate in the sense that, of the hundreds of languages in the world, even many educated people can read only one, and perhaps another one or two stumblingly. But hundreds of millions can read nothing at all. This means that much of the best of human achievement, from all of the cultures in the long march of history, is simply closed to them.

If they happen to live within walking distance of a mighty temple, a great cathedral, a sculpture by Michelangelo, a painting by Da Vinci, if they are ever able to hear a performance of a symphony by Brahms or Beethoven, they are fortunate indeed. Few illiterates are so situated, and the very degrading, dehumanizing social circumstances that may have contributed to their illiteracy make it extremely unlikely that they will even avail themselves of opportunities like those mentioned. For the man who cannot read, Shakespeare might as well have lived on another planet. Aristotle and Aquinas might as well have never been born.

To say that endless reading is the source of many of my ideas would suggest that I simply find in books and articles ideas of others and take them as my own. No, my mind does not simply receive ideas. It talks back to the authors, even the greatest and wisest of them, a response I'm sure they would warmly welcome.

The most stimulating reading is not the kind that deals with romantic escapades, hair-raising adventures, sex, or violent conflict, although these have their obvious excitatory value. It is exposure to ideas, instances of philosophical insight, that occasion the greatest and most long-lasting excitement. But to stop at the point of reception, to simply receive the ideas of others, however valid or brilliant, quite misses the basic point, which is that exposure to the ideas of others properly ought to lead to the creation of one's own.

It is not possible, after all, to plastically accept everything even the greatest minds have believed and propagated. I have an almost feverish respect for Augustine, Descartes, Newton, Locke, Voltaire, Aquinas, Paine, and the other heroes of the pantheon of Western culture. But each made statements that were flatly contradicted by the views of some of the others: So I see the literary and philosophical tradition of our culture not so much as a storehouse of facts and ideas, but rather as a hopefully endless Great Debate at which I am a privileged listener.

Since I am a compulsive reader, I therefore do not have to set aside two or three hours for reading, as the average person might, but read wherever and whenever the physical situation permits. I read, for example, in the bathtub. I read in the backseats of cars, unless there is some particular reason to look out the window or converse with a traveling companion. I read in barber chairs, while standing in line to get into theaters, restaurants, or stadiums, while waiting for my wife to join me so that we can go out to an evening appointment. Since she's usually fifteen or twenty minutes behind schedule, I'm able to cover quite a few pages I would not have read if she were on time. (I heartily recommend this custom to those with a similar problem, since it removes the frustration one ordinarily feels when being kept waiting by anybody.)

I read during meals, unless there is a good reason to pay attention to the food or to enjoy someone's company.

Don't say you can't afford books. They are free for the borrowing at your neighborhood library.

Rule No. 44
Develop the habit of making notes

The memory of humans, compared to the memory of frogs or cattle, is remarkable indeed. Our brains make some sort of recorded impression of an incredible number of bits of information that we absorb during every waking and sleeping moment of our lives. We do not *recall* all this information, of course, since to do so would be pointless. But once Nature and/or God "decided" that not all data would be accessible from our memory files, the door was opened to endless confusion, for it meant that unless very strict criteria and a sharply watchful oversight mechanism were employed at the initial moment we received the flood of sights, sounds, odors, and skin impressions by which we are at all moments inundated, the alternative would be a very catch-as-catch-can sort of process. One consequence is that all of us report that there is "no sense" to what we remember, what we forget, or what made no conscious impression on us in the first place.

Another level of complication arises from the fact that a very small percentage of the impressions we do record are, at a later time, available to the consciousness. Each of us daily has the experience of knowing perfectly well with one part of the brain that we had a particular comb, pencil, or set of car keys with us when, a few minutes earlier, we entered a certain room, but that despite such absolute certainty we are nevertheless utterly unable to recall, at the moment, the circumstances under which the now-missed object left our hand, purse, pocket, or briefcase and moved into the vast domain of Lost Objects.

It would be tempting to say more here on the subject, but this is a book about reasoning, not remembering. I recommend a study of the phenomenon of memory, however. Any good bookstore or library can direct you to fascinating works on the subject. The relevance of this digression is that, precisely *because* the memory is remarkably sievelike, we would be able to think better if we formed the habit of making notes.

Obviously, we don't want to retain references to everything that happens to us. At one extreme there are certain trades or professions in which the making of notes is common: journalists, scholars, psychiatrists, investigators, experienced travelers—all make notes out of self-interest. There is certain information they wish to retain, and they are well aware that they are unlikely to do so if they depend solely on memory.

Some people make many of their notes in the form of letters. Most families, if they are fortunate, have at least one member who is a natural letter-writer and has a good eye for newsy detail.

The importance of making notes obviously increases in proportion to the complexity of the information you hope to retain. If the message is a simple one, such as "Pick up laundry on Thursday," you may or may not choose to rely solely on your memory. But you are poorly advised to do so if the message is one with several factors to it, such as "Please pick up laundry on Thursday, bring it to Aunt Sarah's house, leave it on the front porch just behind the geranium pots and then phone her that evening, after she returns home, and make sure that she noticed the package on the front porch since it will be dark by the time she gets back to the house."

Most people couldn't accurately repeat such a message ten seconds after hearing it—which is the basis of the old parlor game of whispering an even simpler statement along a chain-of-communication. I've used the game as an entertainment-gimmick on my television programs on various occasions over the past thirty years. In no instance did the final version of the message, as spoken aloud by the person at the end of the line, bear the slightest resemblance to the original form. If the given statement was something like, "Snow falls most often during November, December, and January, but not necessarily in all parts of the world," the final message would be as far removed as, "Some people take sweaters on their vacation and others don't use much hair-spray."

In playing the game it is necessary to be sure that each participant hears only that version of the message that reaches him from the person immediately before him in line.

It is perhaps only public figures who accurately perceive the degree to which the factual record is distorted, since they are personally so often the subject of it. An illustrative instance: One night back in 1949 I became involved in a good-natured argument with singer Frankie Laine about the predicament of the average amateur songwriter. "You could write 350 songs a week," I said. "But what good would it do? The important factors concern publishing and recording." Laine took exception to what he thought was an exaggeration and after a brief exchange I agreed to write the 350 songs, within a week's time, just to clarify that part of the matter. The songs were composed shortly thereafter in the window of a Hollywood music store. But now consider Part 2 of the story.

Recently at an airport in Newport News, Virginia, a pleasant young man, having recognized me, approached and offered a number of generous compliments. "But the thing about you that impresses me most," he said, "is that on a bet, or a dare, you once wrote eleven songs on a roll of toilet paper, is that right?"

While the young man's version represented the greatest distortion of the story I had yet encountered, the fact is that inaccurate accounts of the incident have been predominant. I have heard that I wrote 1,000 songs a week, 350 songs a day, that the melodies all had lyrics (none of them did), and many other versions.

The value of setting down on paper the nuts-and-bolts of a problem as they occur to us is that it brings them into sharper focus. The creative process, once stimulated, is by no means prepared to sit idly by and wait for the accumulation of all relevant data. But obviously—all other things being equal—the results will be better if the brain does have available to it, in consciously articulated form, as much relevant raw material as possible. Setting down these particulars also forces us to make selections of certain words, whereas some of our thinking takes place on the nonverbal level, which may have the result of leaving certain areas fuzzy and imprecise.

Lined, legal-sized yellow paper is good for this sort of work, partly because the size of the page makes it possible to jot down a larger number of ideas—keeping all of them visible—than might be possible on a smaller sheet.

It is important to understand that we are not talking here about an either/or, black-and-white situation that involves (*a*) doing all the work in our head, or (*b*) some sort of process whereby the thinking takes place at the end of our pen or pencil. Obviously there is mental activity in both instances. The value of writing things out is that it gives us two methods of approaching the problem rather than just one.

Rule No. 45

Depend on your dictionary

We should use a dictionary frequently. Better yet, we should use several, and the best we can afford. But the contrast between any dictionary at all and none whatever is so great as to be of profound significance.

A dictionary is not merely a book that includes thousands of words and their definitions. It represents the painstaking scholarship of thousands of individual contributors, working over long centuries. An army of benefactors have refined the art of dictionary-making to its present degree of sophistication. So when we open one we benefit not only from the work of Mr. Webster, Mr. Funk, or Mr. Wagnall, but of a great many other word-detectives who have unraveled a seemingly infinite number of fascinating mysteries.

Every word in a dictionary—or in a language—is much more than a series of little black marks on a page, or a combination of sounds from a mouth. Each word is also a puzzle, a mystery from the distant past, a clue to other hidden intellectual treasure.

There is much more to the study of words, and the languages they are used to construct, than "it pays to increase your word power" or any sort of Spiro Agnew memorize-five-new-words-a-day process. The point of adding words to our vocabulary is not to impress others by our superiority in casual or formal conversation. The benefits are primarily internal and only secondarily social.

Increasing our knowledge of words increases our understanding not only of what others are saying but of what we ourselves are saying. It may not have occurred to us that from time to time we really don't know what the hell we're talking about, but I assure you this is the case.

Words are, obviously enough, tools of communication. But on a deeper level they are tools of thought. We must think before we can communicate.

Even occasional casual study of a dictionary, leafing through it just as we might with a magazine, can teach us a great deal by filling in gaps-of-ignorance about the language we speak. But the more common use for a dictionary should become second-nature to us, which is to say, that *whenever we do not know the meaning of a word, we should look it up.*

If we are at such times physically in a location where a dictionary is available—the office, school, or at home—we should search out the needed definition at once. If this is not possible, then we should make a written note of the word, so that we can look it up later.

Knowing the proper definition, or definitions, of a word, and understanding how to use the word, will by no means ensure that on all future occasions when we employ it we will simultaneously reason properly. There are certain individuals who have "a way with words," "the gift of gab," but who do not reason especially well.

Such people do employ their reasoning powers to a modest extent, but their purpose is usually not to determine the facts of a case, to search for truth, but to support a storyline they have already decided upon. The case of the typical disc jockey of the modern sort is even worse. Facts are of little interest to him; he speaks to distract, divert, hypnotize.

Some political leaders, too, have the gift of gab. We can be better protected against their often faulty arguments if we improve our reasoning and vocabulary.

There are few things more fascinating than words. This is primarily because they are symbols that stand for thoughts. Words existed in the form of human sounds, speech, noises made with the mouth, for long stretches of time before people figured out ways of making pictures to represent sounds.

For countless further centuries it apparently never occurred to anyone to wonder where speech came from, and as late as the seventeenth century a Swedish philologist seriously argued that the language spoken by God in the Garden of Eden was Swedish.

That seems funny to us, but Swedes are equally amused by the unspoken assumption by some people that the language of the first men was English. Those who prepare modern translations of the Bible—in any age—are *always* attacked for changing what are somehow considered the true, original words. Some people seem to imagine that our early ancestors and spiritual predecessors spoke the English that was common in the time of King James.

The fact is that the Bible—and all other books worth preserving—must constantly be retranslated. Otherwise they would eventually become unintelligible, because languages evolve so rapidly. None of us today would be able to make any sense out of the Old English language, which was spoken from about A.D. 700 to 1100. We would do little better with Middle English, which was spoken from about 1100 to 1500. What is called Modern English has been heard for only a few hundred years. English, by the way, is not the original language of England; we shall never know what was. In the fifth century invading Teutonic tribes conquered the original Britons—who had been speaking goodness knows what—and imposed their continental speech. The two chief Teutonic tribes were the *Angles* and the *Saxons,* and they came from what is now northern Germany.

The most fascinating fact about the various European languages is that they apparently are derived from one common ancestor language.

Consider, for example, the Modern English words *one, two, three,* and *father, mother,* and *brother.* Notice that they are much the same in the following languages:

English	Latin	Greek	French	German	Dutch	Swedish
one	unus	oinos	un	ein	een	en
two	duo	duo	deux	zwei	twee	tva
three	tres	treis	trois	drei	drie	tre
father	pater	pater	pere	vater	vader	fader
mother	mater	meter	mere	mutter	moeder	moder
brother	frater	phrater	frere	bruder	broeder	broder

One thing we can do with a language is play detective. Pick up words, examine them as clues. They reveal a great deal about the history of a people. The fact that Latin so dominates European languages, for example, tells us something of the power of the ancient Roman Empire and of Roman military conquests; for victors always imposed their language upon the vanquished, whether they consciously attempt to do so or not. We can learn a bit about the Roman occupation of Britain from the year 43 to 410 by such an Old English word as *ceaster,* which is based on the Roman word for camp, *castra.* The word persists in England to this day in such place-names as Chester, Leicester, Dorchester, and Lancaster. Place names ending in the suffix *sex* describe what were once Saxon settlements. Sussex, for example, means South Saxony; Essex is short for East Saxony.

The most interesting book in our home is our dictionary.

Rule No. 46

Keep a daily journal or diary

Like most of the aforementioned rules and suggestions, this one by itself will not notably improve anyone's intelligence. It is, however, an effective way to help keep our minds in order, to retain those impressions that are important, and to carry forward, across time, references to issues of significance in our lives. If we make notations about such things, we do not have to start totally from scratch whenever we reconsider matters of personal importance.

Rule No. 47

Become actively interested
in others and, if you can manage it,
somewhat less interested in yourself

Habits of right reason cannot possibly be developed in a vaccuum. Whatever contributes to our general physical and emotional health will make it easier for us to use our reasoning faculties.

When I say that we should become interested in others, I do not mean to suggest that we should pry into the affairs of our next-door neighbors or in-laws, although there is nothing wrong with our being healthfully involved in their lives. But there are millions in our society who are in serious trouble and therefore require—and deserve—help. We will have no trouble finding them. Many live near us. We will find others in prisons, hospitals, orphanages, retirement homes, mental hospitals, Indian reservations, black and Hispanic ghettos. We may approach such people helpfully either as individuals or within the context of an organization.

In any event, becoming involved with more people, approaching them on a serious rather than trivial or casual basis, will be good exercise not only for our hearts but also for our minds. The old expression, "Travel is broadening," is perfectly sound. But the broadening effect does not come simply from exposure to paintings, statuary, palaces, rivers, mountains, and certain kinds of sunsets. It comes chiefly from meeting new and various kinds of people. They help open our minds, as we will help open theirs. At least the potential for such growth is there. It is not always, alas, realized by some travelers—the phrase "Ugly American" describes one sort—who move about in a sort of intellectual and cultural bubble. Wherever they go, they are determined to make their immediate surroundings as American, or German, or English, or whatever, as possible.

Remember that if we are bored, the source of the problem lies within ourselves.

There is a tendency, in our society, to become endlessly fascinated with things, material objects, and less and less interested in our fellow human beings. Oh, we will be interested enough in them if they have something we need. If we believe they will satisfy our sexual requirements, our need for food, money, for gainful employment, for drugs, or for any other perceived need; then we will become involved with them. But the worst monsters of all time have done that much. What makes us consider some individuals morally superior is largely what they do for others, not what others do for them.

While it is clear that this suggestion is primarily of a moral nature, it is the case nevertheless that we will be more generally reasonable, in a broad sense, if we enlarge the sphere of our narrow interests. To that extent, then, this suggestion, if followed, will provide increased opportunities to demonstrate our reasonableness. There is a connection, you see, between reasonableness and fairness. Being fair with others does not simply mean granting them their justified allotment of material things. It also means granting them what is rightly theirs in the realm of ideas. Just as we should not deal unfairly with others regarding material things, we should also deal with them fairly in discourse.

Rule No. 48

First learn—and then remind yourself every day—that simply because you read something in a book, magazine, or newspaper, it does not automatically follow that it is true

Presented with this suggestion, most people have a tendency to say, or think, "But of course; I know that," after which they behave very much as if they did not know it at all.

The statement, in any event, does not mean that we should disbelieve everything we read. Nor do I assume that there is anyone who either questions or believes 100 percent of what he or she reads. Even children will consider statements false, or at least doubtful, if they contradict something they have already accepted. If young people have been taught that Thomas Paine wrote *The Age of Reason,* then they will not believe the statement: John Lennon wrote *The Age of Reason.*

What we are dealing with is not a simple black-and-white, either/ or situation, but rather one of relative degrees of credulity or skepticism. What is required, therefore, is a constant application of the powers of analysis and judgment as part of the process of reading.

The same is true, of course, of listening. But for our present purposes we may concentrate on reading, since most of us have a degree of respect for the printed word that renders us less prone to skepticism than we would be regarding statements coming from our brother-in-law, a salesman, a stranger, or a politician.

A good many people to whom the reasonableness of this rule is apparent enough will nevertheless partially misinterpret it to mean that we should be particularly careful about statements made by people of whom we are already—rightly or wrongly—suspicious. If, for example, we are opposed to communism—whether for wise or stupid reasons— we may think, "Rule 48 is very good advice because Communists will certainly try to deceive us." But that is not the point. We should reserve judgment about statements from all sides, including our own.

To give a more concrete illustration, a charming little religious magazine, with a generally Christian orientation, published an article recently in which there was reference to the experience of a number of successful people who had overcome early and repeated adversities. The following section referred to my own early experience.

> A small boy born in New York City in 1921 was frequently left with relatives so his vaudevillian parents could go on tour. His abusive mother vented her vicious temper on him. During his childhood, he stayed with dozens of alcoholic aunts and uncles. At age thirteen, he ran away from home to seek an aunt in California, riding his bicycle most of the way until it broke down. He continued his trek on freight trains, eating ant-covered leftovers that wandering hobos had left behind.
>
> After a short term in the army, he began a radio career in the late 1940s and went on to other shows and finally to television. He has since written two poetry anthologies, two short-story collections, and several novels. Also an accomplished pianist and lyricist, he has written more than four thousand songs, including scores for Broadway plays. In addition, he is a popular lecturer and wrote the "Meeting of Minds" series for PBS television.

The author was obviously sympathetic but this brief section of his article contained the following errors:

1. During my childhood I did not stay with "dozens of alcoholic aunts and uncles." The word *dozens* would mean a minimum of twenty-four. I had three aunts and two uncles. Two of the aunts did not drink at all and only one of the uncles was an alcoholic.

2. I did not run away at age thirteen, but at sixteen.

3. I did not run away "to seek an aunt in California." I had no particular destination and was, in fact, vaguely thinking of making my way down to South America. The ultimate choice of Los Angeles was made while en route and involved partly the matter of wanting to move to a warmer climate, since October weather in the Midwest is quite

uncomfortable if one is on the road.

4. I did not ride my bicycle "most of the way until it broke down." I rode it only for about one hundred miles, to the small community of Marion, Indiana. The bike was in perfect condition when I left it there, never to retrieve it.

None of the errors are terribly important. The point merely is that they are typical, that this is how even many professional journalists and book-authors communicate.

Since that is the case, we should always be healthily skeptical of the total accuracy of written reports.

Rule No. 49

After you have done your homework, speak out

Centuries ago, a philosopher coined the play-it-safe maxim: "Of thy unspoken word thou art master; but thy spoken word is master of thee." In other words—don't open you mouth to express deep feelings because you may put your foot in it. The doctrine that silence is golden has many partisans. The idea seems to be that if we react to unpleasantness by playing dead, our private and societal bugaboos will leave us alone.

Don't subscribe to the theory. We should sound off more, though never hysterically or in ignorance. It's not always people's spoken words, but sometimes their unspoken, bottled-up thoughts that master them. An outburst may clear the air and show where you stand. Smoldering anger can build up, turn households into grouseholds.

Express your feelings—in as civilized a way as possible—the moment you feel them. Have the courage of your convictions.

A wonderful thing often happens when you start giving frank and open vent to feelings: (1) the people who matter like you better, and (2) suddenly, you like yourself better.

Folk sayings have an odd way of capsuling psychological truths. It was no accident, for instance, that long before Freud, people sensed the therapy of speaking out, as we see from such sayings as "Get it off your chest," "Let off steam," "Confession is good for the soul."

When I was a boy I was taught that one of the cornerstones of the American political structure was freedom of speech. I knew that such freedom was not an automatic birthright. Communist Russia, Nazi Germany, and Fascist Italy and Spain didn't have it. Then one day, when I was about thirty-five, I realized I had never really availed myself of the privilege.

What to do? Well, first I had to arrive at an understanding of what freedom of speech meant. It couldn't merely mean the latitude to talk about baseball, restaurants, or last night's television shows. Even people living under cruel dictatorships have that much freedom. No, what was involved could mean only the right to criticize. Historian Arnold Toynbee wrote: "The toleration of minority beliefs made the Western world what it is. The difference from Russia is vital."

So I decided to take advantage of my American right to express myself. I had an opinion and put it on record. I happen to be opposed to capital punishment. So I spoke out against the barbarism of hangings, gassings, firing squads, and electric chairs.

What happened? Congratulations? Guess again. Brickbats. Not necessarily because others disagreed with me. Some just disagreed with my right to say it. Many a truth, as the old saying goes, may be contained in a jest. But according to some, a jester has no right to tell the truth—as he sees it. A famous columnist at the time referred to a visit Marlon Brando, Shirley MacLaine, and I made to Governor Edmund Brown of California to discuss capital punishment as "nauseating." Entertainment trade publications suggested that performers should keep their mouths shut. That's nonsense. A politically inexperienced actor named Reagan spoke out and got elected governor and, later, president.

We should do the same at home, too. Being able to discuss differences out in the open is better than pouting in silence. A storm is always followed by clear weather. A good marriage, like a good ship, can weather strong waves better than creeping dry rot.

In the office, we should speak up, though always intelligently and constructively. It may get us a raise. At worst, it will inform others that there's an adult behind our desk.

On public issues, too, we should speak our minds. In the nuclear field, for instance, if Dr. Edward Teller believes there should be more nuclear bombs, he should say so, as he has. If we disagree, we should speak out—as I have. That's the democratic way—to give various sides a chance to contribute to the public dialogue.

There's a military axiom about soldiers who gripe making a healthy army. A citizenry that is free to voice its complaints and aspirations also buttresses a nation in peacetime—spiritually, morally, and physically.

So we shouldn't go around grumbling under our breath. If it's worth gnashing our teeth about, it's worth making noise about.

Again, before we shoot our mouths off, we should do a bit of reading, studying, about the issue. Otherwise we may be defending the weaker side of an argument simply because of our social conditioning or because of nothing more edifying than narrow self-interest. And, for God's sake, we should never lose sight of the possibility that we might be wrong, or we might be right for the wrong reasons. Or we might just be speaking about personal taste and opinion. When we finally do speak up, we should make an earnest attempt to communicate as rationally as possible. We should emphasize reason, not emotion.

Once we've spoken, the reward may not come in the form of dollars and cents. But it will be felt in the more vital area of our emotional bank account—and in the final accounting every one of us must give to his conscience.

Rule No. 50

Begin to accumulate a
personal library of works relating to the
subject of reason and brain-function

The following are intended merely to help start your own collection of these kinds of books.

The Act of Creation, Arthur Koestler.

The Art of Argument, Giles St. Aubyn (Emerson, White Plains, N.Y., 1960).

The Book of Think: Or, How to Solve a Problem Twice Your Size, Marilyn Burns (Little, Brown, Boston, 1976).

Brain Puzzler's Delight, E. R. Emmet (Emerson Books, New York, 1977).

Brain Storms, Wayne Barker, M.D. (Grove Press, New York, 1968).

Coercive Persuasion, Edgar H. Schein (W. W. Norton, New York, 1961).

Conceptual Blockbusting, James L. Adams, (W. W. Norton, New York, 1974).

The Conscious Brain, Steven Rose (Basil Blackwell, New York, 1980).

The Five-Day Course in Thinking, Edward de Bono (distributed by International Center for Creative Thinking, P.O. Box 747, Mamaroneck, N.Y. 10543).

How We Think, John Dewey (D. C. Heath, Lexington, 1933).

Imagination and Thinking, Peter McKellar (Basic Books, New York, 1957).

The Integrated Mind, M. S. Gazzaniga and J. E. LeDoux (Plenum Press, New York, 1978).

An Introduction to Logic, M. R. Cohen and E. Nagel (Harcourt, Brace & World, New York, 1962).

Kindergarten Is Too Late!, Masaru Ibuka (Simon & Schuster, New York, 1977).

The Mind, ed. by Lucy Freeman (Thomas Y. Crowell, New York, 1967).

Passion to Know, Mitchell Wilson (Doubleday, New York, 1972).

Principles of Logic, Josiah Royce (Philosophical Library, New York, 1961).

The Read-Aloud Handbook, Jim Trelease (Penguin Books, New York, 1982).

Reason and Genius, Alfred Hock (Philosophical Library, New York, 1960).

The Story of Man's Mind, George Humphrey (New Home Library, New York, 1932).

Thinking: An Introduction to Its Experimental Psychology, George Humphrey (John Wiley, New York, 1963).

Thinking Is Child's Play, Evelyn Sharp (Avon Books, New York, 1969).

Thinking Straight, Antony Flew (Prometheus Books, Buffalo, N.Y., 1977).

Note that I do not refer to taking books out of the library, reading them, and returning them, although readers may have only this recourse if their financial means are limited. But important books should be retained so that they can be consulted again and again. We would not want to go to a library to check out a dictionary every time we wanted to look up the meaning of a word.

Rule No. 51

If your car has a cassette-tape player, start using your auto as a private university on wheels

Recently I sat, reading, in the slanted sunlight, on a concrete and wooden bench just outside the Second National Bank in the somewhat rundown section at Eighth and Orange, in the center of Wilmington, Delaware. Because there was a trafic signal at the nearby corner, every few minutes cars, encountering a red light, would pause before proceeding. In the overwhelming majority of them, the radios were turned to a painfully high volume. In every one of these cases, the "music" being transmitted was of the "rap" variety. The use of quotation marks is justified, since rap music, by definition, has no melody whatever. It is simply a matter of rhythmic and rhymed chanting to the background of an infectious, danceable beat.

Given the disturbing reality of the pervasive ignorance of many of today's young people, it is interesting to speculate on what difference it might make if those who can scarcely speak coherently, much less read and write, would subtract, let's say, two hours out of each twenty-four now spent in listening to mostly mindless music and instead used their vehicles for listening to radio programs that convey news and commentary, or instructional tapes, the cost of which is no greater than that of the kind that was being played in many of the cars.

For whatever the point may be worth, all of those playing the music were driving late-model cars in good condition.

(An odd factor was that in every car the windows were fully opened. Since the top-level volume could have been as well enjoyed with the windows fully or partly closed—and it wasn't a hot day—it was apparently

261

a matter of some faddish intent to force one's own musical tastes upon all others in the immediate environment.)

There are a number of commercial concerns that sell instructional and self-help tapes and cassettes. If you don't have a playing unit installed in your car, you can use a portable tape recorder for the purpose. You probably already are doing a lot of radio-listening on the freeways but learning very little from most of it.

In addition to newscasts available on commercial stations and networks, as well as programs of commentary and discussion of significant issues, there are—in some cities—noncommercial stations that present even higher quality fare. If you're lucky enough to have a listener-supported station in your area, start taking advantage of it at once.

Also, find out where on the dial your local National Public Radio station or stations are located. Such sources provide points of view and information you're unlikely to pick up elsewhere.

With cassettes, however, we can control the programming. The great advantage of having a cassette is that we can play it over and over again, as often as we wish, and each time we hear it, we may get a new reaction or interpretation.

And you can learn to speak a foreign language much more quickly if you take advantage of driving time to absorb recorded instruction.

If you travel on streetcars, buses, trains, or planes, you're still covered. Portable cassette players equipped with earphones can be used for the same purpose. In fact, doing so will make many an otherwise boring or time-consuming trip much more interesting.

People who say that they "don't have time" to learn about one thing or another are rarely speaking the truth. The fact is they simply don't know much about how *not* to waste time.

Rule No. 52

Rethink your religion

Does this suggestion make you uneasy?

Good. That shows you're paying attention.

I do not suggest that religion itself is irrational. First of all, the phrase "religion itself" is so fuzzy-edged that "it" can hardly be said to be anything, rational or irrational.

But if this suggestion makes you feel uncomfortable, relax. Some of the most intelligent people who ever lived have been affiliated with one religion or another. Of course, millions of near-imbeciles have also been connected with those same faiths.

What I'm getting at is that we are not very intelligent if we simply accept everything our personal religion, if we have one, delivers to us.

Nor would it make sense to reject everything our religion proposed.

To be intelligent, in this context, involves considering the separate components of our faith, one by one.

As a result of that process we may become more committed than we ever were before.

We may also leave our church altogether.

We may leave the Jewish faith and become Christian, or vice versa.

We might leave the Church of Scientology and become Catholic.

It doesn't matter, in this context, whether we make a move or remain where we are. The important thing is to think—to *reason*—about our beliefs. If we arbitrarily assume that there is a God—millions deny it, but let us assume here that there is—it may be argued that reason can take us only so far in speculating about religion and that ultimately we must make the leap of faith, in the absence of conclusive evidence, to maintain one specific belief or another.

Very well. But if reason has limits then let us, for God's sake (interpret the phrase how you will), go to those limits.

While we're thinking about this, incidentally, we should look at a few truths. One of them is that all religions are not equal. Some religions are far more reasonable than others.

The reason it is important to know this is that some people—generally nice, friendly souls—have such a sweet, benign reaction to the word *religion* itself that they somehow feel it is rather marvelous if another individual is "religious," in the absence of any consideration as to what that person's religious views are or what that person actually does as a result of holding such views.

Dumb-de-dumb-dumb.

Some religious opinions are beautiful, moral, enlightening, uplifting. Others are bizarre, crazy, socially dangerous, personally destructive.

Would you personally want to be a fanatic? Of course not. Well, there are millions of fanatics in the world of a specific sort. They are *religious* fanatics.

Some of them act crazy. You wouldn't want them in your house. You wouldn't want your daughter to marry one of them.

The thing is that, in addition to all the fine, admirable things done for religious reasons throughout the long centuries of human life on Planet Earth, there have also been countless evil acts perpetrated by religious individuals *for religious reasons.* There have been murders, pogroms, persecutions, purges, slaughters, beheadings, burnings at the stake, boilings in oil, human sacrifices, instances of genocide, crusades, wars—all supposedly "justified" by their churchly perpetrators.

One of the things we're doing here is conveyed by the old expression "calling a spade a spade." Regarding religion, there are a good many unattractive aspects of its history. It's important to face them—to get them into the sharpest possible focus—as we apply our intelligence to the subject matter.

Again, some religions are rationally superior to others.

That means the others are dumber.

Not many people will argue with the generality. The going gets rougher, however, when we approach specifics. How can we tell one religion is dumber than another?

One way is to ask, What does a given church say about the age of the physical universe?

In the case of a number of them, the answer is forthright enough. The earth is anywhere from five thousand to ten thousand years old.

Let's not waste time here. You may be quite sure—and by no means only on my authority—that a church that teaches any such thing is, at least on this point, guilty of serious dumbth.

Modern scientists—including distinguished Christian and Jewish scholars—know that the physical universe is *billions* of years old.

Another way to separate the dumbbells from the wiser believers is in regard to the question of "the end of the world." For unknown centuries, individuals have been predicting that the end was not only possible but near. In many cases they were so unfortunate as to give a specific date.

All these dates have been passed. Yet there are millions of American Christians who are not simply fearful but absolutely convinced that the world is going to end in the next twenty or thirty years.

Even if the world does end next Tuesday, these people are still dumb, because they have developed their arguments irrationally.

There's a particular sort of error in reasoning common to such would-be thinkers. It is the earlier-mentioned inability to distinguish between *conclusive evidence* and *consistent evidence.* Conclusive evidence really settles the question or proves the point at issue. There is simply no getting away from the fact when evidence is conclusive.

But consistent evidence is of another sort altogether. If certain evidence is consistent, it simply means that so far as this particular bit of data is concerned it does not render the hypothesis impossible.

Let us suppose that you and I were personal witnesses to a murder. A white man named Bob Jones shot a black man named Bill Smith before our very eyes. Bob Jones then ran away. On the basis of our eyewitness accounts of the incident, the police send out an all-points bulletin for the murderer.

The next day, in a neighboring state, a white man named Bob Jones is captured.

Many people—God help us—would immediately assume that because the man is (*a*) white, and (*b*) named Bob Jones, the two factors add up to conclusive evidence that he is the murderer. Stop here and ask yourself the question: Is he?

"No" is also the wrong answer.

There is absolutely no way to know, if all you have to go on are the two factors cited.

What you can say—with absolute certainty—is that these two factors, taken together, are *consistent* with the theory that the captured fellow is the murderer. This cannot possibly be *conclusive* evidence, in the absence of other factors.

The reason they cannot is that there are hundreds of millions of white men on the earth and thousands of them are named Bob Jones.

Now that that simple point has been clarified, let us return to the question of religion.

Assume that in the Bible it is said that in "the last days" purple sunsets will be seen.

Let us assume, secondly, that in 1990 scientists begin to notice a number of strangely purplish skies during the hours in which the sun is setting.

I'm afraid, given the history of religious experience, that thousands of people would close up their business affairs and fall to their knees or rush to their churches, because they were absolutely confident that the world was indeed approaching its end. You and I can perceive that they would be guilty of the consistent-evidence-vs.-conclusive-evidence mistake.

Don't feel so superior to them. You've been guilty of the same error, and often.

And so—upon occasion—have I!

Although my own bias on this question ought to be essentially irrelevant to you, I will satisfy your curiosity on the point by saying that I am among the majority who assume that a God does exist. But can we offer proofs of our assumption? Most Christians, I suppose, if presented with this question, would point to the Bible as their proof. They therefore would be startled to be informed that no theologian or Christian philosopher has ever made such an absurd error. The Bible can no more prove the existence of God than can the Koran, or the writings of Joseph Smith, Mary Baker Eddy, or the Reverend Sun Myung Moon.

The overall point here is not that we should immediately embark on a study of the classic dialogue concerning the existence or nonexistence of God. That we may do on our own time and leisure. The purpose of this rule is (*a*) to interest us in critical thinking itself, and (*b*) to apply it to all our beliefs. If those beliefs happen to be wise and valid, we will end up being better able to defend them. If, as is all too often the case, they are nonsensical and destructive, we should then enjoy the good fortune of being able to toss at least some of them overboard.

Rule No. 53

When possible, spend time
with people brighter than yourself

It is a source of considerable sadness to me that I have spent so little of my time in the company of intellectuals. I hold no contempt for nonintellectuals. One would have to despise the human race if one did. But my soul and mind open up in the presence of highly intelligent people, in conversation with them, to a degree that rarely happens in other theaters of social contact. During my sixty-seven years of life, my seven or eight visits to California's Center for the Study of Democratic Institutions and participation in a dozen or so other scholarly conventions and seminars is the sum total of my activities in my most comforting form of enjoyment.

Once, years ago, I was described by a journalist as a would-be intellectual. But we should all be would-be intellectuals. If we were, some of us would achieve that happy state. In any event, I have always felt very much at home—wonderful phrase—in the company of men and women more intelligent than myself. I have found with them an ease of communication, an openness in exchanging ideas, that I have rarely experienced in normal social contact. It would simply never occur to me to give voice to a philosophical observation in most of the gatherings I attend. But when conversing with intellectuals I sometimes do little else, since it seems the normal mode of communication in such contexts. Such correspondents hardly require my instruction, but my creativity, such as it is, is freed by the simple knowledge that whatever I might say to them will be understood, and I feel a strange sort of comfort, a social ease, and yet one combined with a heightened sense of excitement.

It's as if one were a child with a genetic gift for musical performance or composition and were suddenly introduced to his or her first piano or to a teacher of musical theory. Little—perhaps nothing—in my formal education prepared me for the sort of communication I have described. Nor have I ever assumed, in the company of scholars, that I was properly one of their number. But, again, I felt perfectly at home with them. And if I sometimes held my tongue, it was not for lack of ideas— those were usually tumbling through my mind in incredible profusion— but because I recognized that my position did not permit me to take up discussion time that had been set aside for professional scholars and social philosophers.

I'd come to them, in any event, to learn.

You will naturally apply this suggestion to your own social circumstances. Not all of us have the option to associate with Nobel Prize winners or other distinguished scholars, philosophers, and scientists. But between your own estate and that of such lofty practitioners of the intellectual arts there are many intermediate levels. Undoubtedly you know many people who are less intelligent than yourself, or less well informed about certain issues. It does not follow that you should despise them or forever avoid their company. If you are brighter than they are, the proper response would be to do whatever you can to share your degree of enlightenment with them. But at the same time, in your own social and professional circle, there are those you recognize as brighter than yourself. When the opportunity presents itself, seek out their company.

Rule No. 54

To see how well you think out loud,
make tape-recordings of yourself

It comes as no surprise that there is a loose correlation between general intelligence, however hazily defined, and the degree of coherence in one's speech. Extremely intelligent people are generally recognizable by the ease with which they communicate verbally, while those at the other extreme are often further handicapped by an inability to express clearly even such modest thoughts as they have. But this correlation, oddly enough, does not hold up in all cases.

There are some individuals of quite shallow intelligence who nevertheless have mastered at least some of the tricks of the talkers' trade. Some salesmen, radio disc jockeys, politicians, clergyman, and others are, while not particularly intelligent or well informed, nevertheless able to express themselves with remarkable facility. And it is even more surprising that some highly intelligent people are sometimes weak in either personal conversation or formal lectures.

We can check out our own speaking abilities. Start by selecting any issue or problem of current interest to you. It doesn't matter whether it's an important political or economic question, a personal matter, the possible outcome of the next Super Bowl game, or the problem of actors getting into politics. Simply turn on the machine and force yourself to make a two- or three-minute commentary on any subject.

Then spin the tape back and listen to yourself, repeatedly. Are you speaking, at least for the most part, in complete sentences? Are there at least reasonably smooth connections between one thought and the next? (Pay no attention to such factors as the sound of your voice or the quality of the recording. All you're trying to determine in this context is whether you are speaking in a generally coherent manner.)

It is possible, of course, that you will make one or two common sorts of mistakes in evaluating your performance. If you're a naturally self-confident sort, you might tend to look upon your brief commentary with undue affection. If you're too self-critical, you might give yourself lower marks than you deserve. It could be helpful, therefore, if you arranged for others—family members or friends—to hear the tape.

Needless to say, this obliges you to give careful consideration to the reactions you have solicited.

Another thing you might try is to make a typed transcription of your ad-libbed remarks. Then put that version aside for a couple of days before studying it.

When you do, ask yourself: Do my remarks sound generally sensible? Is my argument (if any) at least fairly well developed? Do the words I use adequately express the thoughts behind them?

If you give yourself relatively low marks on this test don't despair. At least you have become aware of the problem, the existence of which might heretofore have escaped your attention. One of my earlier books, *How to Make a Speech* (McGraw-Hill), might be helpful in this connection since it covers considerably more than the art of public lecturing.

Rule No. 55

Avoid wasting time

Since it is always helpful to define terms, even if only to ourselves, consider for a moment what we mean by the phrase "to waste time." The term doesn't carry a lot of weight until it is applied to specific contexts. Imagine two men lying near the lapping waves on a tropical beach. To an observer they seem to be doing essentially the same thing. But, in fact, one of them is wasting time while the other is putting it to wonderfully productive use. The judgment is made, naturally, based on what the two are thinking of. One's time is wasted in thinking of inconsequential nonsense while the other is considering weighty matters in a reasonable way.

The point is not to suggest that we should avoid going on vacations, playing bridge, attending athletic events, or indulging in other forms of harmless relaxation. But it does mean that in a thousand and one such instances we will have to make a personal decision about whether time is being wasted. In my own case, playing cards, golfing, or going to a rock concert are a true waste of time, because of two factors: (*a*) I have little interest in these activities, and (*b*) during the hours that I would spend indulging in them I could be doing far more important work that would, as a nice plus, also provide a good deal more pleasurable satisfaction. But the time that almost all of us do waste tends to be lost, not so much in long-term activities, but in random, idle moments.

There are many simple ways to avoid wasting time. For example, when waiting to board an airliner, we can sometimes spend several minutes standing in line in the roll-ramp walkway. We should not do that anymore. Assuming we are on a reserved-seat flight, we should

272

simply remain in the lounge until other passengers have boarded the plane. At that point we can walk aboard with an expenditure of no more than thirty seconds. The extra ten or fifteen minutes saved may be used for reading, dictation, note-making, or reflection.

Many travelers essentially waste the hours they spend on airplanes and buses and in trains and automobiles, too, in that they use the time for nothing but transporting their bodies from one location to another. There are any number of things we can do on a public conveyance that are more interesting than staring at the back of the seat in front of us. Reading, writing, engaging in stimulating conversation, listening to tape recordings, working with a pocket calculator or lap-top computer—almost anything we would do at an office, home, or school desk can be done while traveling.

I even put walking-time to extra use by talking into my pocket-size tape dictation machine. And, for centuries before such hardware was available, thoughtful men and women paused occasionally, while strolling, to write a few lines of poetry, make notes for an essay or a letter to a friend, or make entries in a travel journal.

Perhaps because of a character weakness, I find that I am almost literally unable to waste time. For one thing, I do not have as much conscious time available as the average person, because my sleep requirements are greater than the average. The traditional eight hours a night do not suffice; my natural sleep cycle requires that I be unconscious about ten hours a night. I can easily sleep longer if I am especially tired and am not obliged to get up and about. In any event, when awake I simply do not waste the large chunks of time that many people do.

I also play piano in certain odds and ends of time not filled up in a busy day. While there are instances when I may have an hour or two to spend at the instrument, it more frequently happens that just five or ten minutes are available. Since it only takes a few moments to write a song, I often compose music during these fragments of time.

Rule No. 56

Make frequent use of maps

Alfred Korzybski, founder of the General Semantics movement, used the word *map* to mean any verbal or psychological picture of a given reality, as distinguished from the reality itself. When I say we should make frequent use of maps, I mean actual maps.

One reason we should use them is that doing so will make vastly more meaningful the news reports that come to us on radio and television. There are obviously other reasons for using maps. But because in today's world it is important to keep up with significant developments, a map can be wonderfully helpful. In most news about the Middle East, for example, the listener or viewer is bombarded with such terms as *Iraq, Iran, Saudi Arabia, Jordan, Lebanon, Yemen, Israel,* etc. Simply looking at a map of the Middle East while Dan Rather, Peter Jennings, or Tom Brokaw gives you the latest reports will make that information more intelligible.

Television news programs often include visual displays of the geographical areas discussed, but they may be on the screen for only a few seconds and, even then, are exhibited only as background to a foreground image of the newsman talking or interviewing an authoritative guest.

In most large cities there are stores that specialize in selling maps. Bookstores also carry maps, and books and booklets containing maps. Your neighborhood gas station, of course, can provide road-maps of cities, states, and regions of the country.

We should provide our children with a jigsaw map of the United States. Placing the states in their proper position with their own hands will give them a better sense of the geographical makeup of the country than just looking at a map of the traditional sort.

And we should give them jigsaw maps of other parts of the world. And a global map of the earth. The world is not flat.

Rule No. 57

Determine to make your own
contribution to the cause of reason

Merely as an example of what an individual can do to address the dumbth problem, some years ago I developed a thinking game, a table game called "Strange Bedfellows," working with a professional game theorist and educator named Robert Allen (no relation).

Mr. Allen had noticed, in some of my books and speeches, some gimmicks he thought could be used as the basic building block of a thinking game. For example, in one book, *Mark It and Strike It,* I said to the reader, "Let me give you here a couple of examples of Marxist propaganda." Then I quoted two paragraphs that did indeed seem the sort of thing one would expect from a Marxist source, after which I revealed that the author of one paragraph was Pope Pius XII, and the author of the other, Abraham Lincoln. (See Rule No. 81.)

The object of the game, of course, is to encourage analysis of, and response to, certain statements on the basis of their inherent content and to discourage either the enthusiastic acceptance or contemptuous rejection of them purely on the basis of their source.

Thomas Aquinas, one of the most rational thinkers in the history of philosophy, conceded that he learned much from his enemies, by which he meant his philosophical opponents. We seem unable to learn anything whatever from our philosophical opponents.

For yet another example of what an individual can do to address the problem of our deteriorating national intelligence, I began—about thirty years back—trying to get a television series called "Meeting of Minds" on the air. The purpose of the twenty-four one-hour programs of that series is, of course, to introduce American television viewers

275

to some of the important thinkers and doers of history. But at a more basic level, the purpose is to encourage reason and the art of communication.

A third modest contribution was the writing and production of a record album for children called "How to Think." (See page 163.)

Writing this book is a fourth instance.

Try to do something of the sort yourself, in the context of your own social and professional circumstances.

Rule No. 58

Familiarize yourself with the commonly accepted scientific view of the universe

Learning to think better also requires that we develop an at least rudimentary familiarity with the laws of physics; which is to say, the laws that govern the actual world. Doing so will make us less likely to be susceptible to superstition, to become the victim of pseudoscience, or to be guilty of common errors about the natural universe.

We will still have perfect freedom to hold contrary views of our own, but to simply close our minds to the knowledge painstakingly accumulated by hundreds of thousands of scientists over long centuries is to deliberately decide to be ignorant and narrow-minded.

Let's not handicap ourselves at the outset by assuming that some sort of battle line has been drawn, with all of science on one side and all religion on the other. Thousands of scientists, as it happens, have religious views of their own and belong to one church or another.

As Howard Kahane argues in *Logic and Contemporary Rhetoric* (Wadsworth, 1984):

> While some information is completely reliable, some kinds are more reliable than others. The safest kind, without question, if successful application is any guide, is information gained from the physical sciences (and, to an increasing extent, biology, now that the genetic code is being cracked).
>
> One reason why these sciences are so accurate is that science is an organized world-wide, ongoing activity, which builds and corrects from generation to generation. Another is that the method of science is just the rigorous, systematic application of cogent inductive reasoning from what has been observed of the world to expectations about future experiences that can be and are checked

277

up on. No one starting from scratch could hope to obtain in one lifetime anything remotely like the sophisticated and accurate conclusions of the physical sciences.

Grasping the general outline of the scientific picture of the universe, and of the way we fit in it, is doubly valuable. First, that picture can serve as the core into which we can sketch increasingly sophisticated ideas as to how this or that works, so that new information can be systematically integrated with old. And second, it can help us to understand the vital issues of the day (for example, whether we're likely to run out of oil soon if present rates of consumption continue, the consequences of making abortion illegal, whether any "close encounters of the third kind" have actually occurred, the effectiveness of SALT treaties and negotiations, or the risks connected with nuclear power plants), and help us deal with life's day-to-day mundane problems (for instance, whether to take large doses of various vitamins, whether a particular "hair restorer" may actually work, how to choose the best painkiller for the money, how to safely siphon gasoline from one gas tank to another, or which breakfast foods are healthiest).

I strongly recommend Kahane's book. It's one to add to your own library of works about thinking.

After I had completed about 350 pages of the manuscript for this book, friends and strangers began to hear that I was working on it. Some had suggestions of practical value, in that they pointed to the work of others and to the views of scholars already concerned with the teaching of thinking. Peter Schwartz, for example, whom I met in Elmira, New York, sent me two useful books, *Language Awareness,* by Paul Eschholz et al., and Kahane's *Logic and Contemporary Rhetoric.*

I am also indebted to Mort Lachman, the television comedy writer and producer (who worked for many years with Bob Hope). I happened to run into him at a birthday party at comedian Jack Carter's home; and when he discovered I was working on a book about thinking, he asked if I had heard of Edward de Bono. When I told him I had not, he said, "Let me send you some of his books; they will be very useful to you." De Bono's *Teaching Thinking* and *Practical Thinking* arrived the following day. I recommend them.

Rule No. 59

Beware of political rhetoric

It is particularly important to be on your guard when listening to political rhetoric—from any source—and perhaps never more so than when the rhetoric comes from a representative of one's own party; for then the phrases fall so pleasantly on the ear that their very music may blind us to the degree of their inanity.

Do not assume that seeing through political rhetoric to the true reality behind it is easy. Sometimes the task is made even more difficult by the likability or expertise of the speaker. The redoubtable Clare Booth Luce, for example, was a woman of charm and intelligence. These very qualities carried great weight when, speaking as a conservative leader, she defended the Reagan administration against the oft-repeated charge that whatever its other merits, it had demonstrated no compassion for the poor, the unemployed, the old, blacks, Hispanics, Native Americans, and other disadvantaged individuals and groups. Mrs. Luce's defense was, beyond question, clever; it was nevertheless a classic instance of smoke-screening. Speaking in response to the presentation of an award by the United Service Organizations in New York on May 13, 1982, she made no direct reference whatever to the substance of the charge that Ronald Reagan is not known for his compassion. Observe how deftly she responded:

> A truly compassionate administration is an administration that sees first to the security of the country.
>
> The second effect of a truly compassionate administration is to see to the solvency of the country.
>
> Without the security of the nation, all of our wealth—however great—will go down the tubes, together with our liberties and our

279

lives. But without solvency, a country can't raise the monies necessary to defend the nation.

So compassionate politics does reside in, first, a secure country, and secondly, a solvent country.

Now that the comment has been tacked to the bulletin board, so to speak, for our leisurely examination, it will be simple enough for even the most fervently conservative reader to see how Mrs. Luce obscured the issue. Every American administration since Washington's has been passionately concerned about both national security and national solvency. Nor did such concerns come into history only at the founding of our nation; a nation is, by definition, a social entity that must be secure and solvent. To suggest that the administrations of, say, the past three decades—a period during which three of our presidents were Republicans—were *not* concerned with security and solvency would be absurd. Consequently, Mrs. Luce argues nothing of the sort. She does, however, leave the vague implication hanging in the air.

Quite a separate question could be raised about whether the further stock-piling of weapons of mass destruction increases or decreases national security, but it is not necessary to explore that question in the present context. It is perfectly possible to construct a case in defense of the proposition that the Reagan administration was wise in stressing security and financial solvency. But such factors have nothing whatever to do with the perfectly reasonable public debate on whether or not Reagan is a notably compassionate individual. There is a great deal of evidence suggesting that he is not, and very little evidence suggesting that he is. We see, therefore, that by arbitrarily introducing the adjective *compassionate* into a discussion about security and solvency Mrs. Luce obscured rather than clarified the issue.

Note again that Mrs. Luce was a woman of above-average intelligence. Note, too, that she had certain gifts for the exercise of political rhetoric and was one of the more able defenders of the conservative philosophy. Every major philosophical camp has such gifted representatives. So, to return to our central point, we must always be on guard and must develop the habit of reserving judgment when listening to or reading political rhetoric, because its purpose rarely is to participate in the disinterested search for truth. Its purpose is to defend, to advocate.

If you want to know what is wrong with conservatism, the last source to which you should appeal is a conservative, except perhaps journalists George Will and Cal Thomas. If you want to know what is wrong with liberalism, waste little time consulting a liberal. If you want to know what is wrong with Marxist–Communism, you must consult its critics.

Rule No. 60

Remember that much truth is relative

A relative is someone who's related to you. Perhaps you are a daughter. The word *daughter* has meaning only in relation to the words *mother* and *father*.

Suppose today the temperature is 15 degrees below zero, and then tomorrow it goes up to 30 degrees *above* zero. You would say, "It certainly is getting warm."

But suppose the temperature had been 80 degrees above zero and then it dropped to 30. Now you might say, "It certainly is getting cold."

One day we say 30 degrees is warm. Another day we say 30 degrees is cold. The concepts are relative. We decide that things are cold or hot, good or bad, tall or short, big or little, young or old, intelligent or dumb, on the basis of how they relate or compare to something else.

But what about actual, material things, as distinguished from the qualities or attributes of those things? A planet is a thing. Can we talk about its position in absolute terms? No, we cannot. A planet is not located at any particular place. Even if the planets could somehow be stationary it would be meaningless to talk about their separate locations except in the relative context of our own position as observers.

Actually there is little or no argument about this rule, since practically everyone recognizes the relativity of a great deal of truth. The more difficult question is: Are there any truths that are absolute, rather than relative? Given that philosophers hold different opinions on the question, I am hardly about to suggest a resolution here. The truths of mathematics appear to be absolute, but that is partly because they are consistent within the language of mathematics. Suffice it for the moment to say that you should beware of assuming large, arbitrary realms of

282

absolute truth, the authenticity of which cannot possibly be doubted. If there are such categories, then of course we should be able to defend their legitimacy in very precise terms. As an example of the difficulty of doing this, consider the belief of some people that if a statement is found in the Bible it inescapably follows that it is not only true but absolutely so.

Now that is certainly not, on principle, an impossible thing. We can easily conceive of a book—the Bible or some other work—that consisted of nothing but statements with which the entire human race would agree. Unfortunately for consistency, when we turn to the *actual* Bible and consider its hundreds of thousands of particulars one by one, we run into difficulties almost immediately. As regards the question of homosexuality, for example, do you personally think that the proper thing to do with homosexuals, once they have been accurately identified, is to kill them? The answer to that, in today's relatively civilized society, is almost certainly in the negative. But the Bible does state, in the clearest possible terms, that homosexuals, purely as such, deserve the death penalty.

Rule No. 61

Don't be afraid to change your mind

We can't be right about everything. That means we are wrong about some things. So we must try to find out just which of our opinions are mistaken. If new evidence shows that we are wrong, we must respect that evidence. Intelligent people are glad to have new information, even if it forces them to change their minds about something. But people who are not very bright often close their minds to new information, sometimes out of loyalty to opinions they've held for a long time. But the real loyalty we owe is to Truth, not our own prejudices.

One of the reasons we are almost certainly wrong in some of our views is that we may have believed almost everything we were taught, especially during our early years. Unfortunately not everything we were told is true. Some people may have deliberately lied to us. Others may have exaggerated. And some, even when they sincerely meant to tell us the truth, may have innocently passed along information that was incorrect.

A good many things that may seem perfectly sensible are nevertheless wrong. For example:

The sky is blue. No, most of the time it isn't. First of all, if by the word *sky* we mean outer space, it has no color at all and therefore looks black to astronauts and anyone else who is out in it. Even from the viewpoint of the earth, for about half of every twenty-four hours the sky is black, not blue. And what with sunsets and sunrises that make the sky look pink, orange, and yellow, and rain, fog, smog, and snow that make it look gray, the sky doesn't look blue most of the time.

Another thing that many children and some adults believe is that the sun and the moon are about the same size. They look the same, but of course they are not. The moon is much smaller than the earth. The sun is many times larger than the earth. The reason they look the same to us is that the sun is millions of miles farther away.

Even what seems like common sense can sometimes lead us astray. We must be careful, then, in making up our minds about things.

Even after we have made up our minds, we should always admit the possibility that new evidence may make it necessary to change them.

Rule No. 62

Remember that no two things are ever the same

This rule goes against the way most people think about things, and about other people.

Most of us speak about *oranges* as if all oranges were basically the same. Or they speak about Communists or elephants or astronauts as if they were all basically the same. Or about black people or white people as if they were all the same. But the fact is that everything on earth is strictly one of a kind, even though some things will have certain qualities in common with others in its class.

Let's suppose there are two big green things on your kitchen table. They are both called *watermelon*. Are they the same? Of course not. One is no doubt a bit heavier than the other. Or juicier. Or sweeter. Or has more seeds. There will always be differences. Even so-called identical twins are not really identical. *No two things in the universe are exactly the same.*

It's important to understand this, not only when talking about watermelons, twins, or basketballs, but also about different kinds of human beings. Some people use words like *black, Catholic, Jew, Republican,* and *baseball-player* as if all examples were the same. But they are not. No two Republicans are the same. No two Presbyterians are the same. No two things of any kind are exactly alike in every detail. It's all right to put people and things into categories, but we must remember that within each category, or group, the individual people or things are different from all the rest.

Rule No. 63

Know that no one thing remains the same for very long

A watermelon you see on your table on Monday will be different by Tuesday. A little of its moisture will have evaporated. So it will weigh a little less. Perhaps the color will have changed slightly. Even things that seem as if they would never change—hard things, like rocks and marbles and steel bridges, change, too. They wear away or rust. Even though it happens very slowly, they do change—they evolve—constantly.

Even you change, from moment to moment. A picture of you taken at the age of five would look quite different from a picture of you taken at the age of six. You will even have changed a bit by tomorrow at this same time. Your hair and fingernails will be a little longer. You may feel happier than you do now. Or sadder. You may be a little smarter. All sorts of changes are taking place within you at this very moment.

Thousands of years ago a wise man named Heraclitus said, "You can't step into the same river twice." He obviously didn't mean that you can't step into the Nile, the Tigris, the Orinoco, or the Mississippi twice, or fifty-seven times, if you like. What he meant was that, although that moving band of water that you walk into has the same name, at a later time it is very far from the same thing. First of all the actual drops of water you might have encountered on your first wade-in will be so long gone that they won't even exist when, at some later point on the time-scale, you repeat the experiment. The banks of the river may, by the second instance, have moved several feet higher or lower.

In some parts of the world, rivers even occasionally radically change their course if the land through which they flow is level. At certain times the water flow might move quite rapidly and at other times slowly, but Heraclitus, of course, was not really talking about rivers. He was talking about life and all of its experiences. While we might fervently wish that there were more things about life that were permanent and stable, the reality is that literally every single aspect of life is constantly undergoing change.

One thing this means is that it is perfectly possible to make a certain statement today, about a given thing, and have that statement generally be accepted as true. But the very same statement can be false if it is made at a later time, purely because the subject under discussion has changed. To give an extremely simple example, if you walked into the Mississippi river in mid-July you would consider the water on the warm side. Walk into it at the very same point in mid-January and you will describe the Mississippi as cold, which is to say that your once-true statement would now be quite false.

When we recognize such essential truths, we become somewhat more reasonable and less dogmatic.

Rule No. 64

Understand the difference between
the concrete and the abstract

The word *concrete* is easy to understand. One meaning is: that hard stuff they make sidewalks out of. But a more basic meaning is: anything that can be touched. Whatever actually physically exists is considered concrete, such as airplanes, baseballs, roller-skates, trees, people, rocks, dogs, cats.

There are other things you can talk about but can never touch or see. Things like *love, freedom, beauty, democracy, fear,* and *happiness.* You can't hold a pound of *freedom* in your hand. You can't reach out and touch *happiness.* So those are called *abstract.* They're perfectly legitimate, and they are usually ideas or concepts that are important—freedom, for instance.

We can be reasonably certain about concrete things, but often we can't be that scientific or certain about abstract things. Many people forget that difference. And so they argue about abstract words like *freedom, tyranny,* and *religion* as if they were using concrete words like *salami, motorcycle,* and *tennis ball.* Consequently, these people sometimes don't think very clearly about such matters. And because they don't think clearly, they may vote unwisely or do other things that are not good for the country and its people.

Rule No. 65

Don't kid yourself

We should tell the truth, to ourselves as well as to others. As the saying goes: Tell it like it is.

We will think more clearly about something if what we say about it is correct.

Jimmy Jones saw a man about six feet tall take a bicycle that belonged to Jimmy's friend Bob.

When Bob's father asked what the man looked lke, Jimmy said, "He was a great big guy."

Bob said he had seen plenty of tall men himself, so—to try to top his friend—Jimmy said, "But this guy was *really* big. He was about seven feet tall!"

Jimmy didn't intend to lie. He was just exaggerating. There are two kinds of exaggeration; one kind is okay, the other isn't. It's okay when you say, "Boy, this hot dog tastes so good I could eat a million of them!" Or "I'll bet the Los Angeles Rams could beat the New York Jets by a thousand points!"

Exaggerations of that sort couldn't possibly be true, so people understand them for what they are. But if you say that a six-foot-tall man is seven feet tall, that is misleading. If your grandfather gave you two dollars as a birthday present, but you exaggerate and say he gave you four dollars, that kind of exaggeration is actually a lie.

Now it's bad enough for us to mislead others with exaggerations and half-truths, but it's even worse to fool ourselves. So whatever we are talking about, we should always try to state the facts as carefully and correctly as we can.

Rule No. 66

Eliminate trash from your reading

A journalistic form detrimental to the national intelligence is that exemplified by the sensation-and-nonsense papers, sold at hundred of thousands of supermarkets, drugstores, and newsstands. Their circulation is enormous. Since it is impossible for anything human to be totally negative, such papers are not completely without merit. Occasionally one may encounter nuggets of sound medical or psychological advice, an interesting fragment of information, or an unusual narrative, but the bulk of the material published by such papers consists of brain-numbing stories about Elvis Presley, Mick Jagger, Boy George, and other popular heroes of the moment, gossip about entertainers and political leaders, by no means all of it factual, and a generous portion of stories dealing with flying saucers, the occult, and superstition of the grossest sort.

Several years ago, one of these papers ran the following story:

> Steve Allen went berserk in Hollywood—and nearly went to jail. The usually mild-mannered Steverino showed up late one night at his agent's office building and ordered a security guard to unlock the door. The guard refused, so Steve kicked in the plate glass door. Alarms went off, the cops arrived, and a suddenly sheepish Steve said he merely wanted some keys he'd left inside earlier that day. No charges were pressed and Steve's offered to kick in with a new door.

Needless to say, there was not so much as a speck of truth to the story. After my attorney brought this to the attention of the editors, I received an apology and a published retraction. Some such incident had indeed occurred, but had involved a man with a name somewhat similar to my own. Parenthetically, the retraction was run, not at the top of page two—where the false story had appeared—but far back in the newspaper. Consequently we may be certain that it came to the attention of far fewer people than had read the original libel.

As for the propensity of such newspapers to print "twilight zone" stories, there is nothing the least bit wrong in publishing accounts of actual or alleged instances of supernatural or scientifically unexplainable phenomena. Reputable scientists, in fact, conduct research into such matters and issue reports of their studies; it is important that they continue to do so. But such scholarly or impartial rendering of information is of little interest to the editors of checkout-stand publications, for whose tastes there seems to be no story too bizarre or improbable. Photographs are sometimes provided that are interpreted as proof of the story's allegations, with the result that popular but sometimes inaccurate ideas are not dealt with constructively but pandered to. The purpose—as no one would dream of denying—is to make money. Judged by such a standard, the enterprises are eminently successful.

But such periodicals, and the more conventional fan magazines they emulate, sometimes do actual moral as well as intellectual harm. They do this by publicizing, generally in wholly uncritical terms, the depravities or weaknesses of popular figures of music and the cinema. Consequently, while our churches and ethical societies continue to preach the traditional moral verities, the minds of the young and philosophically immature are assailed by messages suggesting that the important thing in American society is to be not moral, not law-abiding, but only successful, in which case anything goes.

These same publications, as they are weakening the moral consciousness of a sizable percentage of the American population, at the same time cater to such popular religious predispositions as can be turned to the publishers' financial advantage. There are, thus, complimentary references to Billy Graham and other religious leaders, endorsements of the power of prayer, the common occurrence of miracles, and so on. Putting these two mutually contradictory messages together, readers by the millions gather the impression that the most perverted or socially destructive behavior-patterns are permissible as long as (a) one continues to assert a belief in the existence of God, and (b) one is successful at selling recordings, attracting audiences in Las Vegas, hitting homeruns, making touchdowns, or becoming a millionaire.

In the field of nutrition, it is obviously not enough to simply eliminate high-calorie, high-fat junk food from our diet; we must naturally replace it with more nutritious fare. Just so in reading, as we eliminate unsubstantial material, we should replace it with something better. Even if we let our reading choices be dictated by our own intellectual circumstances, we should make the firm resolution to read the best sort of material available. If we are Catholic, for example, we should not read extreme right-wing Catholic periodicals, but distinguished journals like *America, Commonweal,* and other such church-related periodicals. The same goes for Protestants, Jews, and others. Why would we deliberately choose to read inferior newspapers and magazines and ignore the best?

And, of course, we should read a good deal more than material that simply conforms to our already-cemented prejudices. If you're an atheist, read high-minded religious literature. If you're a believer, explore the arguments of secular humanists, agnostics, and atheists. If you're of the Right politically, find out what the more responsible representatives of the Left are saying. If you're a leftist, read the better conservative journals.

Rule No. 67

Exercise a degree of control over your emotions

Suppose someone is rude to us. Some people believe that the thing to do in this sort of situation is to "get even." But we can never really get even. Usually by acting mean ourselves we cause more trouble. We may make the other person angrier than he was before, and then he may do something even more harmful. This is not to say that you may never stand up for your rights. But in many instances by acting like a better person yourself you may shame the offender into wanting to behave in a more decent manner. If you act the way he did, then you sink to his level. If you show him a good example, you may lift him to your level, assuming he is not already a professional criminal.

Remember, any dumbbell can pick up a stick and hit someone else over the head with it. But a person who knows how to think, a person who will use his or her intelligence, will usually act in a more human way. Why do I use the word *human?* Because those who let their emotions, from the limbic system, habitually overrule the cortex, are letting the animal part of their natures govern the more uniquely human part.

Such people often tend to become angrier than they should be, to have a great many arguments, perhaps to cry a lot, to be frightened more often than they should be, and, all in all, to cause even themselves a good deal of trouble. Emotions are important, indeed necessary; but we must try to see that the cortex is at least involved in our decision-making and that our emotions don't take over.

We cannot absolutely control everything about our behavior, of course. Perhaps we could if all the workings of the brain were conscious. But even while we are awake the brain is doing some of its work unconsciously, so that we can concentrate on whatever we are most interested in at the moment.

And even though our bodies will do certain things automatically—such as ducking to avoid being hit, blinking to keep out very bright light, and pulling a hand away if it touches something that is too hot—there are things about our conduct that we can control.

Again, emotions have their natural place. If something wonderful happens to us, it's natural to feel elated. If something bad happens, it's natural to feel depressed, perhaps to weep. If something threatens us, it's perfectly natural to feel afraid or angry. But we should still try to let the thinking, reasoning part of our brains take part in the important decisions in emotional situations.

By seeming to contrast reason and emotion, I do not mean to suggest that there is necessarily a hopeless state of war between the two. What one wants is to achieve a balance; life would be dreary indeed among a race of logical but emotionless beings.

Rule No. 68

Understand the difference between fact and opinion

A fact is something that is really true. For example: George Bush, in 1989, is the president of the United States.

But suppose you and a friend are eating banana ice-cream cones and are asked: Does banana ice-cream taste delicious? You might say yes. Your friend might say no.

Both the *yes* and the *no* are opinions. An opinion just tells how you feel about something, whether you like it or not. It would be silly for you and your friend to argue about the banana ice-cream, because both of you are giving your opinion. Nobody is right and nobody is wrong.

It's perfectly all right to have opinions. We all have thousands of them. But we must not make the mistake of thinking that our feelings about things are the same as facts.

Another kind of opinion might be called a wrong fact. For example, it may be your opinion that the state of Florida is just north of California. But it isn't. So you can have an opinion about a fact. And your opinion may be right or wrong. The important thing is: Remember the difference between facts and opinions.

Rule No. 69

Look for the evidence before making up your mind

Scientists, first of all, have been taught how to think—at least about scientific matters. They have been trained not to believe anything unless it is supported by evidence.

Suppose your uncle is arrested—by mistake—because he looks like a man who held up a bank. Naturally your uncle says that he didn't do it. But the judge may suspect he's telling a lie. So the judge says to the arresting officer: "Let's see the *evidence*. Can we *prove* that this man held up the bank?"

Perhaps the officer says: "Well, your honor, several witnesses saw the robber, and they noticed that as he ran away he lost one of his shoes. I have the shoe right here."

The judge says, "What size is it?"

"Size nine."

"Try to put it on the defendant's foot," the judge says.

It turns out that your uncle can't get his foot into the shoe because he wears a size thirteen. So the judge lets your uncle go free because the evidence showed that he was not the guilty man.

If and when they do arrest the guilty man, he too may say that he wasn't at the scene of the crime. Certainly the evidence of the shoe alone will not convict him, because there are millions of men who wear size nine. But perhaps they will find his fingerprint on the lost shoe. That fingerprint would be conclusive evidence that he had handled the shoe.

Don't be quite so ready to accept something as true unless there is some kind of evidence to back it up. For example, millions of people used to believe that the earth was flat. Gradually, scientific evidence showed that it was round. Even then it took a surprisingly long time for the flat-earth people to admit that they had been wrong. They resisted the new evidence for as long as they could. Some still do. This is a very common process. Some people have formed such poor habits of thought that they find it difficult to accept new evidence if it disagrees with something they already believe.

Consider the word *believe*. Belief can be a beautiful, necessary, and comforting thing. But it is not the same as certain knowledge. To know something is to be really sure of it. To believe something is to suppose that it is true. And it may be true. But unless you have evidence to support the idea you are not talking about knowledge.

Rule No. 70

Enjoy the classics

How does it happen that in school we learn how to read—and at the same time we learn to hate to read the things worth reading most?

It's happened to us all—with assignment reading! It happened to me. The teacher assigned *Moby Dick*. I didn't want to read it. So I fought it. I thought I won.

But I lost. My struggle to keep at arm's length from *Moby Dick* cost me all the good things that can come from reading those special few books we call the "classics." I've come back to *Moby Dick* on my own since then. I like it. And I've discovered a new level of pleasure from it with each reading.

What is a classic? A classic is a book that gives you that exhilarating feeling, if only for a moment, that you've finally uncovered part of the meaning of life. A classic is a book that men and women all over the world have kept reaching for, throughout the ages, for its special enlightenment. Not many books can survive such a test. Considering all the volumes that have been produced since man first put chisel to stone, classics account for an infinitesimal share of the total—less than .001 percent. That's just a few thousand books. Of those, less than one hundred make up the solid core.

Why should you tackle the classics? I suggest three good reasons:

1. Classics open up your mind.
2. Classics help you grow intellectually.
3. Classics help you understand your life, your world, and yourself.

That last one is the big one. A classic can give you insights into yourself that you will get nowhere else. Sure, you can get pleasure from a great many different books. But with a great book, once you penetrate it, you reach new heights of understanding. Aeschylus's *Oresteia* was written nearly 2,500 years ago, and it still knocks people out.

Let me offer some suggestions that will help open up this wondrous world. Pick up a classic you've always promised to try. Is it a novel, drama, biography, history? To find out, check the table of contents, read the book cover, the preface, or look up the title or author in *The Reader's Encyclopedia.* Perhaps you shouldn't read it in bed. Classics can be tough going. You need to be alert, with your senses sharp. When you read in bed you're courting sleep—and you'll blame it on the book when you start nodding off.

Don't let a lot of characters throw you. Dostoevsky tosses fifty major characters at you in *The Brothers Karamazov.* In the very first chapter of *War and Peace,* Tolstoy bombards you with twenty-two names—long, complicated ones like Anna Pavlovna Scherer, Anatole, and Prince Bolkonski. Don't run for cover. Stick with it. The characters will gradually sort themselves out and you'll feel as comfortable with them as you do with your own dear friends who were strangers, too, when you met them.

Read in big bites. Don't read in short nibbles. How can you expect to get your head into anything that way? The longer you stay with it, the more you get into the rhythm and mood—and the more pleasure you get from it. Help yourself get into the mood. When you read *Zorba the Greek,* try putting bouzouki music on the record player; Proust, a little Debussy; Shakespeare, Elizabethan theater music.

Read what the author read. To better understand where the author is coming from, as we say, read the books he once read and that impressed him. Shakespeare, for example, dipped into Thomas North's translation of *Plutarch's Lives* for the plots of *Julius Caesar, Antony and Cleopatra* and *A Midsummer Night's Dream.* It's fun to know you're reading what he read.

Read about the author's period of history. You're the product of our time. Authors are the products of theirs. Knowing something of the history of their times, the problems that they and others faced, their attitudes, will help you understand their points of view. Important point:

You may not agree with the author. No problem. At least you were made to think.

Read the book again. All classics bear rereading. If, after you finish the book the first time, you're intrigued but still somewhat confused, reread it then and there. It'll open up some more to you. If you did read a classic a few years back and loved it, read it again. The book will have so many new things to say to you, you'll hardly believe it's the same one.

A few gems to enjoy:

You can find excellent lists of the basic classics compiled by helpful experts, like Clifton Fadiman's Lifetime Reading Plan, the Harvard Classics, and Mortimer Adler's Great Books. Look into them. But before you do, I'd like to suggest a few that can light up your life. Even though some might have been spoiled for you by the required-reading stigma, try them. And try them.

1. Homer: *Iliad* and *Odyssey*. The Adam and Eve of Western literature. Read a good recent translation. I suggest the one by Robert Fitzgerald.

2. Rabelais: *Gargantua* and *Pantagruel.* A Gargantuan romp. I recommend the Samuel Putnam translation.

3. Geoffrey Chaucer: *Canterbury Tales.* Thirty folks on a four-day pilgrimage swapping whoppers. Don't be surprised if the people you meet here are like people you know in your own life.

4. Cervantes: *Don Quixote.* The first modern novel, about the lovable old Don with his "impossible dream." How could you go through life without reading it once?

5. Shakespeare: Plays. Some are flops, some make him the greatest writer ever. All offer gold. His best: *Hamlet, Macbeth* and *Romeo and Juliet.* (See them on the stage or television, too.)

6. Charles Dickens: *Pickwick Papers,* or even *A Christmas Carol.* No one can breathe life into characters the way Dickens can. Did you see the marvelous "Nicholas Nickleby" series when it was telecast in the U.S. in early 1983? The British production company did a delightful thing. Essentially they just *read* the text of Dickens's story and then had performers act the dialogue. It was one of the best television series ever, and it shows that

the vitality of Charles Dickens's characters is such that he continues to appeal to modern audiences.

7. Mark Twain: *Huckleberry Finn.* Maybe you had to read this in school. Well, climb back on that raft with Huck and Jim. You'll find new meaning this time.

Don't just dip your toe into the deep waters of the classics. Plunge in! Like generations of bright human beings before you, you'll find yourself invigorated by thoughts and observations of the most gifted writers in history.

If there's a shop near you that sells second-hand books—particularly used textbooks—drop in and see if you can pick up one of those paperbacks that enable college students to understand important works of literature—novels, plays, poems, etc. For a few dollars you can purchase the *Cliff Notes* series of paperbacks (easily recognized by the bright yellow and black striped covers). There are more than two hundred of them, both fiction and nonfiction. Examples of various "classics" that are available are: *Pride and Prejudice, Jane Eyre,* and *David Copperfield.*

These summaries are extremely helpful as a supplemental aid to a better understanding of the particular work, but do not substitute them for actually reading the works themselves.

Rule No. 71

Don't equate your ideas with yourself

The intuitive, creative powers of the mind will often suggest a hypothesis. Some people make an error in reasoning from that point forward; they make an automatic ego-investment in their creative guess. Right or wrong, the hypothesis may sound rather impressive. We may therefore make the mistake of becoming unduly fond of it. Secondly, to the degree that we are personally insecure, we may further short-circuit the reasoning process by taking any analytical assault upon our theory, however courteously expressed, as an attack upon ourselves. This is one of the most familiar ways in which already-frail reasoning is overpowered. If the ego feels threatened, we push the essential question to a position of secondary importance. The situation deteriorates to a reason-be-damned phase, and an ego-motivated attack upon the attackers will often result.

It will be the lesser of two evils to deal directly with critics' questions or objections. In many instances we succumb to a fit of ad-hominemism. The issue itself no longer dominates. What is important is to win, or—in those who are more naturally aggressive—to defeat the opponent.

Rule No. 72

Remember that you do not think at random but because of motives and reasons

There is a difference between reasons and motives. The word *motive* implies some sort of overall, ongoing plan or interest out of which it would be reasonable to expect certain acts to flow. One may want to further an aim that one perceives as virtuous. One may, for example, act in a certain way because one is a Catholic, Republican, Communist, feminist, atheist, Methodist, or professional basketball player.

A separate category of motives would involve *opposition*. One may perform certain acts because one is opposed, on an ongoing overall basis, to some theory, philosophy, or organization.

Reasons are, as a class, likely to be simpler than motives. A man may, for example, steal a bottle of beer from a liquor store only because he is an alcoholic and at the moment without money to pay for the beverage.

A rapist may strike an unfortunate victim because he is psychologically sick, himself a victim of a mind-set that compels him repeatedly to commit such a vicious act.

A fire-bug may commit his bizarre crime because he is a compulsive arsonist, which is to say a mentally disturbed person of a specific sort that derives intense pleasure from the spectacle of destructive fire.

A psychologically normal person may steal a bag of groceries from a parked car simply because his or her own family has not had food for three days.

But do not conclude, from the citation of such instances, that this section is about alcoholics, arsonists, rapists, poor people, Catholics, Protestants, or whatever. It is about the poor methods of reasoning that all of us are guilty of from time to time.

Rule No. 73

Resolve to get a good, broad-based, general education, even if your formal schooling has ended

There are many among us who have had an intensive but narrowly specialized education, and this too is a contributor to dumbth. Mortimer Adler, in his stimulating *Paideia Proposal: An Educational Manifesto,* wrote:

> But we can and should do something to mitigate the barbarism of intense specialization, which threatens to be as destructive in its own way as the abandonment of specialization would be. We can reconceive the role and offerings of our colleges and universities, made possible by the time saved and the skills acquired that reformed basic schooling will provide.
>
> We need specialists for our economic prosperity, for our national welfare and security, for continued progress in all the arts and sciences, and in all fields of scholarship. But for the sake of our cultural traditions, our democratic institutions, and our individual well-being, our specialists must also be generalists; that is, generally educated human beings.

This returns us to the problem-factor mentioned elsewhere in this study, that our best and brightest are often the best and the brightest in one narrow field, at the expense of general knowledge.

Adler, himself a specialist in the consideration of such problems, is among the many convinced that some such destructive process has taken place. Anyone who is already highly competent at handling computers, pulling teeth, manufacturing airplanes, writing advertising copy, or any of the other thousand and one areas where intense specialized knowledge is obviously required, should resolve to go back to somewhere near the beginning and acquire the knowledge necessary to be a valuable citizen, and a patron of the arts, and a student of the humanities.

Rule No. 74

Look for problem situations in your own experience where you can apply the procedures suggested in this book

The world and its daily trials present us with so many problems that it is difficult—perhaps impossible—to categorize all of them. Some are complex, some relatively simple; some involve mathematics, others concern objects and their mechanical relationships. In any event, categorization is not necessary. You may address each problem on its own terms and, hopefully, arrive at a reasonable solution.

For example on an NBC-TV comedy special—one of the series called "The Big Show"—I thought it would be amusing if Sid Caesar and I did a sketch together that was, in part, a takeoff on the then-popular film *10*. A second relevant factor was that Sid is noted for his ability to do authentic sounding double-talk in foreign languages, including Japanese. On his superb comedy program of the 1950s he frequently did a Japanese character much like that of John Belushi two decades later. Hardly had I combined these two ideas in my mind than it occurred to me that it would be amusing to call our Japanese version "Yen." Then another problem presented itself. I was to work in the sketch with Sid, which naturally required me to speak nonsense Japanese. But while I can speak double-talk in English, I cannot do so in any other language. After considering how I might speak my lines—and inasmuch as the sketch was to involve only a few words in English—a happy solution occurred to me. I wrote down all the Japanese brand names I could think of—*Sony, Toyota, Honda, Mitsubishi, Sanyo, Subaru, Hitachi, Kawasaki*, etc.—and when I had to speak I simply rattled them off at high speed, naturally each time in a different order.

This trivial example is intended to suggest that anyone dealing with problems in his or her own area of activity can employ a similar approach. An alternative solution or fresh idea does not have to be as dazzlingly innovative as Einstein's theory of relativity. But we can all develop the habit of approaching such challenges in the spirit of practiced creative problem-solving and—most of the time, at least—we will get usable results.

As an instance of problem-solving, I submit another example from personal experience:

In December 1984, I received a message from former football coach Pete Elliott, who in his capacity as executive director of the Pro-Football Hall of Fame had called to inquire if I would be interested in writing a theme march that would be permanently used by the Hall of Fame. I immediately accepted the assignment.

So what was the problem? It had nothing to do with the writing of a song, which comes easily enough to most professional composers, and certainly to me, but it had to do with the fact that I had no assurance that the number I submitted would, in fact, be accepted. As soon as the problem itself occurred to me, the solution followed immediately. Rather than offer just one song, which might not be deemed suitable, I wrote six melodies, put them on one cassette and let Coach Elliott know that he and his colleagues could make the choice. Since all the melodies were of professional quality, it was reasonably close to certain that they would not reject all six. The ploy worked. Shortly thereafter I received word that they had narrowed their choice down to two but were having considerable difficulty deciding which of the two to reject.

My secondary solution was to offer them both songs, saying, "If you like, you may use the more spirited march for the opening theme of any films or television presentations you might prepare and the other more patriotic, solemn, more emotional melody as the closing theme."

Recently I videotaped some material for a program called "Inside Your Schools" in the playground of an elementary school in a large eastern city. The area was littered with debris—broken glass, papers, wood scraps, dead leaves, soft-drink cans, etc. Within five seconds after noting the problem, the following solution to it occurred to me: Tell one class of children that for the first ten minutes of their recreation period "we are going to play a clean-up game." Two large trash bags or refuse cans are set up in the middle of the area, and within a limited time period—say, five minutes—the children pick up as many scraps as they can and run to put them into the can. The members of the class could be divided up into two groups so that the element of team competition is introduced. They would be warned not to pick up broken glass. Obviously it would take only a few minutes to tidy up the area.

I do not refer to this solution, God knows, in any boastful sense, since it strikes me that any enterprising eight-year-old could, if asked, suggest the same simple idea. Nevertheless, it had apparently not been thought of at this particular location. The point is that we need not wait for formal tests of our intelligence in order to exercise it.

Rule No. 75

Stop thinking you "don't have time"
to improve yourself

There is some advantage—and I do not mean only the financial one—
that can be derived from almost any situation. Let us assume that we
are convicted of a crime and sentenced to five years in prison. It would
be foolish indeed to waste the time of our incarceration. Think of all
the important books we have wanted to read but "never had time"
for. In prison, we would have the time. We could easily come out at
the end of any extended period able to play the guitar, do card tricks
with professional polish, manipulate a typewriter, or with a much
improved ability to speak foreign languages, particularly if any of our
fellow inmates have spoken them from birth. Naturally we do not need
to be in such extreme circumstances to turn the conditions of our life
to good use.

Rule No. 76

Encourage your own creativity
by studying creativity itself

As mentioned elsewhere in the present work, we are all accustomed to reading about activities we are interested in. Golfers love to read about golf, bridge players about bridge, football fans about football, musicians about music, and so on. If we are aware that we personally have some degree of creativity—either remarkable or modest—we should also know that we can increase it by learning more about creativity and by exercising our talents.

Many of the recent findings about the differences between right-brain and left-brain activity relate to the fact that Nature and/or God have actually programmed our internal computers to function creatively. We literally have brain tissue that specializes in it. For some reason, much of this activity is handled by the right side of the brain.

My own creative abilities seem to have been built into my machinery from the outset, in the same way that the color of eyes or other physical features are largely determined at the moment of conception. If it comes so easily, then it is a fair question whether I am entitled to be proud of it. I happen to be able—for example—to do a trick called playing the piano by ear.

In these remarks I refer largely to my own experience in discussing the mystery of creativity. But I take it as understood that my creative achievements, according to the highest critical standards, are noteworthy from the standpoint of quantity rather than quality. I am no genius, as my wife and children would be the first to tell you. Nevertheless, the process by means of which I, or any other second-rate thinker, conceive of a fresh idea is probably the same as that by which truly great minds turn the trick.

A comment on the subject of *inspiration* is in order. The word in its original sense apparently was meant to convey the idea of a visitation by a consciousness outside one's own. If a man had a startling and valid new idea, it was supposed that God somehow breathed—inspired—the idea into him. On the other hand, in the Middle Ages, those who introduced radical scientific ideas were frequently suspected of owing their inspiration to the devil. There is little point in debating these possibilities, since there seem to be very few people left who believe in either of them.

When we use the word *inspiration* today, we mean to suggest that a creative person is so seized by an emotion that he or she expresses it in some artistic form. It is apparently a popular conception that creative people must somehow be *inspired* to work. But this is not an either/or question. A creative idea may arrive under a variety of circumstances. A person may write a poem in order to sell it and live on the proceeds. Or a writer may pick up some grain of sand in an overheard phrase, an unusual rhyme accidentally noticed, a scenic vista observed, a whiff of perfume—almost anything can be the starting point around which a creative work may be woven.

For example, one day in Los Angeles, as I was looking at an incredibly tall, thin palm tree, it occurred to me that it had taken perhaps half a century to form very much the same design in the air that is formed in an instant by the ascent and explosion of a rocket. First comes the long, narrow perpendicular line and then the umbrellalike outcropping at the top. Such an observation may, as I say, serve as the starting point for a poem. Unfortunately there is no necessary connection at all between the validity, sensitivity, or beauty of the original observation and comparison on the one hand, and the end-product on the other. There are atrociously bad poems based on very sound or sensitive ideas, just as there are delightful or moving poems that start from a rather light premise.

The starting point, again, may be trivial, in either case. I recall one time thinking about darkness, not in the sense of evil or mystery, but merely in the strict sense of absence of light. I remembered experiencing that fear of darkness common to children and probably never totally overcome by adults, save those born blind. Now that is certainly a flimsy enough point of origin; yet a poem can grow out of picking up something common, but finding something fresh to say about it. My contribution was to observe that, contrary to what is widely supposed, most of what takes place on this planet takes place not in the light, but in the dark. This is the poem:

Darkness

When I was very young I feared the dark,
But now I see it's the more natural state.
We come from an eternity of it,
Blink briefly in the light, and then return.

Most of the earth's best work is done in darkness.
And only surface things can know the sun.
The oil, the diamonds, the coal, the iron
Come from the undercrust's eternal night.

The sea's work is done equally by night.
And all beneath the wave is lightless gloom.
The sun has never penetrated seeds;
It touches but the outer skin of fruits.

And you, the best part of you is a stranger
That light nor I will ever know.
It's dark beneath your dress (facetiously)
And darker still beneath your skin. The bones.

The heart works blindly, and the cells
Grope sightlessly among the veins for food.
The blood indeed's so fearful of the light
That at the very sight it starts and freezes.

The Bible tells us that the dark came first.
And also that it shall come last
And when it does the cause may be
That of a sudden there was too much light.

As another illustration of the sort of fragment of experience that can lead to the creation of a poem, I refer to an evening several years ago when, lying half-asleep in my apartment on upper Park Avenue in New York City, I was suddenly startled by that always unnerving sound of tires screeching in the street below. After my initial reaction— wincing, waiting for the sound of a crash—it occurred to me that not only I, but scores, perhaps hundreds of others in the neighborhood must have heard the same sound floating up out of the warm, still summer's night. The combinaiton of the sound, and the reaction to it, led to these lines.

The Sound of Tires

All night long, on dark Park Avenue,
The braking tires screech
Freezing the heart,
Suspending the activity in a thousand apartments,
Shrieking like Mandrake roots the size of a redwood's,
Screaming like the first angel that tumbled into the pit.

With a horrible high fidelity
The squeal cuts sharp across the consciousness
Of diners with pale teacups poised,
Sleepers who make of the sound a lost
    heart's weepy plea for love,
    a nightmare monster's close blood-thirsty shout,
    lovers who are either given
    momentary pause or wildly
    cry harmony back to the
    night's intrusive bleat.

The eye winces, the spirit's shoulders hunch.
The sound has strings. In the dark
    apartments see the puppets twitch.

The songwriter—in any event, if he is seriously professional—could not long function solely on the basis of inspiration; this is particularly true of the lyricist, who often must fashion a product almost in the way that a tailor turns out a suit of clothes—to fit. If you are writing a musical show you must include songs of various types: a peppy opening number, an amusing novelty, a rousing rhythmic number, a tender song of love, and so forth.

Sometimes, in fact, it stimulates the creative juices if you are given a fairly specific assignment, in contrast to just sitting around waiting for an idea to come out of the blue. Some of my best lyrics, I think, have been written to order, to melodies created by other composers, and with titles that originally seemed to me to have a somehow off-center ring.

I don't think any songwriter would ever hope to come up with a number titled "Picnic" for example. It's just not a good title for a song, all by itself. In the unlikely event that you wanted to write a song about a picnic at all, you might come up with a title like "Picnic in the Park," or "I Met You at a Picnic." The simple unadorned word "Picnic" just seems wrong, for the same reasons that would preclude you writing a song called "Ocean" or "Walk" or "Parade." But since I was stuck with the title when I wrote the words for the main theme from the motion picture based on William Inge's play *Picnic,* there was no way out of it.

Picnic

On a picnic morning
Without a warning
I looked at you
    and somehow I knew.
On a day for singing
My heart went winging;
    a picnic grove was our rendezvous.
You and I in the sunshine,
We strolled the fields and farms.
At the last light of evening
I held you in my arms.

Now when days grow stormy
And lonely for me
I just recall
Picnic-time with you.

Another peculiar title is "Gravy Waltz." Ray Brown had written a jazz waltz with that title, and jazz instrumentals almost invariably have abstract titles that tell no particular story and paint no particular picture. But somehow the very oddity of the title forced me to come up with a lyric that I think has a certain freshness—if only because it takes a title that has no meaning and infuses a meaning into it.

Gravy Waltz

Pretty mama's in the kitchen this glorious day,
Smell the gravy simmerin' nearly half a mile away.

Lady Mornin' Glory, I say good mornin' to you.
Chirpy little chickadee told me that my baby was true.

Well, she really ran
To get her fryin' pan
    when she saw me comin',

Gonna get a taste
    before it goes to waste.
This honey-bee's hummin'.

Mister Weepin' Willow, I'm thru with all of my faults,
'Cause my baby taught me to do the ever new
Gravy Waltz.

Lastly, there is indeed inspiration of the sort supposed to be common. Strong emotion—love, despondency, patriotic fervor, sympathy, anger—will sometimes lead people to express themselves in the form of a poem, a song, or an essay, depending on whether the individual is a poet, a composer, or an essayist.

Perhaps I should not be equating songs and poems and essays and novels or what-have-you in this way. A poem rates higher on the artistic scale than does a popular song lyric, although in our culture one may earn a hundred thousand dollars from a song that will shortly be forgotten, while one is unlikely to earn fifty dollars for a poem that might be remembered for centuries. This is odd, too, when you realize that very few can create a really good poem, whereas the woods are full of songwriters.

This ability to create melodies extemporaneously is probably related to the ability to create jokes spontaneously, but I have not the slightest idea what psychological mechanisms are involved. Of course creating combinations of musical notes is a more mysterious matter than creating combinations of words. Words, after all, are merely symbols for things, acts, or concepts, whereas music is not essentially symbolic at all. It may be associative, but in essence it means itself, so to speak.

It is rarely difficult for me to tell where I got the idea or inspiration for a lyric, since one idea leads to another by a generally unmysterious process. But where melodies come from, heaven only knows. When I create them I sometimes figure them out more or less mechanically at the piano, but more often I suddenly hear them in my mind without having made any conscious effort to call them into being. When I am brushing my teeth or driving to work or waking up in the morning, I start to hum or whistle or even just think of a melody, and there it is—another new song has been delivered to me from an unknown source.

Obviously the environment of musical conditioning has something to do with it. A composer tends to create music of the type he has been exposed to: a Chinese composer composes Chinese music, an Indian composer creates Indian music, and an American composer writes American music. But to say as much does not explain the process of creation; it merely limits the field of inquiry. I assume that the creation of music is some sort of semi-automatic mathematical process that the qualified brain engages in when it has been stimulated to a certain necessary degree. Pour numbers into a mathematician's head and they come out in various new and different combinations. Pour music into a composer's brain and he eventually pours it out again, taken completely apart and assembled into a variety of forms so potentially enormous that their extent cannot be comprehended by the average mind.

Another interesting fact about the creative musical process is that my mind seems to build up a sort of tension if I go for several days without relieving myself, so to speak, of the music that is perhaps floating just below the threshold of consciousness. The similarity between this particular creative process and the human procreative function is obvious enough—though this is not to say that there is any connection between the two. But if I let a week or two pass without having written a song, I find that I am almost driven to the piano; and when I finally release the compressed creative energy that has accumulated, what bursts forth is usually not just one song but several. At such times the songs are of the best quality I am capable of. If circumstances prevent my reaching a piano, the songs eventually burst forth anyway; I find myself humming new melodies and jotting down ideas for titles or lyrics.

Although my abilities as a pianist are far below my abilities as a composer, I have noticed that here, too, a period of abstinence charges my creative battery. I usually play with more emotion and originality— if not technical finesse—when I have gone for several days without playing.

It is a common assumption that there is a great deal less creative thinking today than in ages past. When we consider creative giants in the arts, for example, we almost invariably think of the great painters, musicians, sculptors, anthors, and philosophers of past centuries. And, if asked to name a dozen famous inventors, again we would refer largely to history for our examples: Edison, Fulton, Franklin, Da Vinci, the Wright brothers, and Whitney, for example.

As regards the arts—while Saul Bellow is not the equal of Shakespeare, Leonard Bernstein the equal of Beethoven, or Jackson Pollack the equal of Vincent Van Gogh, nevertheless there is far more creative work being done today on a quantitive basis, not only in simple numbers but in terms of the more meaningful consideration of the percentage of the total population involved.

In the technical and scientific areas, while there would be no point in demeaning the achievements of Edison or Steinmetz, the level of sophistication at which our best scientific and technical minds are working today is such that the famous inventors of earlier times would be quite lost if they were to return to earth and be introduced to the new physics and mathematics and the hardware to which they are giving rise.

I am enormously pleased that a formal interest is being taken in the subject of creativity. Think of it; on the one hand the world has progressed almost entirely by the individual creative ideas of a rare handful of inventive individuals, men and women who refused merely to accept what was handed down to them but insisted on questioning what they had been taught and then committed the further radical and dangerous sin of adding to the body of common knowledge. Those civilizations that had a good supply of creative individuals, and permitted them to create and discover, progressed and prospered.

In this historic context it is interesting to consider the popular American attitude toward creative thinkers and intellectuals generally. They are distrusted, called "eggheads," and sometimes accorded precious little respect. Who are we hurting?

But let us assume you have found my observations to this point reasonable and are now prepared to consider ways in which your own creativity may be encouraged.

First suggestion: Stop inhibiting yourself.

Independently I arrived at a working idea that I was later gratified to learn is now a fundamental principle of the art and discipline of encouraging creative behavior. Alex Osborn of the Creative Education Foundation, a pioneer in the field, taught that judgment should be totally suspended while the creative process is flowing.

Although I learned about Osborn's theories fairly recently, I had discovered that my own creative work flowed most freely if I simply decided to delay judgmental decisions until a later stage, at which time I could function as editor of my earlier output. But if I were self-critical at the moment an idea was developing, I could inhibit the full expression of it. Even in group-think sessions, sometimes in the context of television production, I have often instructed my staff people: "Let's just suggest any damn thing we think of at this stage. We can always throw something out later if it's not any good."

It is sometimes thought that there is a wide gulf between creative thinking on the one hand and organized, structured preparation on the other. But this is not the case. Some of my jokes are written in a sheer out-of-the-blue way, but in other cases I can create jokes of equal quality on a more orderly basis. When I first began comedy writing, I discovered a good technique for priming the creative pump was to simply make a list of ideas or concepts commonly associated with the subject in question. For example, if I were writing a western or cowboy sketch I would make a list of related words, such as bunkhouse, sagebrush, critter, Gabby Hayes, six-gun, two-gun, ornery, sidewinder, head of cattle, cactus, purple sage, sheriff, posse, Indian, pony, corral, and so on. Any of these would then be the initial grain-of-sand around which a pearl of a joke might subsequently coalesce, if the figure of speech is not too belabored.

Another thing I discovered early in the joke-writing game was that the collaboration of others in a team process was helpful. Humorous ideas are, it seems to me, somehow structurally different from scientific ideas. In the case of basic science there is something that preexists, in almost a Platonic sense, waiting to be discovered. Newton did not invent gravity; he discovered it. Einstein did not invent his famous formula; he discovered it. Such concepts are already inherent in the physical universe. But jokes not only are the result of new combinations of words and ideas but also grow out of the attitudes of those involved.

I not only seem to be but I literally *am* funnier in the presence of certain people. A good many of those I meet seem so essentially nonhumorous that I become much like them when I am in their company. This is not calculated; it's an automatic social response, an adaptation to a specific environment. But when in the company of other comedy writers, humorists, or comedians, then each of us becomes—in a literal sense—funnier, because of our interaction.

Especially funny people communicate with each other in a markedly different way from the way they communicate with their dentists, grocers, accountants, attorneys, clergymen and—sometimes—their relatives.

Something like the same process is at work when I am performing. An audience, the reader may be surprised to learn, has an actual character or "personality" of its own, before the curtain ever goes up and before an entertainer appears. I discovered this when I was new at the game, in the late 1940s when I was doing a nightly radio comedy program in Hollywood. Each night I would glance through the curtain briefly before starting the show to make sure that the ushers had seated everyone, that house lights had been turned on, and so on. One evening it occurred to me that the audience was particularly lively and animated. People were craning their necks, chatting with each other, looking about, chuckling. This was suddenly contrasted in my mind to audiences from the preceding few days, some of whom had seemed more properly cast for attendance at funerals or civic meetings. In those instances visitors had sat quietly, their faces blank or sober. As one might guess, I was able to make a lively, warm audience laugh much more easily than one that had, for whatever mysterious reasons, come in off the street in a relatively empty emotional state. Any professional comedian will tell you that when an audience is hot, the performer himself becomes literally much funnier. This is most strikingly true of those comedians, like myself, who work in a largely or partly ad-lib context. I more or less play the audience as I might a musical instrument. Just as a pianist will play better on a fine instrument than on an inferior one, so a comedian who works with a degree of spontaneity will perform better to an especially responsive audience.

But what about your own creative ideas? Do worthwhile creative ideas "just pop into your mind" unbidden, or can you order your brain to conceive them?

The question is unnecessarily limiting. It is obvious enough that there are instances where fresh ideas seemingly occur out of nowhere. There are other cases in which the creative portions of the brain seem to be following orders, responding to an exercise in self-programming. But these two categories by no means exhaust the possibilities. To the extent that I may draw a generality from personal experience I find that approximately 90 percent of my usable ideas come about because my mental computer is already programmed by an interest in a specific area. The original motivation may be self-generated—I may simply *decide* to write a specific play, story, book, or musical—or it may come from an outside source; I may be hired or requested to do a certain piece of work. In either case the simple acceptance of the assignment sets the creative wheels in motion. I have little conscious awareness that this is occurring.

Indeed, my consciousness—like anyone else's—tends to be concerned with the thousand and one events and interests that occupy all of our lives: looking for my keys, wondering if I have time to have the car washed before I go to the office, trying to remember if I have answered a particular business letter, making a mental note to buy a birthday present for my wife, and so on. But if our achievements depended only on the powers of the conscious mind, almost all of us, I assume, would still be back in the Stone Age. The creative levels generally do their work subconsciously.

But we can assist the creative process. We can take part in the programming of our own internal computer. If we want to write poetry, we should read good poetry. If we want to write good novels, we should read good novels. If we want to compose good music, we should listen to good music. The point is certainly not to encourage plagiarism but simply to study how the trick has been turned by others, to bring our thinking into tune, onto the same vibratory level, as that which generally prevails in the field of art within which we wish to function.

Perhaps we will choose to program ourselves by appeals to mood changes. I do not mean drugs. Some creative people are rendered calm and introspective at the sight of water—lakes, rivers, seas, or swimming pools. Others are stimulated to heights of creativity by the near-silence of nature, such as one enjoys in the mountains, the countryside, or at the seashore. I once completed a novel with the aid of an old album of Errol Garner piano mood music. Night after night I listened to it again and again, and it never failed to create in me a sort of dreamy reverie-state, which I found conducive to the flow of the kind of ideas dealt with in the book I was writing.

It might be assumed that such distractions as radio, television, or recorded music would be hindrances to creativity. This may be the case with others, but in my own experience a great deal—and perhaps all—of my creative work comes as a matter of response. Oddly enough, the content of what I am listening to, or reading, need have no direct or even tangential relationship to the creative idea that suddenly takes form. But something that I am exposed to—almost like a cue-ball being sent into a group of other balls at rest on a pool table—causes a movement of nervous impulses in those portions of the brain involved with the physical part of thinking.

The specific creative idea that emerges would probably not be forthcoming at all, or at least not in the form that it does, in fact, take, if there had not been some intrusive factor.

At the moment the idea occurs and begins to be expressed, however, what formerly had been a stimulus can become a distraction. At that point I turn off the radio, the record player, or the television set, or put aside the book, and concentrate fully on trapping the idea while it is in fresh condition.

Creativity Is Not the Enemy of Reason

Some people fear that if reason is increased, creativity will automatically decrease. Such fears are groundless. We all have the capacity for both reason and creativity. The one kind of creativity for which I cannot take the slightest credit, nor even give very meaningful information about, is the kind that takes place while one is asleep. I have long felt that a dream—any dream—is, among other things, a creative act. The fact that a good many of our dreams don't "make sense" and that we forget most of them has no relevance to the basic point. If you stop to think of it, a dream involves a tremendously creative process. Your mind calls forth into existence characters—human or animal—places, buildings, vehicles, natural panoramas, colors, temperatures. It is all quite undisciplined, presumably because the ordering or analytical propensities of the brain are suspended during sleep, but the uninhibited, creative parts are observably flowing in a remarkably free way.

If anyone were to present us with a written story, we would certainly consider the account an instance of creativity. Let us assume that the story had a cast of characters, that the persons described perform certain actions, have certain adventures, say certain things to one another, or to themselves. The point is that this is precisely what occurs in dreams. We are unfortunately denied conscious access to the great majority of details of dream-stories, simply because of the weakness of dream-recollection. But, from time to time, a particular dream does impress itself on our consciousness. The wealth of detail is invariably remarkable. Not only are our dreams peopled by distinct characters, but we are able to describe them as we would characters in theatrical, film, or television dramas.

In the case of a play, we might be impressed by the contributions of a producer, a director, a playwright, several actors and actresses, a lighting expert, a scenic artist, and a costume designer. But in dreams the individual dreamer functions as a particularly dramatic example of creative versatility. Each of us, every night of our lives, functions as producer, director, playwright, actor, and assorted technicians.

And the creative supervision, as it were, extends to the minutest details. It is we who decide the colors of costumes, the condition of the weather, the content of conversations, and the size, strength, speed, ferocity or gentleness of animals. That we would extemporize our own remarks in dreams is perhaps no more remarkable than being able to do so in the waking state. Although what is involved in both cases is extraordinary, we simply fail to perceive the wonder of it because it is part of our daily experience. But in dreams we have not the slightest difficulty or hesitancy in creating dialogue for the other characters as well. Even more magically, in dreams we *become* those other characters.

But there is a separate plane of creativity in dreams, in that we are no longer bound by physical laws, no longer limited to acting in time and space as they exist in the real world. In dreams we are able to fly, to exist under water, to walk through walls, to move from one place to another quite distant spot in a moment of time. Indeed, the time-factor of dreams is one of the most mysterious in that not only are we creating the equivalent of a motion picture, so to speak, but we may be projecting that moving picture scene in just a few seconds, whereas in real time and space such a scene might take twenty minutes to take place.

From this, then, I conclude that creativity is not something with which only rare individuals are endowed. It is rather, on the most fundamental level, an identifying characteristic of the human species.

In resistance to this insight, it might be argued that animals appear to dream. Indeed, I assume that they do, since I have witnessed my own dogs occasionally twitching, whining, or moving their legs while asleep, presumably in response to some imagined adventure. It follows that we cannot claim that the creativity of dreams is unique to human beings. But if we do share it with a limited number of animals of the higher orders, this is merely consistent with what is known about the great ancient drama of evolution, in which many of our abilities, insights, and perceptions were not granted in a single moment of time but rather developed over the course of eons beyond our comprehension.

Bertrand Russell, when wrestling with a particularly knotty problem—which in his case might involve mathematical, political, or philosophical concepts—would simply cram himself with as much material as possible and then retire for a good night's sleep. The solution to a problem, he discovered, was often present in his mind, sometimes quite fully developed, when he awakened in the morning. I assume that one thing that happens in the act of sleeping—remaining unconscious for many hours at a time—is that we get out of our own way, so to speak, and let one portion of the mind roam wherever it will, without being inhibited by our conscience or other ego-affecting faculties.

From time to time I write jokes in my sleep, and sometimes songs. Oddly enough, my most successful song, "This Could Be the Start of Something Big," was written in a dream. Thank goodness it occurred just before awakening one morning, since we remember most clearly the dreams we experience at those moments. I jotted down the first few lines of the lyric, which enabled me later to consciously recall the music, and the job was done. It is a source of considerable frustration that in many other instances, although I am perfectly aware, in a dream, that I am creating an attractive melody, I am unable to recall its structure when, hours later, I awaken.

Also, I have learned to pay close attention to my brain in those brief twilight or dawn periods when I am drifting off to sleep or awakening. It is during those moments that the brain will sometimes produce either the resolution to a problem or drop into the slot, as it were, a fairly important factor, one requiring prompt attention but which had been overlooked in the rush of business and personal concerns of the preceding few days. Since I would be surprised to learn that my brain is the least bit unusual in this regard, I suggest to others that they pay the same attention to their internal computers when dropping into or rising up out of sleep.

But if all of this speculation is valid, what a crushing tragedy it is that most people are unable, or at least unlikely, to function creatively in the conscious state. It is certainly the case, after all, that formally artistic individuals constitute a small minority. Not many of us are novelists, poets, playwrights, painters, sculptors, or composers of music.

But creativity is by no means limited to the formal arts and their professional or amateur practitioners. *Proficiency at problem-solving is, beyond question, an exercise of creativity.* Some have greater genetic potential for it than do others. But I assume that all of us, except certain of the mentally handicapped, have some innate degree of potential for such thought, just as we can all draw some sort of picture, create some sort of story, or hum some sort of melody.

I draw comfort—at least as I project such speculation over some expanse of the future—from what appears to me to have been the evolutionary case, which is that consciousness itself emerged *because it had to*. As the conditions of human existence moved from the very basic and primitive into the more socially complex, higher orders of ability became more important. Originally, the physically strongest man in a given family, tribe, or village must have been the natural leader. But, in time, the smartest, wisest individual became more important.

I have earlier referred to a sort of conscious discouragement of undisciplined emotion, which—in many real-life instances—serves to cloud the reasoning powers. But in creative thinking, it is not only permissible to give the emotions free reign, it is probably impossible to think truly creatively without doing so.

This is certainly not to say that all that is required for the practical exercise of creativity is a strong surge of emotion. Emotion by itself creates nothing. When those who paint well serve as teachers to those who at first know little of painting, they do not give their students instructions in how to feel anger, fear, sexual longing, joy, or romantic love. No, they teach them how to mix colors, to hold a palette, prepare a canvas, manage perspective, and experiment with different styles of drawing and painting. The emotions themselves—for better and occasionally worse—come naturally.

Intuition

Intuition is a particularly interesting word. It is not as easy to define as words like *hockey puck* or *pineapple*. It refers to a primarily right-brain activity in which the older, more "primitive," creative part of the brain jumps to a hypothesis apparently *without* having gone through the sort of analytical, logical, or even commonsense thinking of the sort this book is designed to encourage. But is intuition to be devalued simply because "it is not logical"?

I put the last phrase in quotation marks because it seems to me that the evidence for the logicality or illogicality of intuitive thinking is not conclusive. We tend to assume that intuitive thinking simply does not bother with logical steps. But what may be involved is thinking that is quite reasonable but that, for whatever reasons, takes place with such incredible rapidity that all that the *left* side of the brain—the consciousness—becomes aware of is the result: the hypothesis, theory, guess, hunch, or solution. On the other hand, it may be that all—or some—of the ideas developed by intuition do *not* occur as a result of rational processes but rather bubble up out of some sort of semi-mystical creativity with which only humans are endowed.

Consistent with this latter possibility is the fact that much creativity does not seem to require a conscious contribution from the reasoning faculty, something I know from daily personal experience. For reasons I have never understood, some portion of my brain has a prodigious ability to create never-before-heard melodies. I never went to a composing school to learn how to do this. Indeed, I am largely a musical illiterate since I cannot read music well enough to play it. But the gift for composition has been there in my brain since childhood and has, over the last half-century, produced thousands of songs. The reasoning part of my mind—the left-brain activity—is unlikely to have anything to do with this, though it can be involved with writing lyrics.

There is the possibility that the left brain does have some slight input since it is obvious that combinations of notes are never entirely random. If they were, no one would be interested in hearing them, since they would be interpreted as what they were, a meaningless jumble of notes and "harmonies" following in succession but without any possible relevance to the laws of music. I assume that painters, sculptors, poets, dancers, and other creative artists would report largely the same thing about their arts.

Again: I am not in the least concerned with diminishing the realm of the creative or intuitive. The world needs more creativity, not less. But the two are in no sense mutually exclusive. We often hear it said that as individuals practically none of us live up to our potential. It might be more accurate to say that neither our right nor our left brain lives up to its separate potential.

All children are, to one degree or another, naturally creative, precisely because their minds have not been set the way they usually are by the age of, say, thirty. It is no accident, in my view, that many remarkable theories and discoveries in the area of mathematics and physics have been made by men in their late teens or early twenties. Galileo was still a teenager when he made one of his important scientific observations. This is not to say that creativity must necessarily decline in later years, but rather that a young and therefore relatively uncluttered brain may, in some strange sense, have more room to swing ideas about and may be less encumbered by cynical, negative prejudices of the sort that inhibit our own freedom in creative and other areas. It is the relative ignorance of the young that gives them a certain speculative freedom denied those who know so much about a given subject that they are able to bring difficulties and obstructions into clear and immediate focus and thus inhibit—censor—their own creativity.

It was, therefore, with considerable excitement that I read the story about Marvin Minsky in the December 14, 1981, issue of the *New Yorker*. In discussing Minsky's work on computers as a means of resolving certain mathematical problems, among them some that were geometric, the author quotes Minsky as saying: "My machine did not realize that BAC and ABC are the same triangle—only that they have the same shapes. So this proof emerges because the machine doesn't understand what a triangle is in the many deep ways that a human being does— *ways that might inhibit you from making this identification*" (italics supplied).

All of this is consistent with the commonsense observation that creative children sometimes produce solutions to problems that are erroneous simply because they are logically invalid. In these instances the children are in error, whereas the great innovators mentioned were correct in their assumptions. But what the two categories of reasoners have in common is a relative lack of inhibition and a freedom to speculate growing out of youthfulness and ignorance.

To repeat, while it is true that creative thinking and logical thinking are different, both are necessary. Ideally, they complement each other, though sometimes they can be in conflict.

The emotions—even the negative ones of fear and anger—can fuel creative thinking. They rarely stimulate the reasoning process; or, if they do, they may make reason subservient, ultimately forbidding it to control the development of an argument. For *the emotions, as such, have no interest whatever in truth*. They gag on all evidence—however conclusive—that does not harmonize with the preconceived view. They accept all *supporting* evidence. At this latter task the mind of the paranoid may be remarkably ingenious. A personal obsession, a religious or political loyalty or fanaticism, may lead to the production of intricately constructed arguments that are, at one and the same time, remarkably clever and utterly invalid. I have seen more than my share of such material simply because I have been in the public eye for some forty years and have been visible enough and concerned enough about important social questions to have attracted the attention of hundreds of disturbed but ingenious individuals.

Those who send public figures letters and legal briefs outlining their cases invariably have a serious message to impart: "My husband is plotting to kill me." "The Catholic church is slowly, insidiously taking over the United States." "The police department of Los Angeles has been waging a campaign of terror against me for the last ten years." "The world will end in six months." "Only instant, universal disarmament can save us from the coming destruction." "The current president will be assassinated." "The Communists have taken over the Catholic church." "We must deport the Jews because they are stirring up the otherwise naturally peaceable blacks." "The crew members of flying saucers are actually angels sent here to announce the imminent Second Coming of Jesus Christ."

Note that, however preposterous such allegations, they are never constructed *entirely* out of fantasy. I have never received a letter warning me that what we think of as pumpkins are actually named glemps and that they were not intended as food but are, in reality, the Devil's testicles. We are all familiar enough with such bizarre formulations because they constitute the raw material of our dreams. But the conspiracy theories and horror stories outlined in countless letters, which often run into many pages, almost invariably deal with actual individuals and social institutions. The presidents, popes, religions, races, and social groups are real enough, though many of the beliefs and actions attributed to them exist only in the imaginations of the deluded.

A remarkable creativity, then, is often part of the conspiracy-theorist's thinking. He or she stands, in fact, as proof of the danger of creative thinking run rampant.

Some may ask if there is a danger on the other side of the scale, from permitting our creativity to be absolutely dominated by our reasoning faculty. Such fears—I repeat—are groundless because even in those all-too-rare cases in which a conscious attempt to subject creativity to reason is made, it turns out that the emotional, irrational, randomly speculative functions of the brain can never be totally reined in. But we need not be dismayed by this. As I observed earlier, of all of humankind's worthy ideals, absolutely none can be realized. They are not goals for practical achievement. If they were, we would spend our lives berating ourselves for our weakness. Ideals are, again, points on the moral compass. If we want to go west, we had damned well better know where on the compass, relative to our position of the moment, west is. The fact that there is no point on the earth that itself *is* west is obvious enough.

Analogies with facets of religious belief may also be drawn. All of the world's people, as it happens, are not in general agreement about whether there is such an actual place as Heaven. But a belief that there is has no doubt to some extent increased the amount of moral behavior in the world, since it holds up an image of a beautiful, ideal goal and suggests that it may be attained by avoiding sin and practicing virtue.

The creative instinct, in any event, will always retain a measure of freedom. Indeed, it will frequently flirt with anarchy. And when it is dulled, tamed, or crippled, it will never be by *reason*. The unhappy deed will be done by poverty, parental cruelty, exhaustion, monotony, drudgery, sickness, the struggle for physical survival, personal and family obligations, poor education, and the vulgarity and triviality of the cultural marketplace.

Sometimes, too, there is the simple social necessity of following orders and adhering to customary procedure. These are among the restraints that weaken our natural creativity; they are all part of the process of mindless conformity. The creative impulse, which on a rational planet would be welcomed at every turn, must—in this all-too-real vale of tears—overcome the most incredible odds to survive at all.

There is a fascinating, if sometimes depressing, paradox in all this: On the one hand the world survives and is literally nourished by the fresh thinking of creative artists, without whose achievements we would all still be living in the jungle; but creativity must nevertheless justify itself. Each new and worthwhile idea must overcome the objections of new obstructionists. Perhaps this is because the creative thinker forces others to alter their habits. The novel acts and policies may cause ripples in the marketplace. Boats will be rocked, customs and procedures changed, traditional views challenged.

There is even—damn the complexity of life—a justifiable aspect to such obstructionism. After all, not every creative thought is worthwhile. Some new schemes are hare-brained. But in doing the research and writing the scripts for the television series "Meeting of Minds" I detected the common theme that even in the lives of the great personages whose creative ideas were absolutely necessary to human progress, the heavy hand of custom was often raised to bar the path to a better future.

We are not, of course, all equally creative. My own guess is that the general range of one's creativity—not the specific level—is determined at the moment of conception, by a throw of the genetic dice. Subsequent experience can either enhance the exercise of our gift or—as happens in all too many cases—inhibit it. Whatever the philosophical realities, it is clear enough that creativity is a precious asset. It ought not to be wasted.

It is important to reiterate that there is no necessary contradiction or conflict between intuitive, creative thinking and logical thinking. The two are not opposites but stand in harmonious, complementary relationship. While individuals differ in their natural tendency toward one manner of thought or the other, both should be encouraged. Obviously this does not mean that merely by "ten easy lessons," participating in seminars, attending lectures, and reading books we can all become as creative as Leonardo da Vinci and as logical as Bertrand Russell. What it does mean is that we can all think a good deal more creatively and reasonably than we do in the *absence* of special encouragement and instruction. Even those who are most strikingly gifted at certain skills—great athletes, for example—are never totally self-taught. Even such superior individuals require instruction; the wisest usually solicit it throughout their careers. When a champion prize-fighter is at the peak of his form, his advisers still call out suggestions to him throughout the course of a fight, simply because they have other angles of vision than his, as well as certain insights that are denied to participants.

Rule No. 77

Play thinking games and
amuse yourself by trying to answer
puzzle questions that exercise your mind

Before reading the following story, I suggest you get out a wristwatch with a second hand—or a stopwatch. Then read the story and make a pencil notation of the precise time, in seconds, that you reached the end of it.

Next note the exact time at which the solution of the story's problem occurred to you.

On a rainy night in the city of Leipzig, in 1827, a man walked into the shop of a dealer in antique coins.

"I'll get right down to business," he said, as the proprietor welcomed him. "I've recently come into possession of a rare and valuable coin. Ordinarily I wouldn't want to part with it, so great is its historic value, but I find myself suddenly in financial difficulty."

"Very well," the proprietor said. "May I examine the item?"

Without another word the visitor placed upon the counter a bronze coin—apparently ancient indeed. Upon inspecting it closely, the proprietor saw that it appeared to be the sort of coin encountered in those parts of the world that had come under the domination of the Caesars. On the back, clearly visible, was the date "429 B.C."

"I'll have to get back to you about this matter," the proprietor said. "May I have your name and address?"

The visitor gave him the requested information and departed, whereupon the coin dealer walked to the nearest police station and reported the stranger as a would-be perpetrator of criminal fraud.

Question: How did he know the man was dishonest?

Again, note the time. Now put this book aside, for as long as necessary, and speculate about the problem.

Assuming that you have now resumed reading because the solution has occurred to you, I draw your attention again to the question of how the coin-shop proprietor knew that his visitor had attempted to perpetrate criminal fraud.

It may surprise you to be told that he could not, in fact, *know* any such thing, despite the *very great probability* that his suspicions were perfectly valid. There is one other possible explanation for the visitor's actions, and that is *stupidity*. It is entirely possible that he was himself so dumb that he had been hoodwinked by the coin's last owner and honestly believed that the date was stamped on the coin more than four-hundred years before Jesus Christ was born.

This is a simple puzzle that practically everyone is able to answer. But almost all those who do seem invariably to assume that there is only one explanation for the visitor's actions. As we have seen, there are at least two.

There will almost always be more possible solutions to a problem—more alternatives—than those that are immediately self-evident. This is not to argue that all of them will be of equal value. In one of Jim Davis's popular "Garfield, the Cat" books, we see the lovable creature reading a letter that says, "Dear Garfield: How do I avoid the embarrassment of cat hairs all over my house when I have company? Harried."

"Simple," Garfield suggests. "Never invite anyone to your home again."

This would hardly be an acceptable solution to the problem posed, but it is one solution. So keep your own mind open to the possibility that there are more ways to look at a given problem than the one or two that might quickly occur.

The story above, about the "antique" coin, something of a classic in the context of research into the process of problem-solving, is usually rendered with a minimum of detail. I have deliberately introduced such factors as "a rainy night," "Leipzig," and "1827" as a way of bringing the story closer to reality than has hitherto been the case; for when we pare such problems down to the barest possible number of factors, we remove them so far from everyday experience that, in my view, we somewhat weaken their effectiveness as teaching-aids. The problems we encounter in the real world are rarely isolated or simple in their basic construction but are immersed in the ongoing stream of events. What we must often do is sift through a large number of factors to determine those that have relevance to our purposes of the moment.

Here's another problem:

Everyone is familiar with the old trick question, "Who's buried in Grant's tomb?" The tomb is, of course, the final resting place of President Ulysses S. Grant. President John Kennedy, among other chief executives of the United States, is buried in Arlington National Cemetery. Other presidents' remains lie in various parts of the nation, but there are five American presidents who are not buried within the continental United States. Can you name them?

Answer (as of summer 1989): George Bush, Ronald Reagan, Gerald Ford, Richard Nixon, and Jimmy Carter.

Short story: I was doing some research in the chemistry department of one of the nation's leading universities. When I asked one scientist what he was working on he showed me a thick glass beaker containing a foul-smelling purplish liquid. "This," he said, "is the most amazing thing I've ever been connected with. It is an acid that dissolves any and all substances."

Question: How did I know that the man was not telling the truth?

Before referring to the answer—which is given below—pause for a moment, and answer the question yourself.

The answer is quite simple. If it were indeed the case that the powerful acid could dissolve any and all substances, then it would be impossible to find any container to put it into, since whatever the container was made of—whether glass, metal, a ceramic, or anything else—would dissolve.

A Scottish farmer enjoys two freshly laid eggs for breakfast five days a week. But he does not own any chickens; nor does he buy, steal, trade for, find the eggs, or receive them as a gift.

Where on earth do the eggs come from?

Answer: From ducks.

Once you know the answer, the question seems to be an easy one. But it is difficult for almost everyone simply because of the assumption that eggs must come from hens.

Let us assume that it would take five hours for an airplane to fly from New York to San Francisco, or vice versa.

A plane flies out of New York's Kennedy Airport for San Francisco at 10:27 one morning, and at the same time another plane leaves San Francisco for Kennedy Airport.

Question: At the moment they pass each other, which would be the closer to New York?

Answer: Neither. "Obviously" at the moment they pass each other, each would be exactly the same distance from both New York and San Francisco.

The next question concerns the seven Jones sisters. Each sister has one brother. Including the girls' mother and father, how many family members are there?

The answer is not sixteen, although that number is frequently given by those who assume that since each sister has one brother, there must also be seven brothers. But if there were, then each sister would have not one but seven brothers.

The correct answer is ten.

Rule No. 78

Pay attention

There are several puzzle-problems that illustrate the importance of this rule. I have listed just a few on the following pages.

In the sketch below, there are six buckets. The three on the left are filled with lumps of coal. The three on the right are empty.

The object of the test is to rearrange the order of the buckets so that they end up full, empty, full, empty, full, empty.

You must, however, achieve this by moving only one bucket.

At this point read no further but just give yourself a few minutes to work on the challenge.

Whether you have solved the puzzle or failed to do so, let's review the various stages and steps you almost certainly engaged in as part of the problem-solving process.

At first one tends to just stare intently at the sketch and mentally make a few random moves. You have no confidence whatever that any one such move will resolve the matter but are operating on a random, what-the-hell basis. Let's see what happens if I move this bucket. No, that's no good; let's try another one.

Generally, within a minute or two, you reach a second stage in which you may be forgiven for assuming that the situation is impossible, that you cannot, in fact, rearrange the buckets in alternate order by moving only one of them.

But then, either consciously or unconsciously, you may say to yourself, "But it *must* be possible to solve it since people who write books of this sort would not be likely to present puzzles that had no solution whatever."

The fourth stage—and a crucially important one—comes when you say to yourself, "It must be necessary for me to do more than the obvious here, to get outside what *seem* to be the rules of the game."

In my own ruminations, during the approximately two minutes it took me to solve the puzzle, I visualized the buckets not necessarily any longer in a straight line but perhaps some above rather than beside others, or coming up off the page, or receding behind it. Such speculation in itself is very far indeed from the proper solution, but it is a sign that your brain is percolating in a healthy, productive way, inasmuch as it shows that you are prepared to step outside what had seemed to be the normal parameters.

At the last stage, it suddenly occurred to me that the solution might be to empty the contents of one bucket into another and, at that point, of course, my work was substantially completed in the sense that it took only a few more seconds to perceive that bucket number 2 could be lifted and emptied into bucket number 5.

Again, let's review the moral that all such stories present. It is certainly not that they will prepare you to line up objects of two different sorts in alternate order with only one move if you encounter them in the initial configuration given above, since most of us will reach the end of our lives without ever running into any such situation. The lesson to be drawn—so important that it bears frequent repetition—is the value of looking at problems from more than one point of view, refusing to limit ourselves to the approach that comes most readily to mind.

Another riddle asks:

Chapter 7 of the Bible's book of Genesis tells of the number of animals and birds that were to be taken into the Ark. "Of every clean beast thou shalt take to thee by sevens . . . and the beasts

that are not clean by two." How many animals of each species
did Moses actually take aboard the Ark before the Deluge?

A great many people who are not familiar with the Scriptures will
answer this question incorrectly. But, even more surprisingly, so will
large numbers of Jews and Christians, despite the fact that the story
of the Flood that killed almost the entire human population is one
of the basic building blocks of their separate religions.

By way of providing a slightly helpful clue to the answer, I will
say that it could not possibly be figured out by an individual who knew
nothing at all about the Bible and who therefore could not ever have
heard the story of the Flood. Because most readers of this book, however,
will be products of Western civilization, it is reasonable to assume that
all the information they require for answering the question is already
in their possession.

I explain next that the conflicting instructions involving the numbers
two and *seven* are in no way relevant to the deciphering of the puzzle.

To state the case in other terms, *two* is not the correct answer.

Neither is *seven.*

The proper answer is *none,* simply because it was not Moses who
took the animals aboard the Ark; it was Noah.

As in the earlier instance, many of us, on being given this information,
feel a slight sense of annoyance, as if we had been unfairly tricked.
But if we reread the original question we'll see that what brought us
to error was not trickery but our own ineptitude. Most of us know
perfectly well that Noah was the name given in this particular biblical
story and that Moses had nothing whatever to do with it. Despite the
fact that we "knew" this, we nevertheless fell into the trap.

I would be disappointed if the reader simply filed this puzzle-question
away until such time as it could be used to similarly confuse a friend.
The correct answers to such questions per se have little importance.
What is of the most vital importance is to review the means by which
we fell into error. Among the factors that might have been operative,
to varying degrees in individual cases, were: (*a*) our tendency to believe
what we read; (*b*) the Expectancy Illusion, which makes us think we
see what we expect to see; (*c*) our tendency to concentrate on certain
factors of a puzzling situation to the exclusion of elements that are

actually of greater importance; and (*d*) an eagerness to believe that can make us grasp at any fragment consistent with our expectations.

The word *Moses* is obviously not identical to the word *Noah,* but both names are those of characters in Genesis, both include the vowel *o,* and the names of the two start with the letters *M* and *N,* which are similar in sound. Certainly if the question had read, "How many animals, in fact, did Harry Truman take aboard the Ark?" no one would have been fooled by it.

Again, it doesn't matter a damn if you were wrong in responding to the question. It matters a great deal that you consider the sort of carelessness that made your answer wrong.

We have much to learn from an analysis of the ways in which such puzzles lead us into error. Most of us can recall hearing such questions in early childhood.

I believe I was about five years old when I was asked to tell which was heavier, a pound of iron or a pound of feathers. Almost all five-year-olds confidently answer "iron," simply because they have already learned that metal is heavy while feathers are exceedingly light. Of course the error is made *because the question has been misunderstood.* If the question asked was simply which of the two substances was heavier, it would always be correctly answered by anyone who had become familiar with both iron and feathers. Just so, once we understand what the question *is*—as distinguished from what it is *not*—we will, in that case too, have no difficulty in answering it.

Another question of this type, which I heard when I was about ten years old, was, "How many 2-cent stamps are there in a dozen?" If instructed to answer quickly, a good many of us, and by no means only those who are ten years old, will answer 24, since we at once proceed to multiply 12—the number 4 that constitutes a dozen—by 2, the value of each stamp, given in pennies. Others, dividing instead of multiplying, will give 6 as the answer. But again, we give such erroneous answers not because we have the slightest difficulty in manipulating such simple concepts as *two, dozen,* and *stamps,* but because we have misunderstood the question. The question was not "What was the *value* of . . . ?" but "How *many* . . . ? Since we know that there are 12—of anything at all—in a dozen we give the correct answer and are rewarded with a smile or a pat on the head.

There are other trick questions which, unlike the preceding examples, truly are unfair simply because those being quizzed are deliberately led down the path and then loaded with extraneous detail that they try, in good faith, to deep track of. The classic instance of this sort is the old bus-driver story.

> You're the bus driver whose route takes you the length of Wilshire Boulevard and back. At your first stop in the morning 5 passengers get on.
> At the second stop, 3 more passengers are picked up, but 2 get off.
> At the third stop, 9 passengers get on the bus and 4 leave.

The questioner then refers to several additional stops and, in each instance, provides arithmetical information about the number of passengers who got on or off. It is perfectly reasonable, while one is listening to such questions, to assume that the final question will relate to the number of passengers left aboard the bus at the end of its run. Or, if our own minds are somewhat devious, we might assume that we are going to be asked the total of those who had boarded at the halfway point, or something of the sort.

But it turns out that the final question is, "How many stops did the bus make?"

Since there was no good reason to have kept track of such a factor the correct answer cannot come readily to mind.

But even though such questions are definitely unfair, even they have a moral to teach, which is that the factors of a situation that on the face of things seem the most important are not always necessarily so.

One frequently encounters instances of dumbth of a particular kind, a sort that is puzzling because it involves a failure to perceive relevant evidence that, because it is so obvious, ought not to be overlooked.

The following is a word-for-word conversation with a recent temporary housekeeper who had finished serving a simple dinner for one:

HOUSEKEEPER: Would you like some sponge cake for dessert?

S.A.: No, thank you. I believe I'll have some fruit.

HOUSEKEEPER: I'm sorry, there isn't any.

S.A.: (*Pointing to sizable bowl of fruit on table three feet away*) You'll find some peaches and bananas right over there.

HOUSEKEEPER: Oh. (*The fruit had been there for several days.*)

S.A.: Did I understand you to mean that there's also no fruit in the refrigerator?

HOUSEKEEPER: That's right.

S.A.: That's odd. I personally placed a can of figs there just a few days ago. Would you look, please?

HOUSEKEEPER: Sure. (*A moment later*) No, there are no figs there.

S.A.: And no fruit of any other kind?

HOUSEKEEPER: No.

S.A.: (*A moment later, looking in refrigerator*) As you'll see, there's a large strainer full of blueberries, which are fruit. And on the next shelf is a large can of figs. The can I just mentioned.

HOUSEKEEPER: Oh.

What can one say about the woman's failure to see three objects that were plainly in sight? I can only speculate, since I could not embarrass her by interrogating her about the matter, but perhaps in her early years the word *fruit* had applied to particular items, none of which were at hand during our conversation. Let us say that to her the word suggested mangoes and papayas. If that had been the case, then presumably she would have noticed the fruit if it had consisted only of those two kinds. Another possible explanation is that she was simply distracted and not concentrating on the business of the moment. The latter, I think, is more likely to be the operative explanation. Although it may at first seem that such mistakes of simple perception and observation are trivial, they are clearly not so in all cases. If that sort of error is made by the pilot of an airplane, an operating room attendant, or an income-tax advisor, the results can be serious indeed.

Rule No. 79

Realize that everything is open to criticism

As explained earlier, the word *criticism* by no means necessarily implies destructive analysis of the subject matter. As a result of competent analytical criticism, it is entirely possible to construct an even stronger defense of an already firmly held belief, if such is the object of your study. But the vast majority of your assumptions have nothing whatever to do with firm convictions. You will tomorrow, let us say, be exposed to hundreds of separate assertions, running from the important to the trivial. Should you accept all of them? Obviously not, since some will be factually false and others will be nonsense of one sort or another. You already do, in fact, make at least some sort of vague pass at judging what you hear, although, oddly enough, your reasons for rejecting certain assertions may be every bit as invalid as your reasons for accepting others.

But in addition to the new statements to which you will be introduced on the morrow, your mental files are already cluttered with numberless thousands of ideas, some of which were acquired in infancy, others picked up along the way to the present. Obviously your collection of ideas is not a totally random jumble. They tend to fall into certain common categories. Some, for example, will be political. Having been conditioned by the experience of growing up in the United States of America, if you were, you and I will be biased in favor of such political constructs as freedom, democracy, and a representative form of government.

It clearly does not require profound philosophical insight to perceive that, as regards certain specific factors, we Americans are fortunate indeed when we compare our lot to those living in totalitarian Marxist

341

or fascist societies. As regards the rightly respected American separation of church and state, for example, which is one of the reasons for the preservation of our freedom of religious belief, we need only think of the horrors of life in present-day Iran to appreciate our own good fortune.

But as even the casual student of history knows, freedom is by no means the norm in human societies. It is a rarity and as such needs constant supervision and defense. But how can it be intelligently defended by those who understand hardly anything about it? Most of us who consider ourselves defenders of freedom would do very poorly indeed in a casual debate with political philosophers, of the right or left, who differ on this point. The freedom we may be passionately concerned to defend is our own. Many Americans—perhaps the majority—are by no means committed to the defense of freedom for those with whom they differ about certain political, religious, or philosophical questions.

And so it goes with every one of life's important questions, and a good many questions of lesser importance as well. Very few of us will ever subject our assorted opinions and beliefs to even the vaguest sort of critical analysis. The failure to do so classifies us as dummies, in that particular regard.

Rule No. 80

You must become more familiar with history than you are

I state this suggestion as bluntly as possible. This is not something about which we have a reasonable choice, in the way that one might decide whether or not to take up an interest in fourteenth-century Hungarian literature, basket-weaving, chess, or the collecting of Coca-Cola memorabilia. History is in quite a separate and basic category, along with such disciplines as reading and mathematics. Animals, if they could read, might or might not decide to take up an interest in human history, but it would be a very stupid chipmunk who would deliberately neglect the history of his own species. History is, in essence, nothing more complex than the story of the human race.

You are a member of the human family. As such you must become familiar with your family's past.

Rule No. 81

Become familiar with
the General Semantics movement

Around the year 1960, I began receiving letters congratulating me on being a general semanticist. Since I had no idea what a general semanticist was, I began some casual reading in the field by consulting the works of Alfred Korzybski, S. I. Hayakawa, and others. While I will not digress here to outline the theories of general semantics, I nevertheless strongly recommend a study of the field. We will know a good deal more about language and about the delicate, difficult process of human communication after we have familiarized ourselves with such findings and theories.

For example, maps are not the same as territories. This is something "everybody knows," yet in much thinking and communication we proceed as if we knew nothing of the kind.

Another teaching of Korzybski and his followers has to do with the uniqueness of individual instances. One way to put it is to say that Hungarian[1] is not the same as Hungarian[2]. Again, this is something that on one level is evident to all but the mentally retarded, and perhaps even to many of them. But, despite its obviousness, most of us make sweeping judgments about people on the basis of their racial, ethnic, political, or religious background without ever acknowledging that there may be crucial differences between any two Presbyterians, Communists, Republicans, women, tennis players, and so on. What had specifically made some of my correspondents assume I was a semanticist was a gimmick I had employed in some books and speeches. In one instance I said to the reader, in effect: Let me give you here an instance of Communist propaganda. I then offered the following quotation:

344

With the diffusion of modern industry throughout the whole world the "capitalist" economic regime has spread everywhere to such a degree . . . that it has invaded and pervaded the economic and social life of even those outside its orbit and is unquestionably impressing on it its advantages, disadvantages and vices. . . .

Accordingly, when directing our special attention to the changes which the capitalist economic system has undergone . . . we have in mind the good not only of those who dwell in regions given over to "capital" and industry, but of all mankind. In the first place, it is obvious that *not only is wealth concentrated in our times but an immense power and despotic economic dictatorship is consolidated in the hands of a few,* who often are not owners but only the trustees and managing directors of invested funds which they administer according to their own arbitrary will and pleasure.

The dictatorship is being most forcibly exercised by those who, since they hold the money and completely control it, control credit also and rule the lending of money. Hence, they regulate the flow, so to speak, of the lifeblood whereby the entire economic system lives, and have so firmly in their grasp the soul, as it were, of economic life, that no one can breathe against their will.

This concentration of power and might, the characteristic mark, as it were, of contemporary economic life, is the fruit that the unlimited freedom of struggle among competitors has of its own nature produced, and which lets only the strongest survive, which is often the same as saying, those who fight the most violently, those who give least heed to their consciences. . . .

The American reader may think that this, as an open criticism of capitalism and, as a typically Communist diatribe, is scarcely worth attention. But I must confess to having playing a rick; the "Communist" statement is actually out of Pope Pius XI's famous encyclical *On Reconstructing the Social Order.* The author of another quoted "Marxist" statement, I revealed, was Abraham Lincoln.

We have reached such a peculiar pass today that the very idea of reconstructing the social order has a suspiciously "Red" tinge to it. But ideas should be examined and judged on their own merits primarily, and only secondarily on their origin. Knowledge of the origins of ideas may be helpful, but not necessarily. A man widely judged wise and honest is plainly enough entitled to a claim on our attentions not ordinarily granted to the fool, the known liar, or the enemy. Nevertheless, since no one is in possession of the whole truth and nothing but the truth and, conversely, since wisdom may sometimes come out of the mouths of babes, we must force ourselves to evaluate ideas with only secondary regard to their source. For if we judge statements *only* by their source, we will frequently fall into serious error.

There is space here hardly to scratch the surface of the General Semantics philosophy, but you may familiarize yourself with it by attending lectures, by subscribing to *ETC.* magazine (International Society for General Semantics, Box 2469, San Francisco, CA 94126), or by reading books on the subject, to which any librarian can direct you.

Conclusion

An important addendum to my thesis is an idea expressed by Cardinal Newman that, far from being generally troubled by a lack of logic, human beings are actually frighteningly, relentlessly logical. Paraphrasing Newman, Pierre Charles, S.J., in his brilliant exposé of the notorious Czarist, anti-Semitic forgery, the *Learned Elders of the Protocols of Zion,* says:

> The disagreements which separate (men) are not at all derived from shortcomings in reason. They have their origin in an inner zone much deeper than that in which judgments are formed, in what Newman calls "assumptions," that is, orientations at once confused and imperative: there man engages himself as a whole, with his desires and passions, his fears and furies, even his dreams and his resentments. Starting off from these orientations, logic works its way through everything, caring but rarely to adapt itself to reality, but making everything it meets serve the conclusions imposed in advance.

Newman and Charles are right in this. But I argue that applied reason can, nevertheless, be effective against a million and one forms of human error if it is used not as an isolated tool to support arguments for or against any proposition—in the way that lawyers and debaters use it—but rather within the context of *an enveloping, passionate determination to support truth.* This, of course, is not the method of lawyers but of scientists.

We would do well to remain ever mindful of Newman's warning,

347

however. In a modest attempt to reason with American rightists *(Letter to a Conservative,* Doubleday, 1965), I noted that, to me, political conservatives—particularly the more dedicated among them—actually seemed to be a different kind of people from liberals or political middle-of-the-roaders. They did, I thought, have something in common with Communists, Nazis, and fascists. Naturally I do not refer to similarities of specific political beliefs, but rather of spirit, of attitude, and in the approach to problems. I hazarded a guess that we often consciously become conservatives—or, for that matter, affiliates of any other political camp—for reasons that are partly emotional and psychological and have nothing directly to do with economics or politics.

But does not such an ideal as respect for truth run the risk of cutting across lines of loyalty to nation, church, political party, company of employment, school, and other affiliations? Yes it does—and there is some sad irony in the fact. But if from time to time, as in war, for example, we feel obliged to place ourselves in opposition to the truth, then, by God, let us do so knowingly. This is, obviously, an exercise in relative morality, which all absolutists profess to abhor, though they daily practice it. I argue that if we are to commit such offenses against the divine ideal of truth, then it should be done in an attitude of sad, even tragic cynicism, rather than in the sort of mindless fanatical certitude that, ever so willing to be convinced of the rightness of a cause, will so casually proceed from lies and distortions to infringements upon freedom, to cruel invective, to violence, and, in the end, to mass murder. Christ, how many hundreds of millions more will have to be slaughtered before this simple lesson is grasped?

It is easy to assume—once one is introduced to the general idea, however indistinct—that thinking is more or less in the same category as deep breathing, exercise, reading, and other basic survival skills. It is indeed within that category of worthwhile human activities, but it is nevertheless not universally accepted as an unmixed blessing. Along with the obviously good and useful results of thinking, there is also a degree of danger, just as there is in exercising, deep breathing, or reading. The underlying fact is that such activities increase power; and power, however useful and necessary, always carries a degree of risk. That all power is, in part, dangerous is important to know. Even those things needed for our simple survival—gravity and the other physical laws of the universe, sunlight, water, food, air—not only can but, sad to say, do kill people in various parts of the planet every day. I once expressed this insight in a poem.

Everything Can Kill Us

Everything can kill us that we need.
The sun can burn us or by holding back its light
    turn our bones to rubber.
Chaste water can, by being late for
    an appointment,
Shrivel us to dust, then coming
    roistering and drunken
    with its fellows
Wash our ash away
Splashed passionately on impartial rocks.
I need you similarly
and your unnamed force
That flowing full's identified as love
And turned to small degree is known as hate.

As for the danger of thinking, there is no question that an absolute respect for truth and for the weight of evidence will sometimes, as we have seen, be subversive of the established order—whatever that order may be. But more of the order in the world should be subverted, which is to say that it should be responsibly questioned and called to moral account.

Oddly enough, practically every person on earth accepts this view whole-heartedly, until the order of his or her own society becomes the background against which the principle is tested.

But if anything is truly accurate, wise, and reasonable, it will withstand interrogation by responsible reason. In fact, authorities and other defenders of a given status quo often employ honest curiosity by using it to strengthen the established faith, assuming it is defensible and not out-and-out poppycock or tyranny. They sometimes, however, miss such opportunities.

I had the pleasure of attending a Jesuit high school in Los Angeles—Loyola—during my sophomore year. One day a priest was explaining the concept of papal infallibility to us. "The fact," he said, "is that it is impossible for the Pope to be fallible—to be mistaken—on a matter of faith and morals, simply because God, speaking as Jesus Christ, has personally guaranteed that infallibility."

A moment later it emerged, in the combined lecture and open discussion on the subject, that the papacy and its scholarly and administrative arms are extremely careful in issuing formal papal pronouncements on morality and belief and that, in fact, it is not unusual that long years of painstaking study by large numbers of scholars precede the moment of official pronouncement. As soon as I heard that, a question occurred to me. "Father," I said, "you told us a moment ago that God absolutely guarantees that when the Pope speaks on a matter of faith and morals it is impossible for him to make an error. If that is so, then why is it necessary for his advisers to spend years studying and debating about these things?"

Although I was only sixteen at the time, the question was perfectly reasonable. It was not asked out of any Voltairean, skeptical impulse, but on grounds having purely to do with such exercise of reason as I was capable of at that age. Alas, instead of using my question as a base from which to develop a fuller explanation of the dogma in question, my instructor responded with irritation by saying, "Don't ask dumb questions."

In his stimulating *Teaching Thinking,* Edward de Bono observes:

> . . . Sooner or later people are going to start thinking for themselves. There is no way of stopping them, except with a powerful party line which preempts this activity. It may be better to learn to think in an open fashion rather than let thinking be only an expression of emotional discontent. On a recent visit to Australia I was asked by someone concerned with a social studies program why it was assumed that children would be against something as soon as they started to think about it. In his experience, and in mine, the opposite seemed to be the case: when children did think about some aspect of society, they often came to appreciate why things had to be done in a certain way. For instance, when children think about school rules, they often suggest even tougher rules.

Although it is obvious that we should become more rational, we should not expect that the only response to our doing so will be applause. There's a force in humankind that is opposed to the methodical, analytical accumulation and reporting of facts. People seem dimly to sense that there is a natural enmity, for example, between myth and reality. Attack a fact and—even if right—we may merely be laughed at. Attack a myth and we place ourselves in grave danger.

Those who imagine that they are in any sense refuting the thesis of this book by saying, "It is not so much reason the world lacks; it is love," are setting up as opposites or alternatives two factors that in reality are neither. It would be as pointless to say, "It is not so much reason that the world lacks; it is orange juice." The things that are in sadly short supply in today's world, in any event, may be numbered in the many thousands. But there is no reason to choose among them. We should attempt to increase all of them. But beyond this lies the fact that reasonable people will have a clearer perception of the necessity for love than will those who are motivated largely by fear, anger, jealousy, or tribal and ethnic animosities.

It might be assumed that in stressing the importance of reason in the conduct of human affairs, both personal and public, I am coming down unequivocally on one side of a debate that has raged among social philosophers for centuries and which was brought into sharp focus in the eighteenth century. The illustrious French spokesmen for the Enlightenment and their many subsequent adherents were commonly interpreted as suggesting that reason, barring a few inevitably bumpy spots, could produce prescriptions for all social ills. In time, Burkhardt, Le Maitre, and others, speaking partly out of an understandable reaction against the follies and crimes of the French Revolution, emphasized that human nature was far too complex, too nonuniform, ever to be susceptible to even full analysis, much less control, by any purely or largely rational system. In this connection, parenthetically, I heartily recommend Isaiah Berlin's essays in the history of ideas, *Against the Current,* the contents of which will make it easier for the reader of the present work to position my exceedingly modest contribution within the context of this profoundly important debate.

Whether from unusual powers of perception or from the insensitiveness of ignorance, I am able to perceive virtue in "both" camps. The word *both* must be put inside quotation marks because in reality there are not two but various points of view about the issue. But it must first be grasped that there were historic causes not only for the French Revolution but for the philosophical speculation, partly

Voltairean, that emerged at the same point in history. It does not require the expertise of a professional historian to be aware of the numerous injustices and outrages against which men and women of vision and good will were morally obliged to struggle. But all important social movements "go too far" and, whether virtuous or misguided, in time create a reactionary counter-movement. I argue, in any event, that the problem of reason in human affairs is not that there has been too much of it but too little. As for "scientific Marxism," no social system can ever be truly scientific, although systems may have specific components of a partly scientific nature.

Those conservatives are correct who argue that human beings are too spiritually multiform to be directed as wise governors might control a society of robots. There is also the eternally complex dilemma of the contradiction between the two virtuous states of order and freedom. To further confuse the issue, alas, there have been many within the conservative wing, and within the traditional churches, who have argued that one uniform system not only could, but absolutely must, apply to all human beings, including those destined to populate the future.

My point in encouraging reason, however, is not to return to the delusion—if indeed anyone ever in fact so held—that reason itself would somehow lead to nothing but golden social realities. The point is more modest but quite simple: The world and its individuals are better off with reason than without it.

Rationality—or at least rational speech and writing—could do little to stem the tide of irrationality and terror that swelled up from the ugliness of Stalin's Russia and Hitler's Germany. But to say as much can certainly not be used to justify an abandonment of reason. To hold the opposite would be like arguing that sickness proves the folly of being concerned with health, or death proves the uselessness of living. Reason, continuing the analogy, can be viewed as a sort of preventive medicine, although it can cure certain diseases as well as prevent them.

If an entire generation of Americans is ever instructed in the basics of reason, then a sort of conscience of rationality will be developed among us and a set of standards will have been established against which citizens and their leaders may be called to account. Let us not decry the experiment until we have conducted it.

The ignoramuses who people the ranks of the Skinheads, the American Nazis, the Ku Klux Klan, the White Citizens Councils, the John Birch Society, the Posse Comitatus, and other "nuts-and-kooks" groups of the right, to use Richard Nixon's phrase, are themselves possibly beyond redemption, so committed to paranoia and semi-clever irrationality that reason and truth cannot penetrate the armor of their biases, angers, and fears. Their combined mental and moral diseases may be likened to those physical ailments that are in terminal phase, against which even the best modern medicine cannot prevail. But if the clock of history could be reversed just fifty years and the adults who are, in 1990, members of these various morally ill groups were taught to reason, it is safe to say that far fewer of them would have fallen victim to such political delusions as now grip them.

At my dinner table one evening, conservative leader William F. Buckley said of Robert Welch—founder of the John Birch Society— that he had reluctantly come to conclude that there was no political lunacy of which Welch was incapable. Buckley is noted for his delicate sense of language. Words are important to him; he speaks them with some grace. His use of the word *lunacy,* therefore, is careful. We are all wrong at certain times, regarding certain matters. Welch and his kind are frequently, consistently, fiercely wrong, in a patterned way, about certain questions; such states are indeed lunatic.

It is obvious that to solve the long list of troublesome problems that at present plague our society we will have to literally grow bumper crops of individual citizens who are, at the very least, bright enough to understand what the problems are. Those who are capable of conceiving improvements—or if not outright solutions, at least reasonable remedial procedures—will comprise the leadership that so deeply troubled a society clearly requires. But a generation of brilliant leaders and educators—even a replaying of something so unusual as the state of affairs that prevailed at the time of the founding of our nation, when an impressive number of well-educated, thoughtful, philosophical, and courageous men appeared on the stage of world history—would, in the present day, not be sufficient.

To put the point another way, even if we, for a moment, entertain the fantasy that by some divine magic Franklin, Paine, Washington, Jefferson, Adams, Madison, Monroe, and the rest, were actually to return to earth and were given their accustomed positions of power, even they would be unequal to the task that now faces us if the American population had become, at the same time, largely ignorant, apathetic, less able to understand significant issues, less inclined to vote, or were willing to participate in the larger social drama at all only when moved by anger or fear. So that is the primary reason the survival of our free, democratic institutions—indeed, in the long run, the continued existence of our nation as it has been known—literally depends on a new method of education and self-teaching.

In your own walk of life you may think of ways in which the lessons of this book can be brought into play. Perhaps you will think of creative innovations of your own to reduce illiteracy, ignorance, and stupidity. When I spoke at Los Angeles City College some years ago, I met a professor of mathematics named Glen D. James. He mentioned a simple idea that seems to me quite worthwhile: that the producers of television cartoon programs for children begin to add captions— of the sort used in foreign-language films—as an aid to teaching young children to read.

Professor James's suggestion opens up a world of possibilities, because the popular arts—which now serve largely to distract us—could make a vitally important contribution toward our education and general enlightenment. If our society cared half as much about the teaching of reading, geography, and history as it cares about the selling of deodorants and designer jeans, it is difficult to say how beneficial the effects might be. Millions of dollars are spent hiring the best photographers, writers, and directors to create commercials for products that are rarely among life's necessities. The same expertise could easily be directed to the production of programs that taught something worthwhile.

The human mind—once set—is, for a variety of reasons, so impervious to challenging information, so resistant to change, that even the simplest, truest statements must be repeated endlessly if they are to gain any lasting foothold in the public consciousness. Another complicating factor is that there is, in a strict sense, no such thing as "the public consciousness." The term has its usefulness, but we ought to recognize that it applies only to a vaguely defined state of affairs of a mass-psychological nature within a specific time-frame.

Perhaps if God decreed next Tuesday morning at 9:30 that no one living would die but that, on the other hand, no one would ever be born again, we might, in time, be able to apply the term "public consciousness" to something at least approximately constant and measurable. But as for reality, the millions of individual members who comprise the public are constantly being born at one end of the process and dying at the other. Even the wisest among us must die, at which time their accumulated storehouse of information and wisdom blows away in the winds of time, leaving the field to new generations of ignoramuses who must then be enlightened.

Are we not aware—is the evidence not agonizingly clear—that we are now raising a much fuller, richer crop of moral monsters than ever before, perhaps more than any society of the past? And yet we are not born such. We come into the world merely with a remarkable variety of potential, including the potential for good and evil. But something about our methods of nurture is now to a great extent encouraging the evil and discouraging the virtuous, or even the morally neutral.

Whatever the precise means by which the character-shaping is taking place, there is nothing essentially mysterious about it. It is a simple matter of environmental factors impinging on genetically given tendencies. But we must now place the first five years of life under a more powerful microscope than ever before. We must learn to identify the precise means by which millions of adorable, innocent, enchanting children are turned into hard-eyed little burglars, muggers, thieves, rapists, sadists, psycopaths, and murderers.

I would not be surprised to discover that, in fact, we already know the causative factors but that we have somehow managed to blind ourselves to them, perhaps after the unconscious realization that to get them into sharp focus will place us under a fearful moral obligation, or—which some fear even more—a financial obligation.

In the meantime, before the moment when our society makes a firm commitment to address this most fundamental of social problems, we will continue to direct our attention to the symptoms rather than the disease.

The symptoms do of course require our most urgent attention, for they are individually troubling enough. Increases in practically every category of major and minor crime, alarming growth in the prison population (and even greater increases in the numbers of those who ought to be caged for the protection of society), in alcoholism, drug dependence and addiction, child-abuse and wife-beating, and child-pornography—they are all part of a depressing social drama that requires first-hand diagnosis and then radical treatment.

Reason is one factor of the prescription our national sickness requires.

In the end, after the erection of even the best plans and a recommendation of the most appealing hypotheses, we must be wary of uncritical idealism. There is enough unavoidable heartbreak in the world; one ought not to court more.

Even if God empowered me to dispose the affairs of humankind so as to immediately put into practice the recommendations I have here outlined, the improvements in the human condition would at first, I suspect, be modest rather than dramatic.

The most nearly perfect plans can never possibly totally succeed because of one inescapable factor: They must all be carried out by human beings, a notoriously unreliable bunch. *All* grand schemes and policies then—even the most high-minded and virtuous, political or religious— are partly failures, characterized by endless bungling, ineptitude in low and high places, selfish motivation, lapses of memory, moments of inattention, and the thousand and one other factors that make life one damned thing after another.

But, having accepted as much, one must nevertheless, with all possible determination, still set out to encourage what one perceives as socially and ethically necessary.

But what of the argument that it is not only fools, fanatics, and incompetents but our "best and brightest" who have contributed to the present chaos? The answer, partly, is that they were not bright enough.

It is certainly too early to give up on science and the process of universal education, when *they have had little more than a century of opportunity to produce their desired results.* Regardless of which brief segment of time we believe to be the starting point of the modern period, it is clear that it did not begin by making a complete break with its immediate or distant past. The past is never, in fact, broken with, but is eternally dragged, with much of its enormous bulk, into the present and the future. Such a process is even necessary, for a certain proportion of knowledge laboriously accumulated over unknown millions of years by human effort is so worthwhile that it must be preserved and passed along to ages and generations yet to come. Unfortunately, the actual process is more complex; and vast impedimenta of error, superstition, folly, deceit, and foolishness from earlier ages are also brought forward to clutter our pitifully weak attempts to reason our way through the difficulties of the modern age.

If the general situation were no more inherently complex than this, our predicament would be troublesome enough. But there is something more to the drama, the nature of which sometimes inclines even the most hopeful and progressive of individuals to the depression of pessimism; and that is that the mindless, as distinguished from the socially beneficial, aspects of conservatism make it literally dangerous not only to attempt to introduce new knowledge and ideas but to contradict the errors of the past at all, however circumspectly and reasonably one approaches such a task.

So pronounced is this tendency, so powerfully entrenched are its living representatives, that even the right to subject any and all things to rational critical inquiry may be denied. And this, of course, lies at the heart of the age-old story of the thirst for freedom—not just freedom from the Romans, the English, the czars, Hitler's Germans, or the latter-day Russians and Chinese, but true personal freedom guaranteed by law.

Inasmuch as humankind has never found a Golden Key to Utopian perfection, it ought not to be assumed, I repeat, that training a generation of young Americans to think clearly will of itself solve all social and personal problems. Even assuming that we learn to use our reasoning powers far more effectively than we do at present, at the end of any such happy social process a tornado would still be a tornado, a catastrophic disease would still bring personal tragedy, divorce would still have depressing effects on children in whose families it occurs, an alcoholic husband or wife would still be alcoholic, a child born without arms would still be armless, a loved one lost to death would still be gone, and so on. Improving our reasoning powers, nevertheless, will make us much less the victims of life's events than we are at present, will make us less likely to make mistakes, will make us more intelligent as citizens. The point is: We should not expect too much, but count the blessings that are produced by our new labors.

And it is at least conceivable that there are more rational and socially productive approaches to natural disasters and tragedies than those we have so far employed; that creating a generation more inclined to scientific thought would lead to the discovery of cures for more diseases; that there might be fewer divorces; and that death, when it occurred, would be perceived with less irrational fear than has traditionally surrounded it. We can at least be certain that as a result of a greater respect for the ideal of reason there would be somewhat more truth in the world on the one side and less falsehood and dangerous foolishness on the other. We have only to look at the actual world about us now to realize that any such improvement would be no small accomplishment.

Because the point is of such fundamental importance, I stress again that I am not trying to bring about a world—or even a personal lifestyle—in which reason is totally dominant. First of all, any such outcome is impossible. But even if it were possible, it would not be desirable. I am concerned merely to give reason its rightful place, which it certainly does not occupy at present.

But even in the best of circumstances, reason itself is not necessarily supreme. It must be related to other considerations—morality, for example. The best and the brightest, as we have been told, were largely responsible for the conduct of the Vietnam war. They approached it in the spirit of systems analysis, research and development, problem solving, a search for the most efficient means of achieving certain objectives. But the overall wisdom of the operation was, at least for the first few years, hardly questioned. We might recall the lesson of Jonathan Swift's modest proposal for dealing with the twin problems that plagued Ireland in his time: hunger and overpopulation. Swift's bitterly tongue-in-cheek solution: Promote the eating of babies. It was a remarkably creative and, in a sense, rational solution, except for the moral consideration—of which Swift was naturally aware—that the cannibalization of infants is an atrocity.

It does not follow from these few observations that morality—whatever that word might mean—is the only banner under which humans must rally. It might be so if there were only one moral code on Planet Earth, and unanimous agreement as to its contents, beauty, and wisdom. But moral codes—most of which are embodied in religious contexts—are as numerous as religions themselves, which unfortunately number in the thousands. They have their degrees of moral validity nevertheless, which is important. Without it we are animals, and dangerous ones at that. Reason and morality, then, do not have an adversary but a complementary relationship. Reason enables us to evaluate such moral strictures as are suggested to us. Reason tells us that moral codes designed to discourage murder, thievery, rape, marital infidelity, and cruelty are wise and practical, whereas moral rules of a narrowly sectarian or even bizarre nature are decidedly less worthy of respect.

Lastly, having improved our own reasoning powers, we must then become missionaries: Share with others our profound respect for reason, for wisdom, for truth itself. We will presumably choose to do so for purely generous reasons. But there are enough selfish reasons for making such efforts. Obviously, if those around us—the people we live, work, and socialize with—become more adept at reasoning, this will help create a healthier emotional environment for ourselves.

But even in the absence of any such personal campaign we will still be much better off by using our perhaps now largely dormant mental powers. We will be better protected against the not-always-reasonable appeals of salesmen, advertisers, politicians, and others who seek to influence our conduct for their own advantage. It by no means follows that their advantage always equals our disadvantage, but in some cases it does. We can protect ourselves against such encroachments by absorbing the lessons this book imparts, and putting them into frequent practice. It is inspiring to see this happen. I shall never forget the literal thrill I felt when, some years ago at a convention of General Semanticists, I saw some young students—about twelve years old—who, having been instructed by semanticist Katherine Minteer, read aloud and then analyzed for the audience a number of newspaper articles and advertisements. The insight, the clarity, the brilliance with which those children separated hot air from factual, reasonable statements was tremendously exciting. God, if a generation of young Americans could be taught similar lessons, it is difficult to envision the benefits to society that could result.

Resolve to play your own role in the Reason Revolution.